FIREFLY

GUIDE TO SEASHELLS OF THE WORLD

A.P.H. OLIVER

Illustrated by James Nicholls

FIREFLY BOOKS

A Firefly Book

Published by Firefly Books Ltd. 2004

First printing

National Library of Canada Cataloguing in
Publication

Oliver, A. P. H. (Arthur Peter Hoblyn)
    Guide to seashells of the world /
    A.P.H. Oliver ; illustrated by James Nicholls.

Includes index.
ISBN 1–55297–943–1
1. Shells—Identification. I. Nicholls, James II.
Title.
QL404.O44 2004   594.147'7   C2003–907175–8

Publisher Cataloging–in–Publication Data (U.S.)

Oliver, A. P. H. (Arthur Peter Hoblyn)
    Guide to seashells of the world /
    A.P.H. Oliver ; illustrated by James Nicholls.
    – 1st ed.
[340] p. : col. ill. ; cm.
Includes index.
Summary: Guide to over 1,200 species of
seashells from all around the world.
ISBN 1–55297–943–1
(pbk.)
1. Shells — Identification. 2. Shells — Pictorial
works. I. Nicholls, James. II. Title.
594/.1477 22   QL404.O65   2004

Published in Canada in 2004 by
Firefly Books Ltd.
66 Leek Crescent
Richmond Hill, Ontario L4B 1H1

Published in the United States in 2004 by
Firefly Books (U.S.) Inc.
P.O. Box 1338, Ellicott Station
Buffalo, New York 14205

Produced in Great Britain in 2004 by Philip's,
a division of Octopus Publishing Group Ltd,
2–4 Heron Quays, London E14 4JP

Printed in China

Acknowledgements

The information in this book is
gleaned from many sources apart
from personal observation and the
author would like to acknowledge
his indebtedness to many concholo-
gists past and present. While most of
the shells illustrated are from his
own collection, some have been
kindly lent by the National Museum
of Wales, Mr and Mrs T. Pain, and
Messrs W. Karo, F. Mayer and K.R. Wye.

   Thanks are also due to Dr A.J.
Rundle for his assistance with the
bivalves, and to Miss G.M. Warland
without whose help and patience in
turning barely legible manuscript
into typed copy, the project would
never have been completed.
Readers will not need to be told of
the author's very sincere appre-
ciation of the work done by the artist,
Mr J. Nicholls. The encouragement
and help from Mr S.P. Dance, Mr R.P.
Scase and other members of the
Conchological Society of Great
Britain, and the patient and helpful
attitude of the staff of the publisher
who have handled this book are also
gratefully acknowledged.

A.P.H. Oliver

CONTENTS

INTRODUCTION

Tibia fusus

A *Guide to Seashells of the World* – common shells, popular shells, spectacular shells? To choose any group would be difficult and inevitably subjective, so I have given up the struggle and selected those which I should most like to see illustrated. I believe my tastes are fairly typical of the average collector and hope that I shall, therefore, please most readers while accepting that all of them will ask a particular shell has been included or left out.

I have devoted the majority of this book to Gastropoda as I believe most collectors find this the most fascinating class. I have included some of the more interesting Bivalvia, and have given a short reference to each of the other classes of mollusk. I have devoted more space to the most popular families, such as the cowries, cones, volutes and strombs. As to species, I have tried to concentrate on the more common shells but some rare, or at best very uncommon, ones are included because they are known and coveted by many collectors, or even because they are particular favorites of mine. A typical example of a species has normally been illustrated, but occasionally a more unusual variety has been included for interest.

Wherever possible the illustrations are life size, but in many cases it has been necessary to alter the scale. However, shells on any one page are in proportion to each other. In addition, the average large size of each species is given in the text. Distribution areas can only be approximate as every month there is news of one or more species being found in a new location.

A PROBLEM OF CLASSIFICATION

A shell from my own collection is illustrated here (and has been included on page 175) as an example of the difficulties that may be encountered. I acquired it as *Murex radiatus* from west Central America. However, there does not appear to be a shell so named. It is not *Murexiella radicata* Hinds as that has five varices and mine has only three and looks much more like a species of the genus *Chicoreus*. In *An Illustrated Catalog of the Recent Species of the Rock Shells* by Maxwell Smith there is an illustration of a shell not unlike mine which he calls *Murex (Chicoreus) palmarosae mexicanus* Stearns 1897, giving as the locality the Gulf of California. Dr. Myra Keen in

Marine Shells of Tropical West America 1st edition puts this under 'Muricidae of doubtful status' and says 'This is to be rejected for two reasons: first the type specimen seems to be an Indo-Pacific form errneously recorded as from the American coast; second, the name *Murex mexicanus* Petit 1852, was used for a Caribbean form.'!

Dr E. H. Vokes does not list the name in her *Catalog of the Genus Murex Linne; Muricidae and Ocenebridae* 1971. Next, checking with the British Museum collection the specimens most like mine are labeled *M. (Chicoreus) corrugatus* Sowerby 1841, which is found in the Indo-Pacific.

CLASSIFICATION

Classification of living things is essential to any study of animals and plants to enable their relationships to be determined. It is usually based, according to Linnaeus, on anatomical similarities and differences. The first subdivision is into the animal **kingdom** and plant kingdom. The animal kingdom is comprised of **phyla**. The phylum Mollusca, with which this book is concerned, is second only to Arthropoda in number of species. Within each phylum, members are grouped into **classes** according to gross anatomical differences. Mollusca comprises six classes – Gastropoda, Bivalvia, Cephalopoda, Scaphopoda, Amphineura, and Monoplacophora – the main differences between them being in the structure of the shell and foot. Each class is then divided into **orders**, again according to anatomical differences, though less obvious ones. Members of an order are always grouped into **families** and then into **genera**. Intermediate grades such as subclass, suborder, superfamily, subfamily and subgenera are sometimes used. A genus is divided into **species**, members of a particular species being similar enough to allow interbreeding to result in fertile offspring.

Kingdom
Animalia
Phylum
Mullusca
Class
Gastropoda
Order
Neogastropoda
Superfamily
Volutacea
Family
Harpidae
Genus
Harpa
Species
articularis

The classification of such a large phylum as Mollusca is inevitably complex, and des-pite the many books which are available on the subject today, the naming of shells can at times be very difficult even if one is fortunate enough to be able to refer to a well-curated collection at a museum. Taxonomists are constantly finding that species were described under an earlier name than that in current use and the earliest name given is considered to be the valid one.

Also, further study of shells and their animals may show that what have been thought to be two separate species are only varieties of the same species, and *vice versa*.

Scientific name

The scientific name of each species consists of its generic and specific names. These are usually followed by the name of the person who first described and named it (the author) and the date, so that the relevant work can easily be referred to. It has not been possible to specify the dates of the authors' description-tions of some of the species mentioned in this book. Authors' names have not been abbreviated except for Linné or Linnaeus who has been denoted by L.

Kingdom
Animalia
Phylum
Mullusca
Class
Gastropoda
Order
Neogastropoda
Superfamily
Conacea
Family
Conidae
Genus
Conus
Species
arenatus

ABOUT MOLLUSKS

Approximately half of the vast phylum of Mollusca, which contains about 100,000 species, lives in salt water; the other half in fresh-water or on land. This book only deals with the former. These live in all seas, polar and tropical, shallow and deep water. Generally, those living in warm water are more colorful than those living in cold – cold water regions including the deep waters of temperate and tropical seas as well as the arctic and antarctic. The majority of shells covered in this book are found in warm water and any reference to, for example, the Indo-Pacific excludes the extreme south of the Indian and Pacific Oceans and the north of the latter.

Mollusk anatomy

All mollusks have a brain, digestive system and reproductive system. Nearly all lay eggs and some even look after their eggs after laying. The female cowrie is often found sitting on top of her pile of eggs – and should be left there! After hatching, many marine species have a free-swimming or veliger stage before changing into miniatures of their final form.

Excepting the bivalves, they have a ribbonlike set of teeth, the radula, which they use like a file to eat their food. Some of the animals are vegetarians, some are carnivorous and some are scavengers. The cones, augers and turrids kill their prey by injecting poison into it with a harpoon-shaped barb or tooth. While the augers and turrids are not harmful to man, some of the cones can cause considerable pain and a few can be lethal, so care must be taken when collecting such shells alive. The barb can pierce more than the skin so the shell should not be carried about alive in a pocket or bag next to the skin.

Mollusk shells

Mollusks are soft-bodied animals which in the vast majority of cases protect themselves by building a hard covering or shell. This may be in one piece as in the gastropods, scaphopods or tusk shells, and one genus of the cephalopods, Nautilus. The bivalves build a shell in two parts, as the oysters, cockles and mussels. Watering-pot shells start life as a normal bivalve and then construct a long, shelly tube, many times bigger than their original shell, which they incorporate into their new structure. The chiton's shell consists usually of eight plates which overlap and form a cover so that the animal resembles a common woodlouse, though it has no legs. Some gastropods, the nudibranchs in the sea and the slugs on land, and many of the cephalopods, including the octopus and the squid, have no external shell. Some of these have an internal shell, an example of which is the cuttlefish 'bone', often found washed up on the beach and fed to cage birds.

Shelled mollusks have a lobe or a pair of lobes, the mantle, from the edge of which is secreted the material from which the shell is built up. Bivalves grow by adding to the

Mollusks can be found in both warm- and cold-water regions. Those from warm waters tend to be more colorful. *Volutoconus grossi* (above upper) can be found in tropical Australian waters, whereas *Aporrhais pespelecani* (lower) can be found as far north as the coasts of northern Norway.

edges of their valves away from the beak – the place where the valves are joined together by a rubbery like ligament. Gastropods generally grow by adding to the edge of a tube which is coiled, usually dextrally. The limpets and abalones do not, however, produce tubes.

In some families, the Muricidae for example, the animal has a periodic rest in its building. When it has completed part of a whorl it constructs a strong, often heavily reinforced lip before continuing to build. The early lips show as varices on the shells. Most of the Muricidae have three varices per whorl, some up to eight, while the Bursidae often have two. Some shells, such as the members of the genus Lambis, do not build a strong, reinforced lip until they are fully adult, when the lip becomes extended with long, strong spines. The cowries also wait until adult before the lip turns in, thickens and develops 'teeth'. Others, such as the cones, do not modify their lip and therefore give no indication of having reached their maximum size.

Periostroacum and operculum

Many mollusks have a skinlike covering over their shells, the periostracum, often rather furry. This will usually crack and flake off when dry, but can easily be removed by soaking the shell in ordinary household bleach for a few hours and then washing thoroughly with water. This will not damage the shell, and until the periostracum is removed the beauty of the colors will not show. A living animal under water with its periostracum intact looks very different from a specimen with its periostracum either dried out or removed. The cowrie and olive shells have no periostracum. They are as bright and beautiful alive as in a collection – usually more so as they tend to fade, some more than others, when the animal is dead.

Many gastropods have a 'trap-door' or operculum attached to the animal with which they can close the aperture of their shells to protect themselves. This may be solid and heavy as the cat's-eye of the Turbinidae and the Neritidae, or pliant and horny as in the Trochidae and Muricidae. Sometimes, as in some of the cones, it is very small and obsolete and certainly not big enough to seal the aperture. Most collectors like to keep the operculum with their specimens, either tucked inside the shell or stuck on to a piece of cottonwool so that it can be held in its proper position. A horny operculum must not be put into bleach when cleaning off the periostracum as it will dissolve.

Bivalves grow shells in two halves, as opposed to the single shell found in most other classes of mollusk. The example shown here is *Pteria levanti.*

When cowries reach maturity the lip turns in and develops 'teeth'. The teeth thus indicate that the shell has reached maximum size. The example here is *Cypraea maculifera.*

Hints for collectors

The first consideration when collecting should be to collect responsibly. If you are planning to hunt in a particular area, first check with local authorities that collecting is legal and whether any species are protected. Where shelling is allowed, always remember that the number of shells of any species is not limitless. Do not take more specimens than are needed. After turning over rocks or coral slabs to search beneath them, they should be turned back again. Many creatures lay their eggs on the underside of rock and coral, apart from living there themselves, and if left uncovered these are likely to be eaten or die of exposure. Collecting shells has become such a popular hobby in recent years that many accessible reefs have been denuded of most of their molluskan life due to irresponsible shelling.

If you are obtaining shells by exchange or purchase, you should always do your best to check that you are getting your specimens from a responsible and law-abiding collector or supplier.

Cleaning shells

To extract the animal, many species can be brought to the boil in water and then allowed to cool slowly; cowries and olives should not be boiled as their glaze is likely to crack. A piece of bent wire is often the final answer, and an old hypodermic syringe can be helpful in producing a strong jet of water to flush out remains. Burying shells in clean dry sand (but not one above the other) can be effective in hot regions where ants may be helpful – although the smell can be unpleasant.

Acid should never be used to clean off the calcium and coral deposits, as this will clean off some of the shell too, especially the delicate fronds and sculpturing on the Muricidae, which seem particularly prone to such deposits.

Shells should not be varnished or polished. If they become dull, a wipe over with a touch of fine oil will replace the natural oil which has dried out, and do much to restore the original colors and sheen.

Keeping a collection

Collections should not be stored where they are exposed to the light. Strong sunlight, especially, will quickly cause the shells to fade. That is why in a museum the shells on display are usually dull and faded. The main collections are always stored away in light-proof cabinets.

I recommend to a beginner that he or she should decide early on where to specialize. The phylum Mollusca is so vast that one is likely to get more satisfaction from limiting a collection to a few families or to the shells from a particular country or area. Apart from achieving a more 'complete' collection, there is a better chance of becoming knowledge-able in one part of a very wide field.

Three shells highly prized by collectors. *Epitonium scalare* (top), *Spondylus regius* and *Cymbiola aulica* (bottom).

GLOSSARY

adpressed overlapping so as to converge gradually

anal canal channel or opening through which the animal passes waste matter, usually at the posterior end of the lip

anterior end pointing in the direction in which the animal moves; furthest away from the apex

aperture opening in a gastropod shell through which the animal emerges

apex first-formed part of the shell; tip of the spire, usually pointed

axis imaginary line from the apex to the base about which the whorls are formed; adj. axial

base anterior end of a shell, especially the flattened end of a Trochus type shell; also used, though strictly incorrectly, to describe the flat aperture side of cowries

beak see umbo

bifid split into two

body whorl last complete whorl formed 360° from the lip

callus thickening layer of shelly material; adj. callous

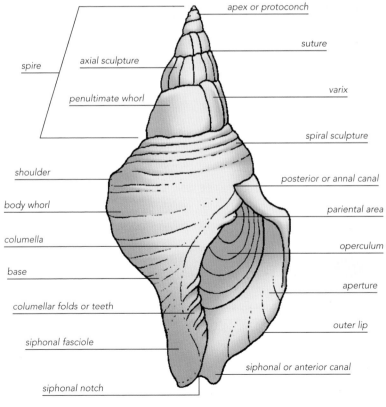

spire

axial sculpture

penultimate whorl

shoulder

body whorl

columella

base

columellar folds or teeth

siphonal fasciole

siphonal notch

apex or protoconch

suture

varix

spiral sculpture

posterior or annal canal

pariental area

operculum

aperture

outer lip

siphonal or anterior canal

cancellate with sculptural cords intersecting at right angles; reticulated or latticed

carina prominent ridge or keel; adj. carinate

columella central pillar of a coiled gastropod shell formed by the inner or axial sides of the whorls; adj. columellar

cord small, round-topped ridge

coronate(d) having nodes or nodules on the shoulder

crenulate having a regularly notched edge

depressed low relative to the diameter

dorsum back of the shell, opposite the aperture

fasciole spiral band built up from the notches in the canal of successive growth stages of a gastropod

fossula shallow, linear depression on the inner lip of some cowries

fusiform shaped like a spindle – i.e., more or less equally pointed at both ends

globose more or less spherical

head scar see muscle scar

height distance from the apex to the base or anterior end of the shell

keel prominent ridge or carina

*Concholepas
peruvianus*

labial area surface around the inner lip or labium from the bottom of the columella to the suture

lamella thin plate or scale; adj. lamellate

latticed see cancellate

length in species of the Patellidae, Acmaeidae or Fissurellidae, the distance from the anterior edge to the posterior edge of the shell; in a species of the Haliotidae, the longest distance between any two points on the circumference of the shell

lip edge of the aperture. The inner lip or labium (see labial area). The outer lip or labrum – the edge of the aperture furthest from the columella. In the following pages the term 'lip' has been used to denote only the outer lip.

lira fine line or groove; pl. lirae, adj. lirate

malleate as if beaten with a hammer

muscle scar or **head scar** mark on the inside of a shell – e.g., bivalve or Haliotis – where the muscle was attached

node small knob; adj. nodose

nodule small node; adj. nodulose

nucleus earliest whorls at the apex of a shell, which were formed during the egg stage of the animal; earliest formed part of the operculum

operculum shelly or horny attachment to the animal with which it can more or less close the aperture of its shell; adj. operculate

patulous expanded or spread

parietal area basal area of a coiled shell on the columellar side of the aperture

periostracum skin of hairy or smooth horny material (conchiolin) covering the outer surface of many shells

periphery widest part of a shell – i.e., furthest from the axis

plica plait, fold or ridge on the columella of some shells; pl. plicae, adj. plicate(d)

posterior opposite to anterior; rear or apical end of a gastropod; siphonal end of a bivalve

protoconch whorls at the apex of a shell, especially where clearly discernible from later ones.

punctate as if covered with pin-pricks

pustule small rounded elevation, smaller than a tubercle; adj. pustulate

pyriform pear-shaped

recurved bent backward; used especially of the anterior or siphonal canal, away from the aperture

reticulate see cancellate

rostrum beaklike extension in – e.g., Tibia and some Cypraea; adj. rostrate

sculpture relief pattern on the surface of a shell

shoulder angulation of a whorl forming the outer edge of the sutural ramp or shelf

siphonal canal channel at the anterior end of a shell through which the animal can extend its siphon, a tubelike part of the mantle for the passage of water

siphonal notch depression or notch in the lip through which the siphon can be extended

spatulate having broad, blunt, fingerlike projections

spiral extending round the whorls more or less parallel with the suture

spire visible part of all the whorls except the last or body whorl

stria fine incised groove; pl. striae, adj. striate

sulcus furrow or slit

suture lines formed by the joining of the whorls

tubercule small rounded elevation; larger than a pustule, smaller than a nodule; adj. tuberculate

umbilicus axially aligned opening within the whorls of a loosely coiled shell where no columella has been formed; adj. umbilicate

umbo or **beak** earliest formed part of the shell of a bivalve

varix thickened ridge formed at the outer lip during a rest period in the growth of a shell; pl. varices, adj. varicose

whorl complete 360° coil of a shell

width widest part of a shell at right angles to its axis

Strombus alatus

11

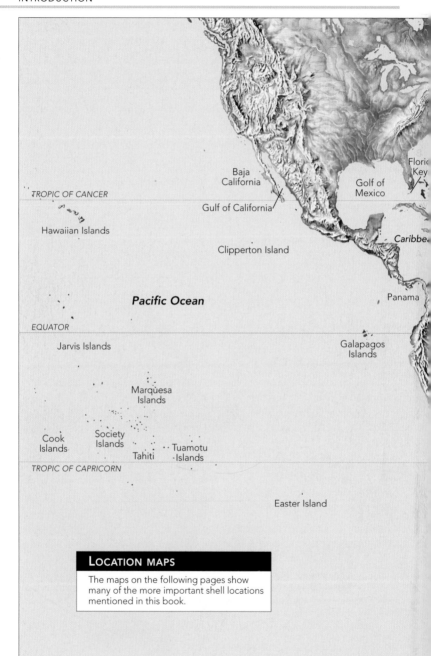

Baja
California

Golf of
Mexico

Flori
Key

TROPIC OF CANCER

Gulf of California

Hawaiian Islands

Clipperton Island

Caribbe

Pacific Ocean

Panama

EQUATOR

Jarvis Islands

Galapagos
Islands

Marquesa
Islands

Cook
Islands

Society
Islands

Tahiti

Tuamotu
Islands

TROPIC OF CAPRICORN

Easter Island

LOCATION MAPS

The maps on the following pages show
many of the more important shell locations
mentioned in this book.

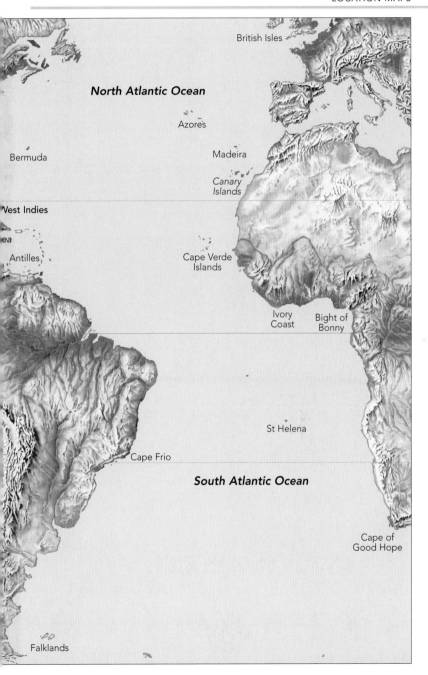

North Atlantic Ocean

British Isles

Azores

Bermuda

Madeira

Canary
Islands

West Indies

ea

Antilles

Cape Verde
Islands

Ivory
Coast

Bight of
Bonny

St Helena

Cape Frio

South Atlantic Ocean

Cape of
Good Hope

Falklands

Mediterranean Sea

TROPIC OF CANCER

Persian Gulf

Gulf of Oman

Red Sea

Arabian Sea

Bay of Bengal

Gulf of Aden

Sri Lanka

EQUATOR

Maldive Islands

Seychelles

Indian Ocean

TROPIC OF CAPRICORN

Mauritius

Madagascar

Cape of Good Hope

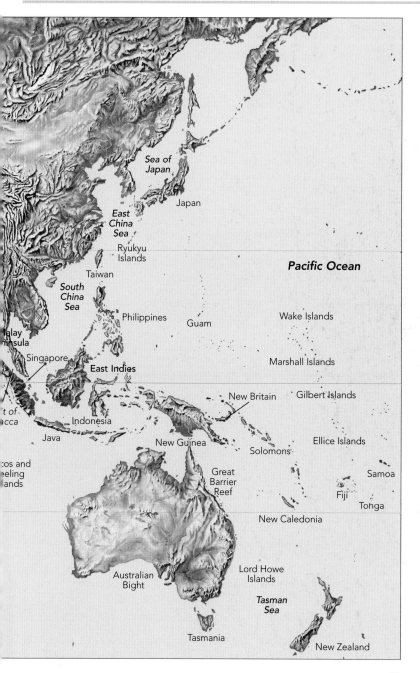

Sea of Japan

Japan

East China Sea

Ryukyu Islands

Pacific Ocean

Taiwan

South China Sea

Philippines

Guam

Wake Islands

Malay Peninsula

Singapore

East Indies

Marshall Islands

New Britain

Gilbert Islands

t of cca

Indonesia

Java

New Guinea

Solomons

Ellice Islands

cos and eeling ands

Great Barrier Reef

Samoa

Fiji

Tonga

New Caledonia

Australian Bight

Lord Howe Islands

Tasman Sea

Tasmania

New Zealand

ORDER: ARCHAEOGASTROPODA

SUPERFAMILY: PLEUROTOMARIACEA

FAMILY: PLEUROTOMARIIDAE

Slit shells get their common name from the slit through which they pass water and waste matter. They were known from fossils and were thought to be extinct until the first recent specimen was found in the Caribbean in 1856. They are of special interest because they are probably the most primitive of all gastropods living today. Since all are deep-water shells they are rare or very uncommon. There are some seventeen known species divided among three genera, *Entemnotrochus*, *Perotrochus* and *Mikadotrochus*. Seven species inhabit the Caribbean area, two off east South America, seven in Japan and Taiwan waters and one off east South Africa. Most are 2in (50mm) to 5in (125mm) wide, but *Entemnotrochus rumphii* grows to over 10in (250mm). Some are umbilicate and all have a horny operculum.

Perotrochus africanus

Perotrochus africanus

Tomlin 1948 *The South African Slit Shell was first found off the Natal coast in 1931 at about 200 fathoms;, about 5in (125mm) wide and 4in (100mm) high.*
A light, thin shell but like all members of the family conical with the characteristic slit. It is orange-yellow streaked with white. Only about a dozen specimens have been found.

P. hirasei

Pilsbury 1903 *the Emperor's Slit Shell from depths of 50 fathoms or more off southwest Japan, 4in (100mm).*
Relatively heavier than the rest of the genus, it is taller and more coarsely sculptured than *P. africanus* above. It is creamy white, heavily overlaid with diagonal streaks varying from pale salmon to a rich orange-red. Where the slit has been filled in as the shell grew bigger there is a stripe which gives the effect of the diagonal lines having been pulled backward at that point. A similar effect can be seen in *P. africanus*. *P. hirasei* is the least rare of the family.

Perotrochus
hirasei

P. quoyanus (not illustrated)

Fischer & Bernardi 1856 *Caribbean, 1.8in (45mm).*
It was the first of the family to be found and is pale brown with yellowish streaks.
Other members of the genus *Perotrochus* are *P. teramachii* Kuroda 1955 which is very variable or is the name given to two separate species, and is from Japan and Taiwan; *P. amabilis* F. M. Bayer 1963, *P. gemma* F. M. Bayer 1965, *P. lucaya* F. M. Bayer 1967, *P. midas* F. M. Bayer 1965, *P. pyramus* F. M. Bayer 1967 all from the Caribbean area; and *P. atlanticus* Rios and Matthews 1968 from Brazil.

Entemnotrochus rumphii (not illustrated)

Schepman 1879 *Japan and Taiwan, the largest of the family, up to 10in (250mm).*
The only other member of this genus is *E. adansonianus* Crosse and Fischer 1861 from the West Indies and Caribbean area. It is the second largest of the family. Both are heavy and solid and have longer slits than members of the other genera. They also have a wide, open umbilicus.

Mikadotrochus beyerichi (not illustrated)

Hilgendorf 1877 *Japan.*
Members of this genus are moderately large and heavy, and have a shorter slit than those of *Entemnotrochus*, but longer than those of *Perotrochus*. Other members of the genus are *M. schmalzi* Shikama 1961 and *M. salmianus* Rolle 1899, both from Japan, and *M. notialis* Leme and Penna 1969 from off south Brazil.

Haliotis asinina

FAMILY: HALIOTIDAE

The family contains only one genus. The shells somewhat resemble a single valve of a bivalve. Rather flat, they cling to rocks with a muscular foot like a limpet. They have a small spiral whorl at the low apex. Body whorl has a series of holes, from four to ten depending on the species, through which water and waste matter is passed, as through the slit of *Pleurotomaria*. Inside of shell is nacreous, iridescent, and used for costume jewelry. The foot is regarded as a delicacy in China, Japan, America, Channel Islands and New Zealand. Known as abalones in America, ormers in Channel Islands, paua in New Zealand, and awabi in Japan. There are some 100 species in the genus.

Haliotis asinina

L. 1758 *West Pacific, 4.75in (120mm) long and half as wide.* Shape gives it the name Ass's Ear. Seven holes open. One of the few glossy members of the genus. Cream heavily overlaid with green-brown triangles and irregular blotches; interior iridescent silver.

H. iris

Gmelin 1791 *New Zealand, 6in (150mm) long, 4.5in (115mm) wide.* Outer surface frequently covered with heavy calcareous deposit; interior richly iridescent silver, blue and green, dashes of gold Muscle scar centrally.

H. discus

Reeve 1846 *Japan and east Asia, 4in (100mm) long, 2.6in (65mm) wide.* Rough, rather uneven surface with bumps and hollows. Surround to holes is elevated; three to five holes open. Green-brown; interior silver. Prefers shallow water.

Haliotis iris

H. ovina

Gmelin 1791 *West Pacific, 2.4in (60mm) long, 1.8in (45mm) wide.* More round than *H. discus*. Ribs run from apex to lip; five to six holes open. Dark green; six, radiating, cream streaks from apex to holes; twenty, narrower streaks from holes to left-hand edge; interior silver.

H. corrugata

Wood 1828 *California and Lower California, 7in (180mm) long.* Higher than most of the genus. Nearly round with highly corrugated surface and scalloped edge; three to four holes open. Green or red-brown, often heavily covered with limey deposit, as illustrated; interior silver, gold, pink, green and blue. Muscle scar. Commonly used for food.

Haliotis ovina

Haliotis discus

H. sieboldi (not illustrated)
Reeve 1846 *Japan, 6in (150mm) long.*
Oval in outline with apex close to margin. Strong radial
ridges of varying widths. Holes large, somewhat tuberculate,
four or five open. Brown or red-brown; interior silver.

H. ruber (not illustrated)
Leach 1814 *South and southeast Australia and Tasmania,
6.25in (160mm) long, 5in (125mm) wide.*
Fine, beaded spiral cords and uneven radial folds. Six or
seven holes open, holes somewhat tuberculate; area
between holes and margin concave. Dark red-brown; narrow
green rays.

H. jacnensis (not illustrated)
Reeve 1846 *Philippines, south and
southwest Pacific, 0.5 in (12mm).*
Very rough, irregular spiral ridges.
Rather scaly. Holes, a little tuber-
culated and rather far apart,
two or three open. Orange-
red; interior silver.

Haliotis corrugata

H. rufescens

Swainson 1822 *The Red Abalone, north and Lower California, up to 12in (300mm).*

It is a large shell, oval and relatively flatter than *H. corrugata*. Its rough exterior has uneven spiral ridges and coarse, radial growth lines. It has three or four holes open. Brick red; the interior is silver and golden brown with a central muscle scar. It is popular as food, although only the larger ones may be taken.

Haliotis rufescens

Haliotis varia

H. varia

L. 1758 *West Pacific, up to 2.4in (60mm).*

A common shell. The uneven spiral ridges are coarse and nodulose. It has strong growth lines and some radial folds. The holes, five or six of which are usually open, are raised. It may be an olive green color or red-brown or mottled with white and/or black. As its name implies it is variable. The interior is silver with iridescent blues and greens.

H. lamellosa

Lamarck 1822 *Recorded as coming from Gibraltar, 2in (50mm).*

The illustrated specimen, however, is from the Greek Islands. It has a rather straight lip and uneven, radial corrugations looking like creases or wrinkles, and fine, spiral striae. It

Haliotis lamellosa

has four holes open. It is a blue-green, almost turquoise color and the interior is silver, blue, green and highly iridescent. It may be a form of *H. tuberculata* L. 1758 (see next page).

Haliotis diversicolor

H. diversicolor
Reeve 1846 *Western Pacific, up to 3in (75mm).*
It is relatively narrower and flatter than the majority of the genus and has rather evenly marked ridges running from the spire to the lip. About nine holes are open. Dark olive green splashed with dark red, brown and lighter green.

H. fulgens
Philippi 1845 *The Green Abalone, California and Lower California, up to about 8in (200mm).*
It is oval with coarse, flattened radial ridges and has five or six open holes and a central muscle scar. The outside is a fairly even dull brown and the interior beautifully iridescent with blue-green, gold and dark brown on silver. *H. fulgens* is fished commercially above a size of 6.25in (160mm).

H. spadicea (not illustrated)
Donovan 1808 *East coast of South Africa, 3in (75mm).*
Perhaps better known under its synonym of *H. sanguinea* Hanley 1841. Rather elongate shell, the exterior comparatively smooth for the genus but with uneven, radiating ribs. Rough spiral ridges, fine growth lines and about nine holes open. Red-brown; interior silver with brown stains near the apex.

Haliotis fulgens

H. emmae
(not illustrated)
Reeve 1846 *South Australia and Tasmania, 4in (100mm).*
Coarse spiral riblets, uneven radial folds and six or seven holes open and raised, with a narrow channel running beneath the holes. Orange-brown with about six, uneven, radial, cream rays; interior iridescent.

Haliotis gigantea

Haliotis tuberculata

H. gigantea

Gmelin 1791 *Japan, over 8in (200mm).*
Although the largest Japanese *Haliotis*, it is not as large as some others in the genus. Its holes are more elevated than any other, being tubercular in shape, and some four are open. The spiral corrugations are uneven and they cross lumpy ridges running at 90° to them. It is a dull brown or red-brown and is prized as a food. The two illustrations show the variation in color and also how the shell becomes rounder in outline as it grows larger.

H. tuberculata

L. 1758 *Mediterranean and northeast Atlantic, about 3.5in (90mm) long and 2.5in (60mm) wide.*
It is prized as food in the Channel Islands, where it is known as the ormer, but is very seldom found north of the English Channel. The spire is raised and growth lines clearly show. It is deeply striated spirally. There are about nine holes open. Variable in color from dull brown, red-brown to mixtures of browns, reds and greens with pale green, zigzag waves. The inside is silver with faint red tinges.

H. australis

Gmelin 1791 *New Zealand, where it is known as the Silver Paua, up to 4in (100mm).*
It has fairly even radial folds across low spiral ridges and growth lines. There are seven holes open. Pale olive green and may have faint red rays; interior silver. It is used for food.

H. midae

L. 1758 *South Africa, up to 5.5in (140mm) long and 4.5in (115mm) broad.*

Haliotis australis

The largest of the South African species and covered with deep irregular wrinkles radiating from the area of the apex. It falls very sharply from the line of holes to the left margin. The holes are numerous, small and about nine are open. It is a dull white with a red tinge; inside it has a central muscle scar and is silver with very pale greens, blues and pinks.

Haliotis midae

H. cracherodi
Leach 1817 The Black Abalone, west USA and Lower California, up to 6in (150mm).
It has a smoother surface than most though the growth lines are clear. About six holes are open. Outside it is a very dark red-brown, almost black, and inside silver with a golden sheen and a central muscle scar.

H. kamtschatkana (not illustrated)
Jonas 1845 North Pacific from Japan, south Alaska to California, 6in (150mm).
Elongate, roughly corrugated and may have weak spiral cords; about four holes open. Gray-brown.

H. elegans (not illustrated)
Philippi 1899 Western Australia, 4in (100mm).
It is elongate with a small spire close to the posterior edge of the shell, somewhat inflated and has strong spiral ribs. Number of open holes is variable-about eight in young shells. Orange-brown with cream rays; interior silver.

H. coccinea (not illustrated)
Reeve 1846 Cape Verde and Canary Islands, 2in (50mm).
It has close-set spiral ridges-sometimes unequal-with fine striae. Holes are close together and five or six are open. Scarlet with cream blotches or rays; interior silver.

Haliotis gigantea juvenile

Haliotis cracherodi

Scutus antipodes

Glyphis elizabethae

Fissurella radiata

Fissurella picta

SUPERFAMILY: FISSURELLACEA

FAMILY: FISSURELLIDAE

The keyhole limpets are flat and round, oval or shield-shaped like true limpets, but generally have a hole in the dorsum – sometimes keyhole-shaped – and often a slit in the margin. There are many small members of the family which includes several hundred species. They cling to rock and coral, mostly in warm seas and are vegetarians.

Scutus antipodes

Montfort 1810 *East Australia from Queensland to Tasmania, 4in (100mm) long and about half as wide.*
As all the genus, it is shaped like a Roman shield from which it takes its name. It is depressed and has fine, concentric growth lines with the apex well off-center. It has no hole and the apex points forward rather than upward. Creamy white outside and pure white within.

Glyphis elizabethae

E. A. Smith 1901 *East South Africa, up to 1.8in (45mm) long and 1.2in (30mm) wide.*
The hole is about one-third of the way from the end and there are eight prominent ridges and numerous small ones of varying sizes between. Gray; interior white.

Fissurella radiata

Lamarck 1801 *Caribbean, 1.6in (40mm) long.*
It has eleven irregular, radiating ribs with finer ribs between and an almost circular hole. Gray; radial ribs lighter; interior white with faint yellow tinge.

F. picta

Gmelin 1790 *South America including the Strait of Mag-ellan, 2in (50mm) long and 1.2in (30mm) wide.*
It has an oval opening forward of the center, and its growth lines give it a rough feel. Twelve dark brown rays alternate with light tan rays of about the same size; interior pure white with the ends of the rays showing round the margin.

F. grandis

Sowerby 1834 *West South America, 2.4in (60mm) long and 1.6in (40mm) wide.*
Much like *Megathura crenulata* in outline, although it narrows more toward the anterior and is much smoother. Very dark brown, almost black, this color forming a narrow band round the inside edge; the rest of the interior is pure white as is the immediate surround to the hole.

Fissurella grandis

Fissurella nodosa

Macrochisma producta

F. nodosa

Born 1778 *Florida Keys and the West Indies, 1.6in (40mm) long, 1.2in (30mm) wide, and high for the genus, 0.8in (20mm).* It has twenty-two ribs which are nodulose, becoming more so toward the margin. The hole is in the shape of a figure eight. White inside and out and usually carries a heavy calcareous deposit.

Macrochisma producta

A. Adams 1850 *Antilles, 1.6in (40mm) long, 0.8in (20mm) wide.* It has much the same outline as *Scutus antipodes* but is relatively higher with a long, narrow, triangular opening running from the apex to within a short distance of the end. White within and without.

Megathura crenulata

Sowerby 1825 *California and the Pacific coast of Mexico, 5in (125mm) long and 3in (80mm) wide.*

A large member of the genus, it has a large oval hole which is a little off-center with a white edge. Numerous fine ridges run from the hole to the crenulated margin across concentric growth lines. Gray-brown; lighter toward the margin; interior pure white.

Diodora graeca

L. 1758 *Mediterranean to southern England, 1in (25mm) long and 18mm wide.* Synonym *D. apertura* Montagu 1803. It has radial ridges, alternate ridges being larger, and very fine concentric cords, giving a slightly reticulated effect. Pink-brown; cords white.

Megathura crenulata

Diodora graeca

25

SUPERFAMILY: PATELLACEA

Some 400 species. The limpets include two main families, Acmaeidae and Patellidae, and a third with few members, Lepetidae. The difference between the former two families is mainly in the animals – for example, the Acmaeidae have gills and the Patellidae have folds on the mantle edge which function as secondary gills. The interior of the Acmaeidae shells are porcellaneous whereas those of the Patellidae are iridescent. Herbivores.

FAMILY: ACMAEIDAE

Acmaea patina
Eschscholtz 1847 *West North America, more common in the north than the south, 2in (50mm) long and slightly less wide.*
Smooth apart from fine growth lines. Gray-green with a blue-gray patch at apex, slightly off-center; then an area where blue-gray color forms a network over base color; on outer third of shell, blue-gray forms reticulations. Interior blue-white with dark brown patch at apex and purple-brown marks around border, corresponding with ends of blue-gray rays on outer side. *A. testudinalis* Möller 1776 in the east is the same species but is smaller, more oval and has a darker brown mark inside.

Acmaea patina

A. borneensis
Reeve 1855 *North coast of Borneo, 1.6in (40mm) long and slightly less wide.*
Rather depressed. Finely striated radially. The apex, a little off-center, is chestnut-colored. The rest of the exterior is black with irregular rays of interrupted, short, white streaks. The head scar is cloudy blue, brown and white; its surround white with a blue tinge and a dark blue-black border. Until recently believed to be a *Patella*.

Acmaea borneensis

A. pileopsis
Quoy & Gaimard 1834 *North New Zealand, Cook Strait, 1in (25mm).*
Numerous small ribs; apex well forward. Red-brown speckled with white; interior with dark brown head scar surrounded by blue-white, shading into dark border streaked with red.

Acmaea pileopsis

FAMILY: PATELLIDAE

Patella longicosta
Lamarck 1819 *East South Africa, 2.8in (70mm).*
South Africa has a particularly fine variety of large and colorful Patellidae. Rough surface. Ten strong ribs end in points like a star, projecting most at the end farthest from the apex,

Patella saccharina

Patella longicosta

Patella caerulea

and smaller intermediate ribs. Dark or light brown; interior cloudy brown and white at the center, with a sharply defined border of orange, bordered by purple then a pale orange tan, and then white. Interior margin has a narrow band of dark blue. It may also be off-white with a darker head scar.

P. saccharina
L. 1758 *Japan, 1.6in (40mm).*
Like a small edition of the above. Seven major ribs and small intermediate ones. Dark brown externally; white inside with dark brown margin and dark center.

P. caerulea
L. 1758 *Mediterranean, northwest Africa, 2in (50mm).*
Rather flat and thin. Irregularly sized, rather flat ribs. Green-gray; white head scar surrounded by a translucent blue-gray through white. Ribbing shows as dark blue rays.

Patella testudinaria

Patella oculus

P. testudinaria
L. 1758 *Philippines, 3.5in (90mm).*
Oval, rather smooth, solid. Very dark, almost black, with rays of red-brown spots; white head scar. Translucent; inside the external colors show through a silvery nacreous layer

P. oculus
Born 1778 *East South Africa, 3in (80mm) long, 2.8in (70mm) wide.*
Rather thin and flat. Some eighteen ribs, not nearly as pronounced as in *P. longicosta*. Dark brown and green circular stripes. Head scar is pale pink-brown bordered with broad white band; outer third dark brown with a little pale clouding.

Patella granatina   *Patella compressa*

P. granatina

L. 1758 *South Africa's western seaboard, 3.3in (85mm) long and rather high, 1.2in (30mm).*

It has about thirty, not very developed ribs and is gray with dark brown mottling or zigzags. The interior has a very rich, deep brown head scar surrounded by a flesh-colored ring and this by an orange-brown or blue-white area edged with a pale purple-brown flecked band.

P. compressa

L. 1758 *Atlantic coast of South Africa, 4.3in (110mm) long, 2in (50mm) wide and 2in (50mm) high.*

It is compressed at the sides and the high apex is slightly forward of center and comes to a point facing forward. When resting on a flat surface, the end margins are both clear of the ground. It is finely ribbed and smooth at the apex. Pale brown-gray or gray-pink, darker toward the margin; interior white or pearly gray edged with a broad pink band.

Patella vulgata

P. vulgata

L. 1758 *The Common Limpet, west Europe, up to 2.8in (70mm).*

Its coarsely ribbed exterior is variable in grays and light browns. Inside, the white or blue head scar is surrounded by dark blue and white rays overlaid with a translucent orange nacre, which may completely obscure the underlying colors.

P. miniata

Born 1778 *South Africa, 2.4in (60mm).*

It has many ribs of varying size, generally large and small alternately. It is gray-white with radial blue-gray streaks. These colors show through the opaque nacre lining the interior except for the white head scar.

Patella miniata   Patella barbara

P. barbara

L. 1758 *East and west coasts of South Africa, 3.75in (95mm)*.
Variable; some flat and others high; some with strong ribs;
some with a few strong but numerous small ribs. White or
off-white externally; brown or red head scar.

P. cochlear

Born 1778 *East and
west coasts of South
Africa, 2.6in (65mm)*.
Pear-shaped and the
exterior is finely stri-
ated radially. White
to pale tan; the in-
terior has a light
chestnut head scar
with a dark blue
surround, a pale
blue outside this,
and an intermediate
blue outside this again;
white margin.

Patella cochlear

P. nigrolineata

Reeve 1854 *Japan, 2.4in (60mm) long
and 2in (50mm) wide*.
May be flat or high with the apex usually well forward of center. Numerous, slightly prominent, narrow, radial
ribs and weak, concentric growth
lines. Blue-green; ribs and growth
lines dark red-brown. Interior silver-
blue with the ribs showing through.
Head scar white, but may be stained
with red or dark brown.

Patella
nigrolineata

Superfamily: Trochacea

Family: Trochidae

The Trochidae or top shells, are flat-based conical shells found in tropical and temperate waters. They have a horny operculum and a nacreous interior. They inhabit the intertidal zone and shallow water and are vegetarians. Some are eaten and some used commercially.

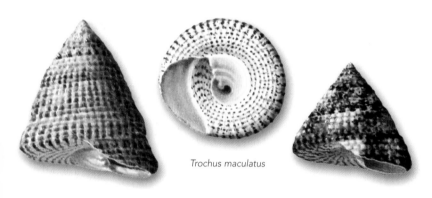

Trochus maculatus

Trochus maculatus

L. 1758 *the Indo-Pacific, up to 2.6in (65mm) high and as tall or taller than it is wide.*
Top-shaped, the shell is sculptured with rows of fine granules and may be either rounded or angular at the base. The base is more finely sculptured than the sides. The umbilicus is nacreous, lirate and edged with five blunt nodules. It is gray or white marbled with blue, green or brown. The shell is highly variable in shape and color, as the two side-view illustrations show.

Tectus dentatus

Cardinalia conus

Gmelin 1790 *Indo-Pacific, 2.8in (70mm) high.*
A heavy solid shell, the lower whorls slightly convex, and with a rounded edge to the base. Spiral rows of nodules on the early whorls disappear on the later whorls, which have strong, radial growth lines. It is white with red, flarelike marbling which becomes long, narrow dashes on the base.

Tectus dentatus

Forskäl 1775 *Northwest Indian Ocean, 3in (80mm) high.*
Finely striated radially, and wrinkled. The sutures have prominent, blunt, solid knobs, up to ten on the last whorl. The base is flat and largely polished with obsolete concentric

Cardinalia
conus

Tectus niloticus

striae near the center. The base is white with a blue-green area near the columella which is twisted forward; rest of the shell is a dull gray.

T. pyramis
Born 1778 *Indo-Pacific, up to 2.8in (70mm) high.*
This is rather shorter in relation to its height than the preceding species. The early whorls have radial lines of small nodules becoming obsolete toward the base. These whorls have small blunt nodules at the sutures, again becoming obsolete toward the base. The base is flat and spirally striated with the columella twisted forward. It is a drab gray-brown marbled with mauve, generally axially streaked.

T. niloticus
L. 1767 *Indo-Pacific, up to 6in (150mm) high.*
The largest of the genus, almost smooth on the later whorls, except for fine radial striae. Above the sutures are angular, tubular nodules on a raised band on the early whorls, both of which disappear on the later whorls. In large adults the last whorl can be swollen, the otherwise straight side becoming concave at the bottom. The base has fine growth lines and axial striae; umbilicate with a smooth columella. White with red-brown axial stripes. A common shell, it has been fished for making 'pearl' buttons and the like.

Tectus pyramis

Maurea punctulata
Martyn 1784 *New Zealand, 1.6in (40mm).*
It is turbinate with spiral rows of tiny nodules, a rounded base and a smooth columella. Illustrated is *M. p. stewartiana* Oliver 1926 which is tan colored.

M. cunninghami
Griffiths & Pidgeon 1833 *New Zealand, 2in (50mm).*
It has a somewhat angular edge and spiral rows of minutely noduled striae. Early whorls are slightly concave and later ones convex. Slightly convex base has spiral lirae, minutely nodulose near the center. Smooth columella. Cream background with light brown striae; base white.

Maurea punctulata stewartiana

Tristichotrochus formosensis
Smith *Taiwan, 1.6in (40mm).*
Slightly concave sides and spiral rows of tiny nodules, the two nearest the suture being bigger. Base is sharply angulate and spirally striate, striae being finely nodulose near smooth columella. Flesh-colored, red-brown clouding and spots on sutural beading; base, the same color with red-brown clouding near columella and spotted at the edge.

Maurea cunninghami   *Tristichotrochus formosensis*

Monodonta canalifera
Lamarck 1816 *West Pacific, 1.2in (30mm).*
Turbinate with flat spiral cords and a curved tooth projecting from bottom of columella. Inside of lip white and lirate; edge of lip shows colors of exterior, dark green, green, and cream spots.

Monodonta canalifera

Tegula regina
Stearns 1892 *South California, 1.8in (45mm).*
Six or seven whorls, axially unevenly ridged, with the lower third angled outwards. Dark purple-brown; base concave with close, narrow, black, radial ribs, cream in the interstices; interior and columellar area gold; columella and the area between the gold and the outer lip is silver-white.

Calliostoma monile

Tegula regina

Calliostoma monile

Reeve 1863 *Australia, 1in (25mm).*
Rounded keel, flat sides and pointed spire. Whorls are finely striate and ridged above suture. Convex base; smooth columella with an obsolete tooth at lower end. Transparent creamy white; the sutural ridge a pure white with mauve spots almost as big as the white areas between them.

Clanculus cruciatus

Clanculus cruciatus

L. 1758 *Mediterranean to Cape Verde, 0.4in (10mm).*
Smooth with obsolete spiral ribs, final whorl inflated. Deeply umbilicate; columella has a tooth at each end, that at the top larger. Lip is strongly ridged within. Dark red-brown except on base around umbilicus where ribs become stronger and are colored with alternate pink and dark red-brown spots.

Clanculus pharonium

C. pharonium

L. 1758 T*he Strawberry Top, Indian Ocean, 1in (25mm).*
Columella ends in a tooth, and has one large and three small folds. Tooth at top of lip projects over the umbilicus. Lip is finely dentate. Spiral rows of fine rounded nodules, mostly rich pink-red, but some are pearl-colored; two rows of dark purple dots on each whorl; base similar, but there is an area round columella and inside lip which is white and ribbed.

Chrysostoma paradoxum

Chrysostoma paradoxum

Born 1780 *Indo-Pacific, 1in (25mm).*
Low spire and large body whorl. Smooth with a shallow groove below the suture. Columella and its callus, aperture and interior all rich orange-gold; rose-brown irregularly flecked with cream.

Oxystele sinensis

Gmelin 1790 *South Africa, 1.2in (30mm).*
Rather flattened with large, inflated body whorl and rather rough surface. No umbilicus. Body whorl deep blue-black, earlier whorls green-yellow; base gray; rose shading to white on smooth columellar edge.

Oxystele sinensis

Monodonta lineata

Monodonta lineata

da Costa 1778 *Great Britain to northwest Africa, 1in (25mm) high and slightly narrower.*
Heavy and coarse, with rough grained surface. Body whorl swollen and penultimate whorl to a lesser extent. Rounded keel; umbilicus sealed with a callus. Apex often worn away in adults, the nacreous interior showing. Columella has a blunt tooth. Dark brown with very small tan flecks; columella white; inside lip dark brown backed by white; interior nacreous.

Umbonium giganteum

Lesson 1831 *Japan, 1.8in (45mm) across.*

Flat with rounded keel and smooth bar faint striae near bottom of last two whorls. Convex base has no umbilicus but has an umbilical callus. Pale blue-green with row of purple dashes below suture, becoming paler on body whorl; keel white with oblique, radial, purple stripes showing as a white and purple band at bottom of early whorls.

Umbonium giganteum

Umbonium moniliferum

U. moniliferum

Lamarck 1804 *Japan, 0.8in (20mm).*
Shaped like preceding species. Cream, heavily patterned with red-brown dots and flecks; base and columellar callus brown. Illustration shows a view of the base.

U. vestiarium

L. 1758 *Indian Ocean and East Indies, 0.5in (12mm).*
Shaped like preceding species. Pattern and color very variable – greens, browns, grays, purples, in dots, spiral lines, tiny axial flames, etc.

Umbonium vestiarium

Cittarium pica

L. 1758 *West Indies, 3in (80mm) high and wide.*
Solid, heavy with rough uneven surface. The shell has a shallow channel below suture, rounded keel and is deeply umbilicate. Smooth columella with a heavy callous deposit surrounding half the umbilicus and a deep notch in the middle. Black with white marbling; base around umbilicus white; interior silvery-white.

Cittarium pica

Angaria delphinula

L. 1758 *Indo-Pacific, 2.8in (70mm) wide.*
The members of the genus *Angaria* have the thin horny opercula of Trochidae but are included by some with the

Turbinidae. Solid, heavy with depressed spire. The encircling, coarse spiral cords have hollow spines on shoulder row, two rows of small ones on periphery, and on base around and inside deep umbilicus. Gray; spines sometimes darker; aperture pearly.

Angaria delphinula

Angaria distorta

Angaria distorta

A. distorta

L. 1758 *South China Sea, 2.6in (65mm) wide, 2in (50mm) high.*
Heavy, solid with large body whorl. Angulate at shoulders with almost flat area from suture to shoulder which carries blunt knobs. Coarse, uneven spiral ridges, some nodulose, on body whorl. Deep umbilicus, opening to which is rough, almost spinous. Various shades of gray from white to black, over pale pink base color.

A. melanacantha

Reeve 1842 *The Imperial Delphinula, Philippines, 1.6in (40mm) high, 2.2in (55mm) wide including spines.*
Sunken spire; suture disappears near aperture when body whorl no longer touches earlier whorl. Small, nodulose spiral ridges and a row of long upward and inward curving spines on shoulder. Six other rows of spines vary in length from row to row and line the umbilicus. Various shades of brown; nacreous, round aperture.

FAMILY: STOMATELLIDAE

Mostly small, they sometimes resemble the Haliotidae in having a depressed spire, large body whorl and aperture, but without perforations. Interior is nacreous. There are about fifty species.

Angaria melanacantha

Pseudostomatella decolorata

Gould 1848 *Philippines, 1.4in (35mm) long, 1.2in (30mm) high.*
Four whorls, the last greatly expanded, with very fine ridges showing more strongly on penultimate whorl. Wide aperture and smooth columella. Pale brown to green; ridges carrying small arrowhead-shaped white marks; alternate dark and light blotches below suture; white crescent-shaped callous area beside columella.

Pseudostomatella decolorata

FAMILY: TURBINIDAE

Mostly fairly large and medium-sized shells, and turbinate as the name suggests. They can be distinguished from the Trochidae to which they are somewhat similar by the calcareous operculum which is flat on the side attached to the animal, and usually spherical, but sometimes with sculpture, on the exterior side.

Turbo marmoratus

L. 1758 *East Indies and Australia,*
up to 8in (200mm).

The largest of the family, it is solid and heavy. The body whorl is very expanded and has three ridges carrying blunt knobs; that nearest the apex very angular and raised, a small one on the middle of the whorl, and one near the base, also angular. The columella is smooth and in adults has a large, rough, wavy fasciole. It is green or brown-green with spiral lines of light green and tan, and on the early whorls lines of dark green and white blotches of varying widths; a band of the same colors below the suture; the interior is nacreous.

Turbo marmoratus

T. cornutus

Lightfoot 1790 *Japan, 3.5in (90mm) high.*
It has four large ridges and about three small ones on each whorl, all becoming obsolete on the body whorl on which the outer two of the large ridges develop hollow horns, growing larger nearer the aperture. It also has coarse growth lines, a wide simple mouth and smooth columella. It is green and brown, the color changing along the growth lines; interior and columella are nacreous with a white area bordering the columella.

Turbo cornutus

T. rugosa

L. 1758 *Mediterranean, Portugal, Azores and Canaries, 1.4in (35mm) high, 1.8in (45mm) wide.*
It bears nodulose spiral ribs and a row of rectangular knobs below the suture, arranged radially. Light brown; the simple columella which is silvery like the interior, is surrounded by a scarlet, callous area.

Turbo rugosa

T. sarmaticus

L. 1758 *South Africa, 2.6in (65mm) high, 3in (80mm) wide.*
The largest South African turbo, it has a large body whorl, two spiral rows of nodules on the shoulder and other uneven ridges. It is dull brown, covered by a green periostracum with one black band above the suture, a second on the inside of the outer lip, and a third bordering the top of the columellar area dividing the nacreous interior from the cream color of the shiny columella; columella bordered by a rich red callous area and pustulate operculum (illustrated) is creamy white.

T. (Ninella) torquata

Gmelin 1791 *Australia, 4.3in (110mm) wide, 2.8in (70mm) high.*
Solid, heavy shell. Whorls have a carina at their widest part which disappears in the body whorl of specimens from east Australia. It has other indistinct ridges, a row of nodules on the shoulder, and is sculptured with fine close axial lamellae. Umbilicus is deep and operculum (illustrated) has somewhat ear-shaped ridges. Pale red-brown and white with some green splashes; columella, umbilicus and operculum white; interior nacreous.

Turbo torquata

Turbo sarmaticus

37

T. (Ocana) cidaris

Gmelin 1790 *East coast of South Africa,*
1.6in (40mm) high, 1.8in (45mm) wide.
Rather depressed, smooth with fine growth lines.
Smooth columella; operculum with white nodules
rather like *T. sarmaticus.* Color very variable, greens
and browns with white markings especially below
suture; spiral bands and dotted lines.

Turbo cidaris

Turbo petholatus

T. petholatus

L. 1758 *Philippines, 2.9in (75mm).*
Highly polished, variable in shape, pattern and color. Spire
more or less high; smooth columella. Various shades of
green, brown, fawn, cream and white, usually with flame-
shaped light markings below suture. Spiral rows of dark
spots and white arrowhead marks, especially evident on
lower half of body whorl; interior nacreous. Operculum is
well-known 'cat's-eye' used in jewelry. Two color varieties are
illustrated. Orange variety shows the 'cat's-eye'.

Turbo cinereus

T. (Lunella) cinereus

Born 1778 *Indo-Pacific, 1.2in (30mm) high, 1.6in (40mm) wide.*
Very depressed spire; fine spiral striae becoming fainter on
body whorl; fine growth lines. Deep umbilicus and somewhat produced siphonal canal giving a peg-top shape.
Cream, heavily mottled with dark brown with green tinge,
though less mottling round the periphery; aperture and
columella nacreous; operculum finely granulated,
white shading to dark at outer edge.

Turbo bruneus

T. (Marmarostoma) bruneus

Röding 1798 *Indo-Pacific, 2in (50mm) long, about*
1.9in (47mm) wide.
Scabrous spiral cords of uneven sizes, largest on the
shoulder giving a subangular look. Very narrow umbilicus. Cream with almost black, slightly wavy, axial flames;
columella and inside of lip nacreous bordered with white, as

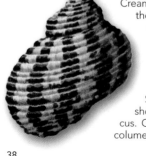

is the interior; finely granulated operculum dark purple on columellar side, becoming pale, almost white, at outer edge.

T. (M) chrysostomus

L. 1758 *Indo-Pacific, 2.8in (70mm) long, 2.4in (60mm) wide.*
Sculptured with coarsely scabrous spiral cords, which on the angular shoulder carry short, broad, open spines; cord on the periphery and another a little lower have much smaller, open spines. Nearly circular aperture; very narrow umbilicus. Creamy fawn with dark green-brown flames from suture to shoulder, and spots and dashes below; interior and columella rich golden orange, bordered with yellow and then white; pale fawn at lip. Operculum almost smooth at center becoming granulate and then striate at outer edge; dark brown in middle becoming golden orange with a white edge toward columella, and flesh-colored with a golden orange edge toward outer margin.

Turbo chrysostomus

T. (M) argyrostomus

L. 1758 *Indo-Pacific, 3.5in (90mm) long, 3in (80mm) wide.*
Bears unequal, scabrous spiral cords, one on the shoulder being especially large and one a little smaller, as far below the periphery as the large one is above, giving a flat-sided effect. May or may not be umbilicate. Pale green-cream with dark red-brown axial flame marks; aperture finely edged with green; columella and lip nacreous, silver, bordered with white; interior white; operculum green and white, granulate.

Phasianella australis

Gmelin 1791 *Southern Australia.*
There are some forty species of *Phasianella* or pheasant shells, which are also turbans. Most are small and all are delicate and richly colored. *P. australis* is the largest, 4in (100mm). Elongate with pointed spire, convex-whorls and no umbilicus. Smooth, highly polished and rather fragile. Operculum is polished, white and pointed at one end. Almost limitless variety of colors and patterns, but generally spirally marked with bands of plain color, arrowhead marks, wavy lines, dots and dashes, greens, browns, reds, pinks, yellows and white. The two illustrations show a 'banded' variety and a young shell with a subaxial flame pattern.

Turbo argyrostomus

Phasianella australis

Astraea tuber

Astraea tuber

L. 1758 *Florida and West Indies, 2in (50mm) high and wide.*
Low pointed spire with squat, rounded axial ribs running
from suture to shoulder of each whorl; knobs on periphery.
Overall diagonal rows of small nodules. Columella has
shallow channel, and fold outside it. No umbilicus.
Operculum has thick comma-shaped ridge. Green-
brown; nodules white; interior nacreous; columella white.

Astraea phoebia

A. kesteveni

Iredale 1924 *Western Australia,
1.2in (30mm) high and wide.*
Very fine spiral striae and growth lines;
base of each whorl unevenly overlaps
suture giving skirted effect. Base has
fine concentric ridges. White; silver-
white interior and columella, latter
surrounded by pale blue; smooth,
uneven operculum is purple, shading
to green-white.

Astraea kesteveni

A. phoebia

Röding 1798 *West Indies and Florida,
2.2in (55mm) wide, 1.2in (30mm) high.*
Spiral rows of small nodules becoming hollow and
subspinous toward aperture. Edge of each whorl bears
saw-tooth spines curving slightly upward. Base with spiral
rows of nodules, may or may not be umbilicate. White;
interior silvery; pale green tinge around umbilicate area.

Astraea calcar

A. calcar

L. 1758 *Philippines and Malaysia, 2in (50mm) wide,
0.8in (20mm) high.*
Depressed spire; low, blunt axial riblets; periphery
of each whorl has long, blunt, dark-tipped spines;
suture of last whorl may be deeply indented. Base
with fine, spiral, scabrous ridges and no umbilicus.
White; white columella surrounded by yellow-green;
interior yellow-green; aperture has orange tinge; band
of white between.

A. tuberosa

Philippi *Indonesia and Malaysia, 1in (25mm) high and wide.*
Low axial riblets; constricted a little below suture. Periphery
has two rows of small spines. Base with spiral rows of fine
lamellae, no umbilicus. White; interior and columella nacreous, pale lavender area around
columella; faintly pustulate operculum, dull
purple, white tinge at edge.

Astraea stellare

Astraea tuberosa

A. stellare
Gmelin 1791 *Australia, 1.2in (30mm) high, 1.8in (45mm) wide.*
Fine spiral ridges; low, small axial riblets. Base of each whorl
has blunt hollow spines open from below. Base has spiral
ridges. White; interior and columella silver-white, latter
bordered by opalescent blue area.

A. heliotropium
Martyn 1784 *New Zealand in*
deep water, 2.8in (70mm)
high, 4.75in (120mm) wide.
Convex whorls with small,
uneven, wavy, scabrous,
spiral ridges; edge
of each whorl
with flat, triangu-
lar, hollow spines
curving up at tips.
Base has five spiral rows of
small, lamellated spines, within which are axial lamellae running into deep open umbilicus. Gray; base light tan;
interior silvery; columella white; operculum ear-shaped,
white, with yellow-green tinge at wide end.

Astraea
heliotropium

Cookia aureola
Hedley 1907 *Queensland, Australia, 2.9in*
(75mm) wide, 2in (50mm) high.
Convex whorls bear oblique rows of small
nodules and short, axial, low, blunt ribs
below suture; final whorl and some of
penultimate whorl carry short, triangular, hollow
spines. Base has spiral, scabrous ridges. Dull brick
red; columella white surrounded by rich golden
orange; interior nacreous.

Cookia
aureola

Guildfordia yoka
Jousseaume *Japan,*
100mm wide including spines,
1.2in (30mm) high.
Slightly pustulate; growth lines; upper
edge of lip 'S'-shaped. Periphery of body
whorl bears nine, long, backward-curved,
hollow spines. Convex base;
shallow umbilicus; white
callus. Light brown; base
paler; columella, interior
nacreous; operculum ear-
shaped, white, finely striate
from an eccentric growth point.

Guildfordia yoka

SUPERFAMILY: NERITACEA

FAMILY: NERITIDAE

Generally small with large body whorl, depressed spire, semicircular aperture. Columella has two or more teeth; callous parietal area is smooth, pustulate or ribbed. Operculum is close-fitting with small projection, locking behind columella, holding it in place. They live in tropical and subtropical areas, in deep or brackish water in mangrove swamps, rivers and seas; on rock, coral and seaweed. Several hundred species. Vegetarians.

Smaragdia souverbiana

Montrouzier *South Africa and Mauritius, 0.9in (22mm).*
Smooth columella with nine teeth, two outer ones large. Finely striate. White or yellow; dark zigzags; parietal area, interior white.

Smaragdia souverbiana

Nerita tessellata

Gmelin 1791 *West Indies, Florida, 0.8in (20mm).*
Broad, spiral cords; two columellar teeth. Black, spotted with dark blue and white; parietal area white, pustulate; operculum black.

N. lineata

Nerita tessellata

Gmelin 1791 *Indo-Pacific, 1.6in (40mm).*
Depressed; spiral cords. Shiny parietal area, underlying plicae. Indented columella has four teeth; lip has twenty, fine teeth. Spiral cords black; interstices dull pink; parietal area yellow; interior cream; operculum with fine granules, purple-green.

N. undata

L. 1758 *Indo-Pacific, 1.6in (40mm).*
Flat, spiral cords; narrow interstices. Plicate parietal area; columella has three teeth and lip has twenty short ridges. Variable color, usually cream, dark green or brown, flames or spiral rows of dashes; sometimes uniformly dark purple-black; parietal area, columella, lip, interior, white.

Nerita lineata

Nerita undata

Nerita textilis

N. textilis

Gmelin 1791 *East Africa, 1.6in (40mm).*
Flat spire; coarse, spiral cords; growth lines. Pustulate parietal area; two columellar teeth; eighteen, long teeth on lip. White; dark blue dashes on cords; parietal area white, green-yellow stain; blue-black, pustulate operculum.

Nerita exuvia

N. exuvia

L. 1758 *Indo-Pacific, 1in (25mm).*
Fifteen, flat, broad-topped ridges overlapping deep channels. Pustulate parietal area; three columellar teeth; twenty long teeth on lip. Ridges beige; channels black; wavy, cream, axial lines; parietal area, interior, lip, dull cream-beige.

N. albicilla

L. 1758 *Indo-Pacific, 1.2in (30mm).*
Elongate; rough growth lines; flat, spiral ribs. Pustulate parietal area; four columellar teeth; dentate lip. Cream or green marbled with dark brown, black or orange; parietal area, lip, pale green; columella, interior, white; pustulate, green operculum.

Nerita albicilla

N. planospira

Anton 1839 *Indo-Pacific, 1.4in (35mm).*
Flat spire; shouldered with spiral cords, deep interstices. Lip starts beyond apex and behind parietal area, which is pustulate and plicate; four columellar teeth. Gray-black maculated with red-brown; lip, interior, columella, parietal area, white; latter with purple spot posteriorly.

N. polita

L. 1758 *Indo-Pacific, 1.6in (40mm).*
Elongate; fine growth lines, smooth parietal area and four or five columellar teeth. Cream, white, green, marbled or lined with brown, green or orange; smooth, green operculum.

Nerita polita

Nerita planospira

Neritina paralella

Röding 1798 *Japan, China, 0.8in (20mm).*
Thin, inflated; fine growth lines; ten columellar teeth; smooth lip. Variable, generally black, axial, wavy lines over olive-brown; smooth, gray operculum.

N. communis

L. 1758 *Philippines, 0.8in (20mm).*
Similar to preceding species, but shorter spire. Color and markings in almost limitless variations.

Neritina communis

Neritina paralella

43

Superfamily: Littorinacea

Family: Littorinidae

The periwinkles are small to medium, occasionally umbilicate and have a smooth columella and horny operculum. They live on rocks, mangroves and seaweed in intertidal areas. Tropical to temperate regions. Vegetarians.

Littorina neritoides

Littorina neritoides

L. 1758 *Mediterranean, UK to Madeira, 0.25in (7mm).*
Pointed spire. Generally olive-gray; purple-brown spiral band; dark aperture.

Littorina littorea

L. littoralis

L. 1758 *North Atlantic from the Mediterranean to New England, 0.6in (15mm).*
Fine growth lines. Variable color, yellows, reds, browns and greens; plain, banded or hatched; columella white; interior and lip brown.

Littorina littoralis

L. littorea

L. 1758 *Same area as above, 1in (25mm).*
Fine, spiral striae and more or less coarse growth lines. Generally dark brown to black, but also green, dark yellow or red, usually in spiral bands; columella white; interior choc-olate. The common European Winkle which has spread across the Atlantic.

L. melanostoma

Gray 1839 *Indian Ocean to South China Sea, 1.2in (30mm).*
Thin; angulate keel; spiral cords. Pale yellow; brown dashes; purple-brown banding; lip and interior pale yellow; upper columella dark purple-brown.

Littorina melanostoma

L. scabra

L. 1758 *Indo-Pacific and round to West Africa, 1.4in (35mm).*
Spiral cords; carinated keel showing on spire. Cream, pale gray or brown, maculated with darker brown flames on lighter background below suture; columella white; interior as exterior but white band within lip.

L. intermedia

Philippi 1845 *North Indo-Pacific, 0.6in (15mm).*
Spiral, tessellated cords and angulate periphery. Tessellations are blue-white on pale chestnut; purple-brown spire; may have darker streaks along some growth lines.

Littorina scabra

L. saxatilis

Olivi 1792 *North Europe and northeast America, 0.7in (18mm).*
Coarse growth lines; faint, spiral cords anteriorly. Yellows, reds, browns, to purple-black; plain, tessellated or banded; columella, inside lip flesh-colored.

Littorina intermedia   Littorina saxatilis   Littorina undulata

L. undulata
Gray 1839 *North Indian Ocean to Japan, 1in (25mm).*
Spiral cords. Dark or light brown dashes on cream, which
may form axial flame marks; violet columella.

Tectarius pyramidalis
Quoy & Gaimard *Japan and
China, 0.7in (18mm).*

Tectarius
pyramidalis

The genus *Tectarius* is nonumbilicate.
Spiral cords; row of nodules on
shoulder, periphery of body whorl
and on spire whorls. Blue-gray
with white nodules and chocolate aperture.

T. pagodus
L. 1758 *Indian Ocean, 2.6in (65mm).*
Coarse, uneven, flat, spiral cords; oblique,
axial cords ending in row of blunt spines; row
of smaller spines on body whorl on which
suture is formed in earlier whorls. Convex
base with spiral rows of blunt nodules and
ridges; smooth columella; spirally ridged inside
lip. Creamy white with brown-gray shading; columella
and interior cream with row of brown dashes level with
large spines.

Tectarius pagodus

Tectarius rugosus

T. rugosus
Wood 1828 *Philippines, 1in (25mm).*
Four, nodulose, spiral cords per
whorl; spiral rows of nodules on
base; interior ridged. Apex colorless; lower three rows of nodules
through white, straw yellow to
orange at lip; lower row pale pink to
dark purple; base, aperture white;
columella pale brown.

Echininus cumingii

Echininus cumingii
Philippi 1847 *Pacific, 1in (25mm).*
This genus is umbilicate and has
nodulose, spiral cords bearing short
spines. Blue-gray; umbilicate area
white; interior brown.

SUPERFAMILY: CERITHIACEA

FAMILY: TURRITELLIDAE

There are over fifty species in this family which live in the tropics in shallow, muddy places. They have a long, pointed spire with many whorls, no umbilicus and a horny operculum.

Mesalia brevialis

Turritella
crocea

Turritella
communis

Turritella
rosea

Turritella
bicingulata

Mesalia brevialis

Lamarck *Portugal to Senegal, Atlantic Islands, 1.5in (37mm).*
Solid with only slightly flattened, convex whorls and up to five ridges below the suture, the strongest anteriorly, the weakest posteriorly. It is minutely spirally striated with a curved and smooth columella and a subcircular aperture. Cream or white with light brown axial flames, generally darker below the suture.

Turritella crocea

Kiener *China Seas, 3.5in (90mm).*
Twenty or more convex but rather flattened whorls and about seven, spiral ridges with fine threads in between. Brown whorls with a pale area below the indented suture.

T. communis

Risso 1826 *Europe, 2.4in (60mm).*
Convex but flattened, with eighteen whorls and about ten, spiral ribs of varying sizes; convex base. Light brown to white.

T. rosea

Quoy & Gaimard 1834 *New Zealand, 2in (50mm).*
Flat-sided whorls and fine, spiral ridges overall, two ridges near the base of each whorl being twice as big as the others. Keel sharply angulate and base also finely ridged. Brown; lighter below suture.

T. bicingulata
Lamarck 1822 *Canary and Cape Verde Islands and west Africa, 2.6in (65mm).*
Eighteen, finely striated whorls. Constricted at the suture, then sloping out to two flattened ridges with a shallow channel between them. Cream with fine, axial, pale red-brown lines overall, but tending to disappear in the channel, and with dark purple-brown flame marks from the suture to the first ridge, and on the base which has three or four, flattened ridges.

T. duplicata
Lamarck 1816 *Indo-Pacific, 6in (150mm).*
About eighteen whorls, the early ones being convex with many, fine, spiral ridges. After the first six whorls a central ridge becomes elevated into a strong keel, most of the others tending to disappear. After about ten whorls a second elevated ridge begins to appear, but less prominently, and over the last two or three whorls both of these gradually become less conspicuous. The whorls at each end are therefore rounded and those in the middle are sharply angular. The upper half of each whorl is a medium-dark brown and the lower a pale cream-brown.

T. terebra
L. 1758 *Indo-Pacific, 5in (125mm).*
About twenty-five rounded whorls with a very thin, sharp spire. It has six sharply developed spiral ridges and fine cords in the interstices. Deep sutures; four spiral ridges on the base. Dark or light brown.

T. leucostoma
Valenciennes 1832 *Gulf of California, 4.5in (115mm).*
About twenty, flattened whorls, each with five, spiral ridges expanding from the constricted suture to the lowest ridge. Cream with many axial red-brown flames; earliest whorls dark brown.

T. gonostoma
Valenciennes 1832 *Gulf of California, 4.5in (115mm).*
About sixteen whorls; flat-sided, but beveled at each side to a constricted suture. Whorls may have fine, spiral cords or may be almost smooth. Cream with heavy, dark purple-brown mottling; on earlier whorls cream only shows at suture.

Turritella duplicata

Turritella terebra

Turritella leucostoma

Turritella gonostoma

*Architectonica
maxima*

FAMILY: ARCHITECTONICIDAE

The sundial shells, about forty species, live in tropical or sub-tropical, mostly shallow, waters. Depressed and circular, with a flat or slightly convex base. Deep, open, usually crenulated, umbilicus; small aperture and horny operculum.

Architectonica maxima

Philippi 1849 *Indo-west Pacific, 2.4in (60mm) wide.*
Convex spire and a narrow, incised suture below which is a flat ridge, a narrow groove, a second ridge and a slightly wider groove. Both ridges have numerous axial striae, deeper on early whorls, making a tessellated pattern, and are fawn or flesh-colored, with red-brown marks below the suture. These are followed by two ridges divided by a wide channel which have alternate dark red-brown and white blotches. Base from periphery inward; ridge; channel; smaller ridge; somewhat plicate, wide area; channel; finely nodulose cord; and finally a denticulate ridge lining the umbilicus. Apex mauve; base fawn, with brown radial mottling.

A. perspectiva

L. 1758 *Indo-Pacific, 2.4in (60mm).*
From deep, very narrow suture outward: narrow ridge with brown line; white band; deep very narrow groove; broad convex area with red-brown band; broad gray-brown band becoming fawn on last whorl; narrow, dotted, brown and white band; deep groove in which lower whorls form suture; small ridge white with pale-brown spots, hidden except on last whorl.

*Architectonica
perspectiva*

Overall fine, axial growth lines. Base flat or slightly convex. From periphery; ridge; channel; cord; plicate area; channel; row of nodules; groove; denticulate ridge lining umbilicus. Base fawn, with brown dots on outer ridge and inner edge of plicate area; nodules white and denticles stained brown.

A. nobilis
Röding 1798 *Central America, 1.8in (45mm).*
Like *A. maxima* except that first two ridges below suture are not divided by a groove. Where *A. maxima* is fawn, *A. nobilis* has a pink tinge.

Architectonica nobilis

A. perdix
Hinds 1844 *North Australia to Malaya and Sri Lanka, 1.2in (30mm).*
From suture outward: minutely spirally striated band; narrow groove; broad striate convex band; narrow groove; broad ridge; channel; narrow ridge hidden under suture except on last whorl. Overall fine growth lines. Broad band pinky flesh; other bands and ridges white with chestnut spots; apex mauve. Base has two ridges divided by channel at periphery; broad, smooth (excepting growth lines) area; groove; row of nodules; groove; then denticulate ridge lining umbilicus. Outer ridges flecked with brown; opaque, blue-white, broad band; white umbilical ridge.

Architectonica perdix

A. laevigatum
Lamarck 1816 *India, 1.2in (30mm).*
Five, roughly equal, flat ridges and axial growth lines overall. Top band is fawn with a few brown blotches; second and middle bands mauve toward aperture, becoming pale blue like apex, and indistinct pale brown dots; bottom bands fawn with large pale brown marks. Base sculpture as *A. perdix*, fawn with a blue tinge on broad middle area, brown radial markings near periphery.

Architectonica laevigatum

Philippia radiata
Röding 1798 *Indo-Pacific, 0.9in (23mm).*
Relatively high and smooth with obsolete, spiral striations and two, very small ridges above suture. A brown band below suture sometimes has oblique axial rays spreading from it over the white background. Rather convex base with groove at periphery and white umbilical area. Fawn-flesh with brown specks on rim.

Philippia radiata

Heliacus stramineus
Gmelin 1822 *India, Philippines, New Guinea, 1in (25mm).*
Whorls becoming rounded to an almost circular mouth; fine spiral grooves between deep narrow suture and periphery; three ridges between periphery and base; small cord between lower two ridges; spirally ridged base, rather narrow, minutely denticulate umbilicus; oblique growth lines overall. Color tan; darker at apex.

Heliacus stramineus

FAMILY: PLANAXIDAE

Small, solid, conical shells rather like the Littorinidae, and living in the same habitat. There are marine and freshwater members of the family and they are found in warm waters worldwide.

Planaxis sulcatus

Born 1780 *Indo-Pacific, 1.2in (30mm).*
Solid, heavy, high-spired and sculptured with spiral cords, about ten on the body whorl. Finely denticulate or smooth columella. It may have a narrow umbilicus. Lirate inside lip. Purple to brown with light gray or cream spots on the cords, profuse or sparse; inside of lip has brown stains.

Planaxis sulcatus

FAMILY: MODULIDAE

Somewhat similar in shape to the genus *Angaria* of the Trochidae family, they have a single tooth near the base of the columella and are narrowly umbilicate. They inhabit sandy, weedy areas.

Modulus tectum

Gmelin 1791 *Indo-Pacific, 1in (25mm).*
Solid, depressed spire, angulate shoulder with strong axial ribs. Body whorl expands rapidly to a wide mouth and has spiral ridges, some nodulose. Columella smooth, prominent tooth at bottom. Lirate interior. Dirty white, some ridges with black specks; outer edge of columella and tooth deep purple-brown; a line of the same color may run into interior at top of columella.

FAMILY: VERMETIDAE

Modulus tectum

Unusual shells which are long tubes, evenly spirally coiled at the apex and then loosely and irregularly so. The genus *Siliquaria* has a narrow opening along the top of the tube.

Vermetus tulipa

Vermetus tulipa

Chenu 1843 *Panama, west Central America., Early whorls small, 2-3mm diameter, growing to a length, if stretched, of some 2.4in (60mm).*
The whorls are acutely angulate where they are joined to the substrate. Surface of tube is wrinkled. Cream or brown with gray or brown shading.

V. arenaria

L. 1758 *Mediterranean.*
Generally fairly even spiral coils. Somewhat flattened tube with a slight ridge on the upper surface; coarsely wrinkled. Shades of gray.

V. cereus
Carpenter 1856 *Philippines.*
Rather flattened tube, smooth apart from growth lines and closely coiled. Light brown. The specimen illustrated looks remarkably like a trilobite.

V. tokyoense
Pilsbury 1895 *Japan.*
Slightly flattened tube with the end becoming free of the substrate and turning up. Rough surface. Light brown. The illustration shows the shell attached to a piece of dead coral.

Vermetus arenaria

FAMILY: SILIQUARIDAE

Vermicularia fargoi
Olsson *Florida and Caribbean.*
Tightly coiled spire; coils then open and become haphazard. Has three coils on tube, conspicuous on early coiled part but tending to disappear toward mouth. Brown, early coils paler. Sometimes found crawling about on mud.

Vermetus cereus

Siliquaria ponderosa
Mörch 1860 *Australia.*
Early whorls closely coiled then growing haphazardly. Whorls rounded except at the top where flattened. At the outer edge of this area is a narrow slit running the length of the shell except at the flattened apex. Pale tan or dirty white. The slit, or a series of holes, is common to the genus *Siliquaria.*

Vermetus tokyoense

Siliquaria ponderosa

Vermicularia fargoi

Terebralia sulcata

Terebralia palustris

FAMILY: POTAMIDIDAE

One of two families of horn shells, they are long, tapering and have many whorls, usually large apertures and horny opercula. They inhabit muddy places, mangrove swamps and estuaries, and are vegetarians.

Terebralia sulcata

Born 1778 *Indo-west Pacific, 2.4in (60mm).*
Axial ribs; spiral grooves. Expanded lip joins body over short, tubular siphonal canal. Blunt, axial rib above siphonal canal. Gray or gray-brown; tessellations darker; obsoletely lirate interior; columella and inside of lip callous, shiny and gray-brown.

T. palustris

L. 1767 *Indo-Pacific, 4.75in (120mm).*
Coarse axial ribs and three, deep, spiral grooves. Flared lip curved over short siphonal canal. Obsoletely grooved aperture; columella, parietal area and lip callous. Dark brown; interior purple-brown; lip fawn, anterior purple; parietal area and columella chocolate, latter white centrally.

Cerithidea cingulata

Gmelin 1791 *Indo-west Pacific, 2in (50mm).*
Oblique, axial ribs and two, deep grooves form three rows of blunt nodules per whorl. Lip very expanded at each end Blunt rib above siphonal canal. Nodules dirty white, interstices brown; interior white.

Cerithidea cingulata

C. obtusa

Lamarck 1822 *Indo-west Pacific, 2in (50mm).*
Small, coarse, spiral cords; axial ribs. Expanded, recurved lip; short canal; apex usually eroded. Light brown or dirty white; brown markings; interior, lip, columella white.

Telescopium telescopium

L. 1758 *Indo-west Pacific, 4in (100mm).*
Straight-sided with four, unequal, flat, spiral ridges per whorl; last whorl rounded at base which has one large, many small cords and a wide, shallow channel around the strongly twisted columella; lip extended anteriorly. Dark brown or black; interior shiny blue-black; columella mauve-brown.

FAMILY: CERITHIDAE

The other family of horn shells, they are similar but generally more colorful, and have simpler apertures. More or less distinct varices. The opercula are not circular as in Potamididae and nucleus is off-center. They generally live in clearer water among coral, and prefer sand to mud.

Cerithium nodulosum

Bruguière 1792 *Indo-Pacific, 4.75in (120mm)*.
Coarse, spiral cords; blunt, heavy nodules, eight on last whorl, one nearest aperture very swollen; three, large, nodulose cords on base. Expanded lip curves in front of short siphonal canal; lirate aperture. Columella ridges, bordering anal and siphonal canals, run into interior. White; blue-black, spiral dashes on nodules and base; interior, columella, lip, canals, white; interior sometimes with blue-black shading.

C. aluco

L. 1758 *Indo-Pacific, 3in (80mm)*.
Smooth or obsolete fine ridges and a row of six, short, blunt spines on upper part of whorls. Aperture like *C. nodulosum* except siphonal canal bent back 90° and aperture lirae obsolete. White; profuse purple flecks and blotches; lip and columella opalescent, purple flecks anteriorly.

Cerithidea obtusa

Rhinoclavis nobilis

Reeve *Philippines, 5in (130mm)*.
Straight-sided; first eight or nine whorls spirally ridged, last three of these axially ribbed, and prominent ridge at base. Expanded lip; siphonal canal recurved 90°; smooth columella; reasonably developed anal canal. Cream; profuse, small, pale tan flame marks; aperture opalescent.

| Telescopium telesopium | Cerithium nodulosum | Cerithidea aluco | Rhinoclavis nobilis |

53

R. vertegus
L. 1767 *Throughout Indo-Pacific, 2.6in (65mm).*
Solid, narrowing anteriorly; uneven, deep sutures. Spiral ribs, axial cords, obsolete on last two whorls. Few early varices; slightly expanded lip; siphonal canal at 90° to axis. Small anal canal; callous columella, central fold; shallow groove around callus. Light brown; apex, early whorls, aperture white.

R. sinensis
Gmelin 1791 *Indo-Pacific, 2.6in (65mm).*
Row of blunt nodules below suture, then spiral rows of small nodules. Fine axial and spiral threads between rows and between shoulder nodules. Axial swelling between siphonal canal and suture. Faint early varices. Expanded lip; columella with central fold; siphonal canal at 90° to axis. Cream; faint clouding, spots of purple-brown especially on large nodules; varices whitish; aperture off-white.

Rhinoclavis vertegus

R. bituberculatum
Sowerby 1865 *Western Australia, 1.8in (45mm).*
Four rows of blunt nodules on each whorl; fine axial and spiral striae between. Expanded lip; siphonal canal at 90°; columella with callus and one tooth. Flesh-colored; dark blue flecks especially on last whorl, where they form spiral lines of dashes which show on interior; aperture white.

R. asper
L. 1758 *Indo-Pacific, 2.4in (60mm).*
Three, spiral cords (four on body whorl); oblique axial ribs; sharp nodules at intersections. Lip only slightly expanded; columella with central fold; siphonal canal at 90° and almost opposite lip. Cream or white; sometimes brown stains; aperture white.

Rhinoclavis
sinensis

Rhinoclavis
bituberculatum

Rhinoclavis
asper

Rhinoclavis
fasciatus

Clypeomorus
traillii

Cerithium
erythraeonense

R. fasciatus
Bruguière 1792 *Indo-Pacific, 3in (80mm).*
Deep suture; fine, axial riblets and faint, spiral striae, both obsolete on last whorls. Slightly expanded lip. Siphonal canal bent back 90°. Callous columella has one fold. White or fawn; two or more light brown or chestnut bands obscure white; bands showing on interior and lip; columella, callus, interior, lip white.

Clypeomorus traillii
Sowerby 1855 *Indo-west Pacific, 1.2in (30mm).*
Stubby; fine, spiral striae; fine ridges, some nodulose. Early varices; expanded, thickened lip; short siphonal canal at 45°; distinct anal canal. Creamy brown; some nodules dark brown; aperture white; interior may be spotted brown.

Cerithium erythraeonense
Lamarck 1822 *Red Sea, 2.8in (70mm).*
Spiral, fine ridges; angulate whorls; ten ribs form short, pointed nodes at periphery; very large rib above siphonal canal. Expanded, thickened, crenulated lip curved to cross strong siphonal canal at almost 90°. Smooth columella; distinct anal canal. Fawn; gray-brown markings; aperture white; lip fawn.

C. caeruleum
Sowerby 1865 *Indian Ocean, 1.6in (40mm).*
Fine spiral striae; rows of nodules on body whorl, two on earlier whorls; one row with larger nodules than others forming angulate shoulder. Blue-gray; apex pink; nodules, lip and short, backward-curved siphonal canal, dark purple-brown; rest of aperture white.

C. vulgatum
Bruguière 1792 *Mediterranean, west Africa, 2.9in (75mm).*
Fine, deep, spiral striae; axial ribs; restricted below suture, then angular; ribs form short spines at the angle. Slightly flared lip; distinct anal canal; short, slightly recurved siphonal canal. Variable. Gray or brown; wavy, axial, darker lines; interior similar; columella white, color showing through.

C. ruppellii
Philippi 1848 *Red Sea, 1.8in (45mm).*
Narrow. Three spiral rows of nodules, five on body, striae between. Early, white varices; expanded lip; long, straight canal. Pale gray-brown; aperture white; interior gray-brown.

Tymphanotonus aurita
Möller *west Africa, 2.2in (55mm).*
Finely spirally ridged with rows of rectangular, oblique nodules in middle of whorls, and rectangular aperture. Chocolate-brown; nodules often worn to white.

Cerithium caeruleum

Cerithium vulgatum

Cerithium ruppellii   *Tymphanotonus aurita*

SUPERFAMILY: EPITONIACEA

FAMILY: EPITONIIDAE

The wentletraps or staircase shells, are found worldwide, often among soft coral or sea anemones, in shallow water. There are some 200 species. They are rather delicate, conical, with many, often loosely coiled, whorls, on which are slightly oblique, axial lamellae or varices which were formed as the reflected outer lips at earlier pauses in the growth of the animal. Some are umbilicate. They are usually white, but a few have brown tinges or markings. Their opercula are horny, with few whorls, and the nucleus is nearly central.

| Cirsotrema zelebori | Epitonium multistriatum | Epitonium lamellosum | Epitonium pallasi | Epitonium perplexa |

Cirsotrema zelebori

Dunker 1866 *New Zealand, 0.9in (22mm)*.
Thin with about nine whorls which have oblique, rather closely set lamellae, fifteen per whorl. There are low, spiral ridges, nine on the last whorl, which form blunt nodules on the lamellae. White.

Epitonium multistriatum

Epitonium scalare

Say 1829 *South-east USA, 0.5in (12mm)*.
Narrow and very pointed; about fourteen, axial lamellae per whorl. Shining white.

E. lamellosum

Lamarck 1822 *West Indies, 0.8in (20mm)*.
Eight whorls, twelve lamellae on last whorl. A pale fawn, darker at the suture; lamellae, apex and aperture white.

E. pallasi

Kiener 1838 *Australia, Philippines, China Seas and Mauritius, 1in (25mm)*.
Rather broad at the base compared with the preceding species. About eight whorls often joined only by the lamellae, of which there are about ten per whorl. It has a deep umbilicus. Shiny pale orange-brown apex; lamellae and aperture white; interior pale orange-brown.

E. scalare
L. 1758 *East Asia and Australia, 2.6in (65mm).*
The Precious Wentletrap, for long prized by collectors, is the largest of the genus, about half as wide as it is high. Whorls joined only by the lamellae, eight per whorl. A deep umbilicus. Very pale flesh color; lamellae white. This species was once very rare and fetched high prices. Copies were made in China of rice paste, which are reported to have deceived collectors. If they were on the market today they would probably fetch a higher price for their interest's sake than the real shell.

Epitonium dubia

E. perplexa
Pease 1860 *West Pacific and Indian Ocean, 1.6in (40mm).*
About seven whorls with twelve lamellae per whorl. White or pale fawn; may have a purple band below the suture after the early whorls; lamellae, apex and aperture are white.

E. dubia
Sowerby 1844 *Australia and East Indies, 1.6in (40mm).*
Very thin and delicate. Deep suture; expanded whorls; minutely spirally striate; small lamellae on the early whorls become thin, small ridges on later whorls. White.

Clathrus clathrus   *Clathrus clathrus*

Clathrus clathrus
L. 1758 *The Common Wentletrap, Mediterranean to the North Sea, 1.4in (35mm).*
Rather narrow; about fifteen whorls with nine lamellae per whorl. It is cream or fawn in color. Often there are two or three, spiral, pale purple-brown bands which show most clearly where they cross the lamellae. Both color forms are illustrated.

Amaea raricostata

Amaea raricostata
Lamarck 1822 *Mauritius and Sri Lanka, 1in (25mm) high and over 0.8in (20mm) wide.*
Stubby; cancelled by fine axial ribs and spiral cords. The shell has occasional, heavy, thick varices especially on the last whorl. White.

A. magnifica
Sowerby 1847 *China Seas, up to 4in (100mm).*
A very thin, delicate, and high-spired shell. Spirally finely ribbed, with low, thin and irregularly spaced lamellae. White with a mauve apex. This is a relatively rare shell and is a collectors' item.

Amaea magnifica

57

Janthina globosa

Janthina exigua

Janthina janthina

FAMILY: JANTHINIDAE

The violet snails live in all warm-water seas. Very thin-shelled, they produce a float of gelatinous bubbles to which they remain attached and move where the winds and currents take them. They live on plankton and emit a violet fluid when attacked. About thirty species.

Janthina globosa

Swainson 1822 *1.6in (40mm)*.
Globose with rounded whorls, deep suture, depressed spire and extended columella. Wide lip with a restriction in the middle which shows in the V-shaped growth lines; fine spiral striae. Violet spire, paler on last half of body whorl, very pale just below suture.

J. exigua

Lamarck 1816 *0.8in (20mm)*.
Relatively high spire; whorls with V-shaped striae, the 'V' lining up with an indentation on lip; long columella; lip produced anteriorly. Purple; white band below suture.

J. janthina

L. 1758 *1.6in (40mm)*.
Globose; angulate whorls; depressed spire; fine growth lines. Flat base, spirally striate; columella produced and twisted anteriorly. Early whorls pale blue, body whorl white; base, columella violet.

SUPERFAMILY: HIPPONICACEA

Capulus
ungaricus

FAMILY: CAPULIDAE

Cup-shaped, they are parasites, preying largely on other mollusks.

Capulus ungaricus

L. 1758 *Europe, 2in (50mm)
wide, 1.2in (30mm) high, but variable.*
Hooked apex points downward and inward; radial striae; coarse, uneven growth lines. Thick, dark brown periostracum; dirty white; interior pink.

SUPERFAMILY: CALYPTRAECEA

FAMILY: CALYPTRAEIDAE

The slipper limpets often have a shelf or cuplike projection internally. Very variable in shape, depending on their substrate.

Crepidula
fornicata

Crepidula fornicata

L. 1758 *The American Slipper Limpet, North America and accidentally introduced to Europe around 1900, 2in (50mm)*.
Recurved apex; strong growth lines; about half the aperture

covered by 'shelf'. Dirty white, fawn and cream. Very variable. Often grouped one on top of another.

Crucibulum lignarium
Broderip 1834 *Indonesia, China Seas and west tropical America, 1in (25mm).* High and cup-shaped with coarse growth lines and radial striae. Interior cup attached at apex and on one side. Light brown.

Crucibulum lignarium

Crucibulum auriculatum

C. auriculatum
Gmelin 1791 *Central America, 1.2in (30mm).*
Round and depressed with pointed, recurved apex and spiral threads covered with short, sharp spines. Cup attached at one side; ear-shaped. Creamy white with pale purple-brown axial rays more clearly seen in the shiny interior.

C. scutellatum
Gray 1828 *Gulf of California and Panama, 2.6in (65mm).*
Coarse large radial ribs. Cup attached at apex. Brown; pink interior.

C. extinctorium
Lamarck 1822 *Malaysia and China Seas, 1.6in (40mm).*
Very variable, flat or elevated; sharp apex, usually recurved; coarse spiral striae. White with very pale pink rays. Illustrated attached to a *Natica*.

Crucibulum extinctorium

Trochita trochiformis
Born 1778 *West Central America to Chile, 2.4in (60mm) wide and 1.2in (30mm) high.*
Depressed and conical. Whorls carry coarse, oblique, radial ribs. Thin, wavy-edged aperture runs from center to near edge of shell, almost opposite end of last whorl. Pale brown flesh; base lighter and shiny.

Crucibulum scutellatum

Trochita trochiformis

FAMILY: XENOPHORIDAE

The carrier shells owe their popular name to the animals' habit of attaching empty shells – if bivalves, inner side upward – pieces of coral, stones or grains of sand, to their shells. In most species this only occurs during their young state and the attachments are only on early whorls. In others such as *X. pallidula* and *X. neozelanica* it continues throughout growth. They live in tropical seas, in shallow and deep water; those from shallow water are the most enthusiastic 'collectors'. They are active and move quite quickly.

Xenophora pallidula

Xenophora pallidula

Reeve 1843 *Japan, Philippines and South China Sea, 4in (100mm).*
Conical; spiral striae; coarse growth lines. Slightly concave base, free of any attachments, has coarse growth lines – almost folds – and narrow umbilicus which may be covered by callus on inside lip. White or light brown; base light brown and cream; aperture callus rich brown fading to white at edge.

X. crispa

Koenig 1831 *Mediterranean, 1.8in (45mm).*
Somewhat depressed and narrowly umbilicate, with oblique growth lines and generally axial, small, wavy riblets. Wavy, uneven periphery. Base has oblique radiating rows of small nodules; striated around umbilicus. Shells, stones and so on attached to suture and periphery. Cream; base cream to fawn, darker around umbilicus.

Xenophora crispa

X. corrugata

Reeve 1843 *Indo-west Pacific, 1.6in (40mm).*
Depressed with deep suture and uneven surface like rough hewn marble. Base has small, oblique, radiating ridges with coarse growth lines, some dark brown. Usually hidden under empty shells, stones etc.

Xenophora calculifera

Xenophora corrugata

X. calculifera

Reeve 1842 *Japan to Philippines, 2.8in (70mm).*
Rather thin with uneven surface, fine oblique striae. Suture barely perceptible where not obscured by attachments which are small and only on the suture. Base cancellate with small, radial, curved ribs and spiral striae. Wide, deep umbilicus. Cream-gray, yellow staining; base the same.

Tugurium indicus

Gmelin 1791 *Australia, 3.3in (85mm).*
Very thin, delicate, rather depressed,
with suture only a faint ridge. Outer
edge of shell wafer thin. Surface is
sculptured with close-set, fine,
radial riblets which are crossed by
oblique, radial, uneven striations.
Small pieces of stone debris
attached only to first two or three
whorls. Concave, deeply umbilicate
base. Outer edge of aperture forms a
flat ridge, about 2mm wide, with fine
growth lines/folds running from ridge into
umbilicus. Outside the ridge is a thin, smooth,
shiny, irregular skirt, very jagged at edge. Suture, visible
through skirt, is further from apex than ridge of lip. Cream to
pale fawn; base ridge to umbilicus white; skirt fawn.

Tugurium indicus

Tugurium exutus

T. exutus

Reeve 1842 *west Pacific,
1.8in (45mm).*
Depressed and similar to
O. helvacea but sculptured
with fine, oblique, axial
ridges; broad, wavy ribs run
at 90° to these. Ridge on base
has four rows of minute
nodules. Open umbilicus is
carinated with striae running into it; ridge to carina smooth
with a few faint concentric threads and growth lines.
No attachments, or a few grains of sand near apex. Fawn,
darker at apex.

Stellaria solaris

L. 1767 *Philippines, 2.9in (75mm).*
Low spire; somewhat convex
whorls with hollow, protruding
spines at periphery of whorls,
hiding suture. Surface uneven
with fine, generally spiral
threads; oval aperture.
Base concave and umbili-
cate with strong, wavy,
uneven, nodulose, oblique,
radial cords. Ends of spines
curve along edge of base,
forming continuous strong
ridge. Light brown; aperture
smooth, shiny, darker brown.

Stellaria solaris

61

*Tibia
fusus*

SUPERFAMILY: STROMBACEA

FAMILY: STROMBIDAE

The family includes the genera *Strombus, Lambis, Tibia* and *Terebellum. Tibia* contains only six species and two in the subgenus *Rimella*. All are from the Taiwan to Red Sea area. None are common, though they may not be rare locally. Most are collectors' items. *Tibia serrata* Perry 1811 is a 'lost' shell – its locality is unknown. They are high-spired, long, have an extended siphonal canal which is generally smooth, except in *Rimella*. Sculpture is confined to lip and early whorls, and color to shades of brown. They generally inhabit deep waters.

Tibia fusus

L. 1758 *Philippines, 8in (200mm) long and 1.4in (35mm) broad.* Very high-spired with eighteen whorls. Early whorls have narrow radial ribs and spiral ridges. Ridges disappear first, about six whorls from the base, the ribs three whorls later. Last three whorls are smooth apart from fine growth striae and spiral grooves on base of body whorl. Very long, narrow, delicate siphonal canal. Lip has five, fingerlike projections outlined by a low ridge which forms a half circle on penultimate whorl and disappears at other end on siphonal canal. Columella with tooth posteriorly and callus extending under curved end of the ridge, together forming anal canal. Horny, leaf-shaped operculum. Shiny tan-fawn, lighter at apex; ridge on the fingers red-brown. Rather rare shell and highly prized by collectors.

T. martinii

Marrat 1877 *Philippines and Taiwan, 6in (150mm).*
Rare. Lightest of the genus; microscopic axial and spiral striae; slightly constricted at suture. Five, short, stubby projections – two or three obsolete ones – on lip, outlined by small ridge which continues on siphonal canal. Light brown; some darker shading, especially below suture; fingers white; ridge red-brown; columella and callous inside lip white; interior gray-brown. A form, *melanocheilus* A. Adams 1854, has a broad purple-brown band inside lip and other minor differences.

T. insulae-chorab

Röding 1798 *Indian Ocean from Red Sea to Philippines, 6.25in (160mm) long, 1.8in (45mm) wide.*
Early whorls axially ribbed with microscopic spiral striae between, later whorls smooth. Short siphonal canal often curves up slightly toward aperture; five, short, stubby fingers and a ridge from siphonal canal outlining lip, fingers, siphonal and anal canals. In the form *curta* Sowerby 1842 this ridge ends on penultimate whorl instead of on antepenultimate whorl (see illustration). Both forms have strong columellar callus, with blunt tooth posteriorly, continuing toward apex forming anal canal with ridge. Shiny light

Tibia powisi

brown; form *curta* with darker band below suture; axially rather streaky.

T. powisi
Petit 1842 *Japan and Philippines, 2in (50mm).* Smallest of the genus with ten whorls. Spiral ridges with interstices pitted. It has the usual five fingers, short siphonal canal and very short anal canal. Lip has deep furrow behind fingers. Columella with small callus, inner edge of lip has thick, callous ridge with lirae which continue into aperture. Light brown, some purple areas; columella, interior, ridge inside lip, white.

Rimella (Varicospira) cancellata

Rimella (Varicospira) cancellata
L. 1758 *Indian Ocean, Philippines, north Australia, 1.4in (35mm).* Solid with axial ribs and spiral grooves giving it a cancellate sculpture. Short siphonal canal. Thickened crenulate lip, backed by deep furrow, is produced toward apex over two or three whorls. Columellar callus follows lip to form long anal canal. Irregularly placed varices. Lirate lip and interior. Cream, exterior of lip, varices red-brown; columella, interior of lip white.

T. (R.) crispata (not illustrated)
Sowerby
From the same area as and very similar to *R. cancellata* but extension of lip turns back sharply.

form curta

Tibia martinii

Tibia insulae-chorab

GENUS: STROMBUS

The conch shells are found throughout the tropics. They are large and small, generally solid, with an expanded body whorl, narrow aperture, thickened outer lip and short siphonal canal. A characteristic of these shells is the `stromboid notch', an indentation near the bottom of the outer lip through which one of a pair of tentacles, each carrying a well-developed eye, protrudes. The operculum is horny, long and narrow, with the nucleus at the anterior end. The foot is very muscular and can turn them over or move them along remarkably quickly. They live in shallow water on sand or sandy mud and are vegetarians. Some are edible.

Strombus pugilis

L.1758 *The West Indian Fighting Conch, Caribbean, 3in (80mm).* It has about eight whorls with about nine short spines on the shoulder of the body whorl projecting from just above the suture in earlier whorls; those on the penultimate are longest. All but last two whorls have spiral cords and blunt ribs which end in the spines. Spire concave and about a quarter of the length of the shell. There are a few spiral cords from the suture to the spines and at the base of the body whorl. Outer lip thickened and projected at posterior end; strong stromboid notch; short siphonal canal; columella, fasciole and inside lip callous. Light tan, almost white at apex; red edge to siphonal canal; callus golden brown; interior white.

Strombus canarium
form turturella

Strombus pugilis

S. alatus

Gmelin 1791 *The Florida Fighting Conch, Florida and adjoining coasts.*

Same size as *S. pugilis* and rather similar in shape but the outer lip is not projected, and the spines are reduced to five short ones on the latter half of body whorl and elsewhere to blunt knobs. The spiral cords which extend from the apex to the suture of the final whorl are stronger. The color, however, is a rich chocolate streaked with white on the spire; white at the apex; fasciole and inner edge of lip orange-red; parietal callus and columella dark red-brown; interior brown-mauve.

S. canarium

L. 1758 *India to northeast Australia, the Philippines and Japan., Variable in size up to 4in (100mm) but generally nearer 2in (50mm).*

Spire may be short and smooth or high with angular whorls, cancellate sculpture and varices. Body whorl striated at the base and either smoothly rounded or with faint ridges and shouldered; both varieties illustrated. Swollen outer lip; stromboid notch not strong; short siphonal canal; callous and very shiny columella. Color either plain white with pale fawn stains and axial streaks, or dark brown on intermediate colors; it may have an overlying fine network of darker brown; interior and columella white; parietal wall sometimes metallic looking. The plain color form has been named *turturella* Röding 1798 and *isabella* Lamarck 1822.

Strombus canarium

Strombus alatus

S. gigas

L. 1758 *The Queen Conch, Florida and the West Indies, 12in (300mm).*

Moderate spire. Short, strong spines at the shoulders of the whorls. Coarse, flat, spiral ridges; spiral cords; axial striae; coarse axial ribs and folds especially on the parietal wall. Flared lip is produced posteriorly to almost level with the apex, and lip edge is wavy and simple. Narrow but deep stromboid notch. Heavily callous, smooth columella. Wide and glazed parietal area. Short, open and recurved siphonal canal. Cream and white; aperture a rich, shining rose pink with yellow shading. This species is taken in huge quantities for food and sometimes produces a pink pearl.

Strombus gigas

S. latissimus
L. 1758 *West Pacific, up to 8in (200mm)*.
A remarkably heavy solid shell. The carinate early whorls
have small blunt knobs, which on the penultimate and body
whorls become fewer in number, larger and very rounded,
one on the shoulder farthest from the
lip particularly so. The thick lip
flares out beyond the apex,
and opposite the columel-
la is thickened even more
into a ridge, sometimes
forming an overhang.
The stromboid notch is
well toward the anterior
and is narrow and deep.
Heavily callous columel-
la. It is cream heavily mottled with brown, generally
axially. Interior and inside
of lip dirty white, col-
umellar callus light
brown as is the area of
the lip on and outside
the ridge.

S. goliath
(not illustrated)
Schröter 1805 *Brazil,
up to 12.5in (320mm)*.
The largest of the strombs.
Heavy with rather short, concave, pointed spire. Adpressed
suture. Inflated body whorl with rather
rounded shoulders carrying five, heavy,
blunt knobs on the dorsal side, and five much
smaller ones on the ventral side under the parietal
glaze. This glaze covers the ventral side of the body whorl.

Strombus latissimus

The dorsal surface is somewhat malleate with coarse, broad,
flat, spiral ridges having shallow, fairly narrow grooves
between. The lip flares very widely, the edge making a
smooth, sweeping curve, and the posterior end forming a
nearly perfect half-circle, and extending well beyond the
spire to hide it completely from the ventral side; it ends
posteriorly on the suture above the body whorl. The
aperture is relatively narrow. The cross-section of the inside
of the lip is almost 'L' shaped, there being a strong ridge
parallel to the straight, smooth columella. A narrow groove
runs from the posterior end of the columella across the top
of the parietal area where the lip joins the body whorl.
Stromboid notch is almost nonexistent. Short, open and
slightly twisted siphonal canal. Cream with axial, wavy,
purple-brown lines on early whorls; aperture and callus white
to pink-white; interior darker. Periostracum is tan and shows
faintly through the parietal glaze.

S. galeatus

Swainson 1823 *Gulf of California to northwest South America, 8in (200mm).*

It has a pointed, concave, rather depressed spire, with spiral striae and axial riblets. These disappear on the last whorls giving way to broad, rather flat, spiral ribs. The lip is expanded and the stromboid notch not particularly well developed. The body whorl is white, the earlier whorls orange or brown; interior brown and orange. Young specimens have brown or orange mottling or bands and the interior is white. The shell has a thick, brown periostracum. The animal is popular as food, and it is fished in large numbers in the Gulf of California. It is closely allied to the Brazilian species. *S. goliath* (see page 67).

S. costatus

Gmelin 1791 *The Milk Conch, West Indies and Florida, 7in (175mm).*

Very solid and heavy. Crenellated spire with shouldered whorls and two spiral cords above the suture and below the shoulder knobs. The solid outer lip is thick and ridged at the edge of the aperture. Columella, parietal area and outer lip heavily calloused and glazed. Creamy white; parietal area and outer lip metallic looking; base of columella with a brown tinge.

S. oldi (not illustrated)

Emerson 1965 *Somali coast of east Africa, 4.3in (110mm).*

Due to its restricted range, a rare shell. Rather similar to *S. tricornis* (see page 70) from a little farther north on the other side of the Horn of Africa. The body whorl is narrower, the angle of the spire is less and the posterior

Strombus galeatus

Strombus costatus

extension of the lip is flatter, more
open and less pointed. The knobs on the
shoulder are smaller and more numerous. The body whorl
has about ten, coarse, rounded, spiral ridges which extend
on to and become bigger on the flared lip. There are small,
spiral threads between the ridges. Narrow and deep stromboid notch. Straight columella; glazed parietal area. Short,
open and slightly twisted siphonal canal. Cream, heavily
mottled with dark brown; knobs generally white; inside of lip
white becoming dark brown within the aperture.

S. listeri (not illustrated)
Gray 1852 *Bay of Bengal and northwest Indian
Ocean, 6in (150mm).*
Until very recently a rare shell, but found in some numbers in
the last few years. Light but strong. High, pointed spire;
long, narrow body whorl. Early whorls with many axial ribs,
which become obsolete on the last three whorls. The latter
with strong but rounded shoulders. Constricted suture.
Expanded lip, the edge roughly parallel with the columella
and extending posteriorly in a round-ended projection
about level with the suture above the penultimate whorl on
the ventral side. Thickened outer third of lip. Very wide and
deep stromboid notch. Smooth columella and narrow
aperture. Extended, open siphonal canal curves away from
the lip side. White profusely covered with brown, axial
streaks; body whorl mostly brown on the dorsal side, lighter
on the ventral, with four spiral rows of small, white, chevron-
shaped marks; aperture white; thickened part of inside lip
and interior stained with brown.

S. tricornis

Humphrey 1786 *Red Sea and Gulf of Aden, 5in (125mm).*
Solid with fairly high spire and knobbed above the suture. Body whorl is shouldered with blunt knobs, the one on the dorsum being large and elongated axially. Flared outer lip is produced anteriorly to about level with the apex, thickened and slightly inverted close to the aperture. Strong stromboid notch; heavily callous columella, parietal wall and outer lip. Cream with more or less heavy mottling of light or dark brown; callus a dirty yellow-brown, with rather a metallic look. It lives in shallow, sometimes very shallow, water.

Strombus tricornis

S. gallus

L. 1758 *The Rooster-tail Conch, West Indies, 6in (150mm).*
Fairly high spire and small, blunt knobs above the deep suture. Spiral cords on the early whorls become low, flat ridges below the knobs on the shoulder of the body whorl. There are about seven knobs becoming progressively larger to the penultimate knob; final knob small. The outer lip is flared and very produced posteriorly, slightly outward and backward, to give the 'rooster-tail' which curves in on itself to become channeled. It also flares out to obscure in part the spire. The outer lip is not thickened but is slightly frilled and has a deep stromboid notch. The siphonal canal is produced and curved backward and then forward and to the right. White with orange-tan mottling; interior white; inside of the lip, columella, parietal wall and siphonal canal shades of pale orange-brown; inner edge of outer lip is slightly metallic looking. This species is rather uncommon.

Strombus gallus

S. peruvianus

Swainson 1823 *Peru to Mexico, 6in (150mm).*

Rather similar to *S. tricornis,* but bigger, and the top of the posteriorly extended lip is more recurved. Rather concave spire and spiral ridges with small nodules above the suture. Five blunt knobs on the shoulder of the body whorl, the penultimate being by far the largest. The body whorl has low flat, spiral ridges, about fifteen in number, and a second row of very rounded knobs or swellings below those on the shoulder. Outer lip is thickened and produced with the outer edge curled back. Stromboid notch is wide and lirate below the notch; short, sharply recurved siphonal canal. Columella with about eight plicae, the anterior ones bifurcated, and a well-defined channel running from where the lip joins the shoulder to the last whorl and down into the aperture. There is also a channel running from the produced top of the lip into the interior; this opens up into a deep 'well' which is the interior of the last of the knobs on the shoulder. Creamy white to light brown with mottling showing through the blue-white glaze on the parietal wall; interior and columella fleshy pink; the 'well' white; the thickened lip has a metallic look. It has a thick brown periostracum which, like those on other strombs, flakes off when dried.

Strombus peruvianus

Strombus dentatus

Strombus fusiformis

Strombus erythrinus
rugosus

Strombus erythrinus
var. elegans

S. dentatus

L. 1758 *East Africa to Polynesia excluding north Indian Ocean, Japanese mainland and Australia, 2.2in (55mm).*
Smooth, glossy, inflated, and bluntly axially ridged below suture on last three whorls; early whorls have small varices. Lip is slightly expanded with six blunt teeth; interior of lip strongly lirate. Columella shiny and smooth except for four long folds at posterior end and five short ones anteriorly. Thick callus; short, recurved siphonal canal. White maculated with brown, generally axial flamelike marks; siphonal canal with purple stain; teeth on lip, anal canal and columella white except for anterior folds; lirate area on inside lip rich dark purple, showing through on body whorl. Generally found in shallow water in or near coral reefs.

S. fusiformis

Sowerby 1842 *Red Sea, Gulf of Aden, east Africa and Madagascar, 1.8in (45mm).*
Spiral band below suture and varices on early whorls. Two, low, blunt knobs on shoulder of body whorl, which is faintly spirally ridged except close to lip where ridges become prominent, and on lower third of body whorl where they are prominent throughout. Lip slightly expanded and strongly lirate within; shiny columella, ridged at each end; fairly shallow stromboid notch; short siphonal canal. Cream; sparse brown dots and blotches of light red-brown; columella, interior white. Generally found on sandy coral bottoms in deeper water.

S. erythrinus

Dillwyn 1817 *Indo-Pacific from east Africa and Red Sea to Hawaii, Samoa and Tonga, 2in (50mm) long and 17mm wide.*
Angular, ribbed and with some early varices. Spiral cords become bigger anteriorly and near lip; ribs become six, blunt knobs on dorsal half of body whorl. Constricted at suture. Lip slightly expanded, thickened, backed with a groove, lirate internally. Stromboid notch not strong; short siphonal canal; columella with plaits at each end. White, banded on body whorl and clouded with pale or dark yellow-brown; inside of lip, inner half and bottom end of columella, rich dark purple-brown. It is variable, and two varieties are illustrated. The variety *elegans* Sowerby 1842 is from Noumea in New Caledonia. The variety from Fiji, Tonga, Samoa and the Ellice Islands is given subspecific rank as *S.e. rugosus* Sowerby 1825 and has a coarser sculpture, the columella and aperture pure white.

S. sinuatus

Humphrey 1786 *West Pacific, 4.75in (120mm) long and 2.8in (70mm) wide.*
High-spired with body whorl two-thirds of total length. Whorls somewhat constricted below suture and spirally corded. Angular shoulder just above suture has row of blunt knobs, biggest on middle of dorsum. Lip wide, flaring and thickened, with sharp ridge running parallel to columella; lip joins spire of shell partly obscuring it; posterior edge of lip has four or five spatulate projections. Deep stromboid notch; short, recurved siphonal canal. White or cream mottled with yellow-brown; inside of lip pink; columella light golden brown; interior rich dark purple-brown. Lives in rather shallow water.

S. marginatus

L. 1758
Divided into four subspecies:

S. marginatus marginatus

L. 1758 *North and east Bay of Bengal to north part of Strait of Malacca, 2.2in (55mm).*
High-spired with varices, spiral cords, axial ribs and sharply angular shoulder. Ribs disappear on last two whorls leaving nodulose keel on shoulder. Base of body whorl striate. Thickened, sharp-edged lip ending posteriorly on keel of penultimate whorl. Shallow stromboid notch; short siphonal canal. White maculated with dark or light brown; four white spiral bands on body whorl; inside of lip lirate, white; columella with faint plicae anteriorly; interior white.

Strombus
sinuatus

Strombus
marginatus
marginatus

Strombus marginatus
robustus

S. marginatus robustus

Sowerby 1874 *Strait of Malacca, around South China Sea to south Japan, 2.6in (65mm).*
Much shorter spire than above and rounded shoulders without keel. Strong axial fold at outer side of parietal area. Posteriorly, lip ends on or above suture of second whorl.

73

S. marginatus succinctus (not illustrated)
L. 1767 *Southeast India and northwest Sri Lanka, 2in (50mm).*
High-spired and rather narrow. Large blunt knob on dorsum of body whorl. Color paler.

S. marginatus septimus (not illustrated)
Duclos 1844 *Ryukyu Islands, Philippines, New Guinea, Solomons and New Caledonia, 1.9in (48mm).*
High spire. Like *S.m. succinctus* but without knob on dorsum; sometimes with two or three small ones instead. Lip a little more flared. Dark brown; five, narrow, spotted, white bands.

S. maculatus
Sowerby 1842 *East and north Pacific, 1.4in (35mm).*
Moderate spire with former varices and with rounded, faintly knobbed shoulders. There is a narrow constricting groove below suture which disappears on body whorl. Shoulders on dorsal half of body whorl with about five, very blunt knobs, corded on bottom half of body whorl and near outer lip; latter swollen and turned in. Well-developed stromboid notch; short, almost straight siphonal canal; strongly lirate aperture; columella usually lirate with a smooth, central area, but may be lirate its entire length. Cream or white with usually very pale yellow-brown banding and mottling, but variable; aperture with pink tinge.

Strombus *variabilis*

Strombus *epidromis*

Strombus *maculatus*

S. variabilis
Swainson 1820 *Central Indo-Pacific from Indonesia and Malay Peninsula to the Marshalls and Samoa, 2.4in (60mm).*
High-spired; finely spirally ridged on early whorls and base of body whorl; former varices on early whorls, which are also axially ribbed and angular, ribs becoming knobs on shoulder of body whorl. Flaring lip is recurved anteriorly and extends posteriorly to end on the penultimate whorl. Siphonal notch is not very deep; slightly recurved siphonal canal. White with brown mottling, mainly wavy, axial streaks, and areas of cross-hatching; about five, more or less indistinct, spiral, white bands show on lip; interior and columella smooth and white. Those specimens from the west of its range generally with a dark brown rectangle halfway along edge of columella; those from east without.

S. epidromis

L. 1758 *New Caledonia to New Guinea, the Philippines, Indonesia and Singapore and north to Taiwan, 3.5in (90mm).* Angulate and axial ribs which disappear on the last two or three whorls and give way to small knobs; spiral striae and varices on early whorls. Flared lip is thickened and recurved at edge, posterior end joining shell above suture of penultimate whorl and forming anal canal. Moderately deep and wide stromboid notch; slightly recurved siphonal canal; smooth and heavily callous columella and broad parietal area. White with faint, pale brown, axial mottling; interior and columella shiny white; lip edge and columella with metallic look. Lives in rather shallow water.

S. mutabilis

Swainson 1821 *Indo-Pacific except Hawaii, 1.6in (40mm).* Very variable. Rather short spire. Rounded, blunt, axial ribs, becoming heavy knobs on dorsal half of body whorl. Faint, spiral cords becoming much sharper on base and near lip. Deep, spiral, narrow, constricting groove below suture. Lip flared, thickened, with a short, blunt projection at shoulder forming outer side of anal canal. Shallow stromboid notch; short, only slightly recurved siphonal canal; lirate aperture and columella. White or cream mottled and spotted with light and/or dark browns generally in axial streaks and spiral bands. Often has a central light band on body whorl and sometimes up to seven, narrow, light bands. Columella and lip white or pink; deep interior sometimes mottled as outside. Color form *zebriolatus* Adam and Leloup 1938 from Kenya has dark brown, wavy, axial streaks on body whorl.

Strombus mutabilis form zebriolatus

Strombus mutabilis

Strombus mutabilis

Strombus mutabilis (Red Sea)

Strombus mutabilis (New Guinea)

75

S. plicatus
Röding 1798
Divided into four subspecies:

S. plicatus pulchellus
Reeve 1851 *west Pacific, 1.4in (35mm)*.

High, concave spire; varices, spiral cords, axial ribs; cord below suture more prominent especially on earlier whorls. Axial ribs become nodules on shoulder of last two whorls. Three or four blunt knobs on dorsum of body whorl; penultimate knob biggest. Corded on bottom of last whorl and near lip. Flared, slightly recurved lip, extending to suture of penultimate whorl. Wide, moderately deep stromboid notch; short, reflexed siphonal canal; lip lirate and columella also, though almost smooth centrally. White or cream; light brown maculations; four, narrow, white spiral bands with brown spots on body whorl; both sides of lip white; columella white or cream; interior with purple-brown lirae; end of siphonal canal mauve.

Strombus plicatus pulchellus

S. plicatus plicatus (not illustrated)
Röding 1798 *Red Sea, 2.4in (60mm)*.
Colorless aperture and lip; some of columellar lirae brown.

S. plicatus sibbaldi (not illustrated)
Sowerby 1842 *Gulf of Aden to south India and Sri Lanka, 1.4in (35mm)*.
Similar to *S.p. plicatus* but stubbier body whorl. Columellar lirae purple-brown; interior and lip white.

S. plicatus columba
Lamarck 1822 *east Africa, Madagascar and Seychelles, 1.8in (45mm)*.
Purple-brown or brown blotch posteriorly on columella, latter strongly lirate; one or two blotches well inside lip.

Strombus plicatus columba

S. microurceus
Kira 1959 *Java to south Japan, Samoa and New Caledonia, 1in (25mm)*.
Similar in shape to *S. mutabilis* but the columella is yellow-orange on its outer half and dark purple-brown with yellow striae on the inner half; the interior is white; band of purple-brown with white spiral lirae within lip; siphonal canal has purple mark.

Strombus microurceus

S. terebellatus
Sowerby 1842 *east Africa and west Pacific, 2in (50mm)*.
Elongate, narrow, rather fragile, inflated and smooth. Narrow band below suture on early whorls. Oblique groove on bottom of body whorl. Lip slightly thickened behind edge. Wide, very shallow stromboid notch; smooth, thinly callous columella; siphonal canal short but extending

Strombus terebellatus

beyond end of lip. Cream maculated with light or dark brown; darker below suture; brown lirae inside aperture; columella white, brown marks showing through callus.

S. urceus

L. 1758 *west Pacific from the Solomons to Malay Peninsula and Sumatra, 2.4in (60mm).*

Rather narrow with high spire of angular whorls, spirally striate and ribbed. The ribs become more or less heavy knobs on shoulder of dorsal side of body whorl; spiral ridges on base of body whorl. Thickened lip; stromboid notch sometimes deep, sometimes hardly apparent; columella smooth in the middle and lirate at each end; aperture usually strongly lirate. It is, however, a very variable species. White, cream or brown, with spots, flecks, bands or axial streaks of light or dark brown; columella and inside of lip may be dark or pale pink; interior white or purple-brown or deep rich purple; the whole columella, lip and interior may be almost black. Illustrated are: a brown, orange-mouthed specimen from the Philippines; a deep-water specimen, light in weight and color and with more rounded whorls from the south Philippines; and *ustulatus* Schumacher 1817, the white with black mouth variety, often bigger than average, from Singapore. The latter form is found less commonly elsewhere around the South China Sea.

Strombus urceus

Strombus urceus
form ustulatus

Strombus urceus
(deep water)

77

Strombus minimus

Strombus fasciatus

*Strombus vittatus
vittatus*

S. minimus

L. 1771 *west Pacific, 1.6in (40mm).*
High spire; spirally ridged and axially ribbed, ribs replaced by knobs on body whorl. Narrow band below suture. Flared, thickened lip is lirate within, projecting posteriorly to top of antepenultimate whorl. Broad, shallow stromboid notch; callous columella, callus extending posteriorly forming, with lip, the elongate anal canal; short, almost straight siphonal canal. Light or dark brown; tiny cream spots; sometimes spiral row of white dots on body whorl; aperture yellow; columella white or pinkish.

S. fasciatus

Born 1778 *Red Sea, 2in (50mm).*
Solid with low spire and sometimes narrow band below suture which disappears on last whorls. Knobs, increasing in size, developing on penultimate whorl, about ten on body whorl, largest on middle of dorsum. Slightly flared lip; wide, moderately deep stromboid notch; slightly curved siphonal canal; smooth columella; small fasciole. White; five to nine, narrow, irregular, broken, spiral lines of very dark brown-black; columella yellow; interior yellow-orange; ends of spiral lines show just within lip and lines themselves show faintly through lip and sometimes under columellar callus.

S. vittatus

L. 1758
Divided into three subspecies:

S. vittatus vittatus

L. 1758 *South China Sea to New Guinea and Fiji, 3.3in (85mm).*
Stout, pointed spire with axial ribs. Groove below suture forming band on which ribs form nodules; below groove, ribs become obsolete on middle whorls; also two, fine, spiral cords on this band. On body whorl only cords remain. Area below suture concave. Spire may have former varices. Shoulder of body whorl has one or two slight 'lumps' and one blunt nodule in middle of dorsum. Base with up to twenty, spiral grooves. Expanded, thickened, lip curling in a little; broad but not deep stromboid notch; inside of lip finely lirate, lip ending on suture above penultimate whorl. Columella smooth centrally, pustulate posteriorly, with up to five weak lirae anteriorly, and bounding short, straight siphonal canal. White; mottled with light or dark brown, especially on subsutural band, lip and last part of body whorl; in latter area fine, axial, minutely zigzag, brown lines, and about five, spiral bands; columella, interior and inside of lip white. Illustrated is high-spired form named *australis* Schröter 1805.

S. vittatus campbelli (not illustrated)

Griffith & Pidgeon 1834 *north and east Australia, 2.6in (65mm).*
Similar to above but knob on dorsum bigger, and band below suture has strong nodules.

S. vittatus japonicus

Reeve 1851 *south Japan, 2.6in (65mm).*
Lower spire; fine, spiral cords and small, axial ribs.

S. lentiginosus

Jousseaume 1886 *tropical Indo-Pacific, east Africa to Society Islands, not generally on Asian coast except south India and Malay Peninsula, 4.1in (105mm).*
Solid and heavy with short, pointed spire and spiral striae. Axial ribs nodulose on shoulder of later whorls and bearing eight knobs, longer axially than broad, on dorsal side of body whorl, antepenultimate in middle of dorsum very large. Body whorl with five rows of much smaller nodules, three other coarse ridges without nodules, coarse striae at base. Slightly flared lip is greatly thickened opposite columella and extended and curved posteriorly, to join spire on suture above antepenultimate whorl; this part of lip has two notches, one quite deep. Deep stromboid notch; short, recurved siphonal canal; straight, smooth columella is heavily callous, as is parietal area which extends over two whorls above body whorl and, with end of lip, forms deep, long anal canal; White, heavily speckled with dark brown-gray; interior and columella pink-cream; lip edge with about seven, spiral, purple-brown stripes; parietal area somewhat metallic.

Strombus vittatus japonicus

Strombus lentiginosus

S. gibberulus
L. 1758
Divided into three subspecies:

S. gibberulus gibberulus
L. 1758 *Indian Ocean, Malaya and northwest South China Sea, 2.8in (70mm).*
Moderately elevated spire; spirally corded; earlier swollen varices. Penultimate whorl is expanded and bulges over suture on dorsum of body whorl; latter also inflated at shoulder, and with cords disappearing except at base where they reappear on lip. Lip expanded, thickened before its sharp edge; posterior end on inflated part of body whorl, well below suture. Moderately deep stromboid notch; siphonal canal long for the genus and somewhat recurved. Smooth columella. White heavily marked with broken light brown axial lines; more or less faint, narrow, white spiral bands; columella pinky white, sometimes with mauve inner side at bottom; lip white with deep mauve lirate band about 3mm inside; interior white with mauve tinge; anal canal mauve; siphonal canal white.

Strombus gibberulus gibberulus

S. gibberulus albus
Mörch 1850 *Red Sea to Kenya, 2.2in (55mm).*
Smaller than *S. g. gibberulus.* White with very pale fawn markings and purplish broken band below suture; columella white; same purple band on inside lip.

S. gibberulus gibbosus
Röding 1798 *southeast South China Sea and outward to Society Islands, 2.2in (55mm).*
Smaller than *S. g. gibberulus,* and markings usually darker browns and yellows. Columella white or yellow, sometimes rich chocolate brown. Spiral cords on lip rather weak.

Strombus gibberulus albus

S. aurisdianae aurisdianae
L. 1758 *east Africa to Ryukyus and the Solomons, 2.9in (75mm).*
Solid; moderately high spire; spirally corded and axially ribbed. Somewhat angulate and with short blunt spines on shoulders. Below suture is a strongly beaded band. On body whorl

Strombus gibberulus gibbosus

the blunt spines become quite large. Two cords near middle of last whorl have short blunt knobs. Lip expanded, thickened, but coming to a sharp edge, with two or three uneven folds on outside before the thickening; a short fingerlike projection from posterior end of lip and a deep stromboid notch at the other. Siphonal canal deep, slightly twisted to the right and recurved almost through 90°. Lirate anal canal; columella pustulate at top, otherwise smooth and callous; wide parietal wall, callus almost extending to apex. White or pale brown mottled with darker brown; lip with about eight pale red-brown spiral bands; columella and parietal area light brown at anterior end, creamy white at the other; inside lip pinky white; interior orange.

S. aurisdianae aratrum

Röding 1798. *This is a subspecies of the above from northeast Queensland, Australia and from the east coast of Malaya and perhaps areas between, 3.5in (90mm).*

It is bigger, more elongate, has a sharper spire and the projection on the lip is about twice as long. Siphonal canal is also longer and a little less recurved. Spines and knobs bigger and fewer. Color is tan, similarly mottled; stripes on lip, projection and edge of lip are deep purple; columella and interior are rich shiny orange-brown, and upper half of parietal area is dark brown; inside of lip fades to pink.

S. bulla

Röding 1798 *Indonesia, Philippines, Taiwan, the Ryukyus and New Guinea east to New Caledonia and Samoa, 2.8in (70mm).*

Similar to *S. aurisdianae* but much smoother; spiral cords barely raised; subsutural cord obsolete; knobs smaller; projection from lip longer and narrower; no lirae on anal canal; callous area covers about half the shell and some-times whole of spire. White, heavily mottled with light brown; callus white, pink-brown anteriorly; interior rich shiny orange-brown.

Strombus aurisdianae aurisdianae

Strombus aurisdianae aratrum

Strombus bulla

Strombus pipus

S. pipus

Röding 1798 *east Africa and south and east tropical Pacific, 2.8in (70mm).*

Rather short spire, slightly angulate, spirally corded and axially ridged with early varices. Body whorl a little inflated with four spiral rows of small knobs on middle and one near base; each knob has a dark purple-brown spot on its lip side. Expanded lip is thickened before sharp edge which is curved inward and extends onto penultimate whorl, with two notches at posterior end; inside of lip faintly lirate. Deep stromboid notch; very short, recurved siphonal canal; smooth, callous columella; parietal wall has clear glaze. White with tan-brown mottling; inside of lip, anal and siphonal canals rich purple-brown; edge of lip white crossed by bands of the same color; columella, lower end of parietal wall and deep interior white.

S. luhuanus

L. 1758 *Strait of Malacca to south Japan, the Line Islands, Fiji and east Australia, 2.8in (70mm).*

Conical with low, smooth or ribbed, concave spire and last whorl sharply angulate. Lip curved inward, faintly lirate within. Deep stromboid notch; short, almost straight siphonal canal; smooth columella. White or cream; broken, brown, axial, zigzag streaks forming six, broad, spiral bands on body whorl; inside lip and aperture rose pink; columella with broad, straight band of very dark brown callus.

Strombus luhuanus

S. decorus

Röding 1798 *north and east Indian Ocean, 2.8in (70mm).*

Similar in shape to *S. luhuanus.* Conical with depressed spire and pointed nipplelike apex. Shoulders bumpy rather than knobbly, one large 'bump' on dorsal side of body whorl. Expanded lip has thin edge. Deep stromboid notch; almost straight, short siphonal canal; smooth columella. White; broken, axial, wavy streaks of dark brown forming seven, spiral bands on body whorl; columella, inside lip, both canals white; interior apricot. Young specimens, before the lip develops into its final shape, can very easily be mistaken for a species of *Conus.*

S. latus

Gmelin 1791 *west African coast from Rio d'Oro to Angola and Cape Verde Islands, 6in (150mm).*

The only known *Strombus* from the eastern Atlantic region. Solid and heavy with moderate spire. Spirally striate on the early whorls and axially ribbed; ribs forming knobs on shoulder. Seven large blunt knobs on body whorl, increasing in size near the lip; second row of smaller with blunt knobs; and a third and fourth, smaller still, below these. The body whorl has rough, axial, uneven ridges. Expanded, thickened lip; wide, deep stromboid notch; short, almost straight siphonal canal; and smooth, heavily callous columella.

Strombus decorus

Strombus latus

White, heavily mottled with brown; inside lip and interior pink; thickened edge of lip is metallic pink; columella and around notch with orange tinge.

S. granulatus

Swainson 1822 *Ecuador to the Gulf of California, 2.9in (75mm).*
High spire; spirally striate, angular shoulders, ribbed on very early whorls then bluntly spined and restricted at suture. Body whorl has nine, quite large, spinous knobs and three spiral rows of small knobs; axial cords begin on penultimate whorl and grow stronger toward lip which has fine, axial growth striae, and thickens before curving inward to a sharp edge. Lip is pustulate within. Deep stromboid notch and short siphonal canal, recurved through 45°. Columella has six faint ridges anteriorly. Parietal wall callous anteriorly. White heavily clouded with light and dark brown; inside lip, interior and columella white with pinky tinge in stromboid notch and siphonal canal; parietal wall pinky, a little metallic at base, clear glaze on upper half.

S. gracilior (not illustrated)

Sowerby 1825 *Peru to the Gulf of California, 2.9in (75mm).*
Very similar to the above but sturdier spire, and less well-developed knobs; lacks the pustules inside lip.

Strombus granulatus

83

Genus: Lambis

The genus *Lambis*, known as the spider or scorpion shells, includes nine species all of which are found only in the tropical Indo-Pacific. None are small; they all develop long projections on the outer lip of the adult shell, have a long siphonal canal and the characteristic stromboid notch. Some are divided into subspecies. The female is often bigger than the male.

Lambis lambis ♀

Lambis lambis ♂

Lambis lambis

L. 1758 *east Africa and Red Sea to the Marshall Islands and Tonga, 8in (200mm).*

Pointed spire of about eight whorls, spirally and axially striate, with sharp angular shoulders carrying small knobs. Body whorl has fine, blunt knobs; that nearest the parietal wall a mere lump; the next not much bigger; the third well-developed; the fourth, the largest, and the fifth are joined; a second row of much smaller knobs and a third on which they are barely apparent. Lip flares widely and is spirally and axially corded; edge of lip forms six long spines, posterior two being the longest, one lying against spire. In the male, which is about forty percent smaller than the female, the anterior three spines are quite short and are only slightly recurved, whereas in the female they are at least twice the length and curved up at about 50° to 60°. Long siphonal canal is curved beyond plane of lip. Inner edge of lip is callous between base of spines, which are formed by the folding inward of the edge of what would otherwise be broad, spatulate projections. Very deep and wide stromboid notch and smooth columella. Parietal callus covers half body whorl and up to, but not contiguous with, the apex itself. Small ridge on columella and on inside of lip at end of anal canal; aperture itself is very narrow. Creamy white, heavily mottled with brown, or brown and purple-brown; spines retain the periostracum even when dried; columella, parietal area and interior flesh-pink.

L. millepeda

L. 1758 east Indonesia and the Philippines, 5.75in (145mm).

Rather short spire with about eight whorls, spirally ribbed and angulate with blunt spines on shoulder, restricted at suture. Body whorl has a row of three large and one small knobs and two rows of small knobs. Narrow aperture; lip has three long projections posteriorly and six, short, hooked ones opposite columella. Very deep stromboid notch and only slightly curved siphonal canal.

Lambis millepeda

Inside lip strongly lirate except at edge and columella smooth in the middle, lirate at each end. Parietal callus wide and extending to first projection, ending just short of apex. Cream with brown maculations; suture stained purple; inside lip, columella and callous area mushroom-colored; lirae white, interstices purple; two white teeth at base of anal canal.

L. crocata

Link 1807 Indian Ocean to the Ryukyus, Marshalls, Samoa and northern tip of Australia, 6in (150mm).

Moderate spire of about twelve whorls; spirally and axially corded with a row of beads above suture. Body whorl has one spiral row of about four knobs, the last two large, and two other rows of more and smaller knobs. Lip has six spines which are longitudinally corded. Wide and deep stromboid notch; long siphonal canal is curved through 90° in two planes. Cream maculated with yellow-brown; inside lip, interior and columella pinky-orange. There is a subspecies from the Marquesas Islands, L. c. pilsbryi Abbott 1961 which is twice the size of L. crocata, with the smaller projections less curved.

Lambis crocata

L. truncata
Humphrey 1786
The species is divided into two subspecies:

L. truncata truncata
Humphrey 1786
Indian Ocean, 15in (400mm).
All spire, except for last three whorls, is very depressed, almost flat, giving a truncated effect; spirally corded and fine, axial cords. Whorls with angular, coarse, large knobs on shoulder; body whorl has especially large hump on high point of dorsum and other smaller humps and knobs. Lip has six, rather open spines; deep, wide stromboid notch has crenulated edge. Siphonal canal is as long as average spine, a little reflected backward and toward aperture. Heavily callous, smooth columella; parietal area spreads over part of body whorl but is 'indented' at shoulder of whorl. Cream; brown maculations; aperture, inside of lip, columella and canals pink; darker on parietal area.

*Lambis
truncata
truncata*

L. truncata sabae (not illustrated)
Kiener 1843 *Red Sea and Gulf of Oman and from Indonesia east to the Tuamotu Archipelago, up to 12in (300mm).* Differs from the above in size and in having a pointed, not truncated, spire.

L. chiragra
L. 1758
Divided into two subspecies:

L. chiragra chiragra
L. 1758 *Sri Lanka eastward to Tuamotu Archipelago, north to Ryukyus and south to northern Australia. Female form much bigger, up to 10in (250mm),*
and differently marked from the male. Rather low spire of nine whorls; spirally corded, becoming very coarse on body whorl. Whorls angulate with row of nodules on shoulder, bearing four, large knobs on body whorl, the last a double one and very long; three or four other rows of knobs. Lip is posteriorly curved through 90° across top of columella and behind apex but covering nearly half the spire. Five, long, strong spines on lip, tips more or less pointing posteriorly - one at end beyond top of columella; one at end of anal canal; three on lip, one of which is below the deep stromboid notch - and a sixth projection at base of body whorl. Columella lirate,

*Lambis chiragra
arthritica*

Lambis
chiragra chiragra ♀

inside of lip faintly so; wide parietal area. At top of columella and further into aperture than end of anal canal is a ledge or flange, 0.4in (10mm) to 0.6in (15mm) long. White mottled with brown; lip, columella and interior shades of pink; interstices of lirae and lip edge darker.

The male, which was once thought to be a separate species named *L. rugosa,* is up to 175mm, similar to female but smaller with five knobs on body whorl. Columella lirate throughout, strongly at each end, and lip also lirate. Aperture, interior, lip and columella pinky-red; lirae white with interstices; bottom of columella purple. It has the same sunken shelf at the top of the columella.

L. chiragra arthritica
Röding 1798 *Western half of Indian Ocean, 8in (200mm).*
Female only slightly larger than the male, and the species is remarkably similar to male form, *rugosa,* of *L.c. chiragra.* Lip and columella strongly lirate, more so than in *rugosa.* Lirae white, interstices purple over a rich red-brown or pink background. The main structural difference is no 'shelf' within aperture at top of columella. Instead there is a rounded projection from top of columella (not so deep in aperture) over which the lirae from columella continue and which forms one side of very narrow anal canal.

Lambis
chiragra chiragra ♂

87

L. digitata

Perry 1811 *East Africa to Samoa, 5.5in (140mm).*

High spire; spirally striate; low ribs ending in sharp knobs on angular shoulder of whorls. Body whorl has spiral row of six knobs, biggest in middle of dorsum and three rows of small knobs. Lip, flattened at edge and extending as narrow ledge over inside of lip, has eight projections, two long ones posteriorly-one joined to and projecting beyond spire and tending to bifurcate - and six short ones opposite columella. Deep, wide stromboid notch with scalloped edge as is rest of thickened lip below. Moderately long, almost straight siphonal canal. Columella, narrow parietal area and inside of lip strongly lirate. Outer end of columellar lirae sharply defined and forming a ridge. Narrow ridge on each side of inner end of anal canal ends in deep well. White, heavily maculated with brown; inside of lip white or pinky white; lirae on lip and columella white, interstices dark purple-brown; interior yellow.

Lambis digitata

L. scorpius

L. 1758 *Strait of Malacca to Ryukyus, north Australia and Samoa, 6.75in (170mm).*

A subspecies *L.s. indomaris* occurs in the Indian Ocean. Short spire; spirally corded including lip; angular shoulders with small knobs; beaded band below suture. Body whorl has row of five large knobs, two rows with smaller knobs, and a fourth with still smaller ones anteriorly. Posterior end of lip curves round to engulf half of spire and forms rounded, triangular flange on far side of first projection; three posterior projections are long; three opposite columella short and hooked; all six point posteriorly. Deep stromboid notch with scalloped edge, as is remainder of lip. Quite long, curved siphonal canal is sealed at end. All projections are coarse, lumpy and of irregular width. Strongly lirate columella and aperture. White and pale gray; sparse brown spots and clouding; inside of lip pink; lirae white; interstices, interior purple-brown.

Lambis scorpius

FAMILY: APORRHAIDAE

Pelican's foot shells. About six species all from north Atlantic and Mediterranean.

Aporrhais pespelecani

L. 1758 *Mediterranean to north Norway, 2in (50mm).*
High spire; spirally corded and angular with axial ribs across last three whorls. Body whorl with second row of riblets, concave between the rows, and a beaded cord. Very

Aporrhais pespelecani

expanded, thickened lip with coarse growth lines, bearing four projections - one short and squat partly attached to spire, a second longer, a third short, a fourth forming siphonal canal. Wide, shallow stromboid notch. Two biggest ridges on body whorl form 'backbone' of middle two projections. Smooth columella; callous parietal area. Dull gray-brown; lip lighter; aperture dirty white.

FAMILY: STRUTHIOLARIIDAE

The ostrich foot shells. Six species; *S. papulosa gigas* Sowerby 1842; *S. papulosa papulosa* Martyn 1784; *S. pelicaria vermis* Martyn 1784; *S. pelicaria tricarinata* Lesson 1880 from New Zealand; *S. scutulata* Martyn 1784 from Australia and one species from the Indian Ocean.

Struthiolaria papulosa papulosa

Martyn 1784 *3in (80mm).*
Solid; very angular and carinated at shoulder of last four whorls; spirally corded. Rather flat-sided body whorl has coarse growth lines. Expanded lip, almost semicircular columella, and heavily callous lip and parietal area, lower half swollen. Short, curve siphonal canal. Gray; axial, indistinct, brown streaks; aperture white; interior light brown.

S. pelicaria vermis

Martyn 1784
North Island, 1.4in (35mm).
Similar in shape to above but smooth except for faint, low nodules on shoulders and sometimes fine, beaded, spiral cords. Variable color, purple through brown to yellow.

Struthiolaria papulosa papulosa

Struthiolaria pelicaria vermis

SUPERFAMILY: CYPRAEACEA

FAMILY: CYPRAEIDAE

The cowries are probably the most popular shells with collectors because of their beautiful glossy state when taken and their gorgeous colors. They are found in tropical and semitropical waters, and are herbivorous, feeding on algae. They grow spirally like other gastropods until they reach adulthood when the outer lip turns in, thickens and teeth are formed on both the lip and columella. They are active during the night and hide during the day. They prefer hard coral reef and shallow water. There are, however, exceptions to nearly all these generalizations.

Cypraea isabella

L. 1758 *Indo-Pacific, 1.2in (30mm)*.
Rather cylindrical with short, fine teeth. Fawn-gray with more or less profuse, interrupted, black, longitudinal lines; orange-red tips and spire; white base. *C. isabella mexicana* (not illustrated) Stearns 1893, found in west Central America, is very similar but has brown, callous sides and the tips are more produced and brighter.

C. hungerfordi

Sowerby 1888
Japan, 1.6in (40mm).
The commonest of the endemic Japanese cowries and lives in deep water. Specimens believed to be of same species recently found in deep water off Cape Moreton, Queensland. Pyriform with strong teeth. Flesh-colored base and slightly callous sides merging into whitish band with dark brown spots which edge a broad, longitudinal, dark band of close, gray-brown stippling; darker transverse bands showing through faintly. Other endemic Japanese species are *C. teramachii, C. hirasei* and *C. langfordi*.

Cypraea isabella

Cypraea hungerfordi

Cypraea cinerea

C. cinerea

Gmelin 1791 *Caribbean and down east coast of South America to Bahia Blanca, 1.2in (30mm)*.
A little swollen; teeth quite strong. Gray-brown with two, light, transverse bands; base lighter with rosy tinge; margins and extremities marked with minute spots and dashes of black as if dipped in ash. I have a beautiful specimen taken from a fish's stomach off Brazil

which is smaller than those from the Caribbean, with a lighter base, finer teeth and dashes of rich red-brown all over the dorsum.

C. tessellata
Swainson 1822 *Hawaii, 1.2in (30mm).*
Rare, but one of the most beautiful. High dorsum and strongly callous margins. Fine teeth. Blue-gray background with three darker brown-gray bands; rectangular red-brown and white spots on the sides and extremities. Base brown-red with white spots spreading over to teeth on each side.

C. lurida
L. 1758 *Mediterranean and east Atlantic from Azores in the north to St. Helena and Angola in the south, 1.8in (45mm).*
Rather light, ovate. Fawn-brown; three darker bands with two dark brown spots at each end; pinky-red tinge at each end of aperture; base white; cf *C. pulchra.*

C. pulchra
Gray 1824 *Red Sea, Gulf of Aden and south coast of Arabian Peninsula to Gulf of Oman, 2in (50mm).*
Superficially similar to *C. lurida*, but the latter is much coarser. *C. pulchra* is less swollen, smoother, glossier and lighter in color, and lacks the red tinge at ends. Its teeth are very much finer, are red-brown and in the middle of the columella they extend about one-third of the way across the base. Straighter aperture than in *C. lurida*. It is also a much more solid shell and as one of the most beautiful cowries is aptly named. Rare.

Cypraea tessellata

Cypraea lurida

Cypraea pulchra

C. chinensis

Gmelin 1791 *Indo-Pacific from Tahiti westward to the Strait of Malacca and from south Japan to the north coast of Australia, and also the east coast of Africa from the Cape of Good Hope to Aden, 1.2in (30mm).* The callous sides give the shell a somewhat angular look. Teeth strong especially on the outer lip. The dorsum is mottled light brown to green; sides, which are more or less heavily callous, are cream dotted with mauve spots; base and teeth are creamy white with orange between the teeth. May be more elongate than the illustrated specimen.

Cypraea chinensis

C. coloba

Melville 1888 *Southeast India and Sri Lanka, the Bay of Bengal, and central Indian Ocean from the Andaman Islands to the Chagos Islands (i.e., mainly the area between the two in which C. chinensis occurs, to which it is very closely related), 1in (25mm).*

It is more depressed than *C. chinensis* and has extremely callous margins and very heavy, coarse teeth especially on the outer lip. Background color is fleshy pink; dorsum covered with minute green-brown spots and with larger dark brown spots where the dorsum and margins meet; base pink-brown.

Cypraea coloba

C. onyx

L. 1758 *South Africa up the coast of Africa to Kenya; Madagascar, Mauritius, north Indian Ocean, Indonesia, Philippines and northward to south Japan; northwest Pacific including the Marshalls, Gilberts, Solomons and north New Guinea;, 1.6in (40mm).*

Base and sides are very dark brown to black, contrasting strongly with the pale blue-white dorsum through which two yellow bands are conspicuous on a young shell and show through faintly on the adult; the dorsal line is dark brown, revealing the yellow bands. In the variety *adusta* Lamarck

Cypraea onyx

1820 from east Africa the dorsum is a very deep rich brown
with a faint lighter dorsal line. The variety *succincta*
(not illustrated) L. 1758, from India and Iran, has a
rich red-brown on base and dorsum with two faint
pale lines across the latter; teeth lighter.

C. pyrum

Gmelin 1791 *Mediterranean and west
African coast to Cape Frio, 1.8in (45mm)*.
Pyriform with fairly strong teeth. The
wide margins, base and extremities
are orange-red; teeth and interior
white; dorsum brown; mottling nearly
obscures cream background, but
three narrow cream bands are more or
less conspicuous.

*Cypraea onyx var.
adusta*

C. mus

L. 1758 *This is not by any means a common cowrie as it
appears to be restricted to the north coast of South
America from the end of the Isthmus of Panama to the
Gulf of Venezuela, 1.8in (45mm)*.

It is a broad, somewhat angular shell with a humped dorsum.
Moderately strong teeth. Its light fawn back-ground is
overlaid with darker fawn-gray wavy lines running from the
dark brown teeth on the outer lip over the wide margin;
these lines show only at the edge of the margin on the
columellar side, and the teeth, also dark brown on that side,
are covered by a dark brown band running the length of the
shell; dorsum is speckled with the same fawn-gray stippling
and the conspicuous pale dorsal line is marked on both
sides with very dark brown spots tending to run together at
the posterior end of the dorsum.

Cypraea pyrum   *Cypraea mus*

Cypraea ziczac

C. ziczac
L. 1758 *Indian Ocean from east Africa, east and north through the China Seas to south Japan, and south to northwest and north Australia and the Great Barrier Reef, then east across the central Pacific to Tahiti including New Guinea, the Solomons, New Hebrides, Fiji, Samoa and Cook Islands, 0.8in (20mm).*

Pale brown; three bands of very light blue-white chevrons; base is light red-brown with black spots which spread on to the paler margins and encircle the extremities; small, dark spot on the sunken spire.

C. diluculum
Reeve 1845 *East Africa from Durban to Aden, the Seychelles, Mauritius and Reunion, 1in (25mm).*

Somewhat similar in pattern to *C. ziczac* though larger. Ivory white background; three bands of dark gray-brown between which are chevrons of the same color – the illustrated specimen has less color than is typical. Margins and base are spotted with the same color except in the variety *virginalis* Schilder and Schilder 1938 which has no spots and is found together with the more common variety. The sunken spire carries a small dark spot.

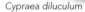

Cypraea diluculum

C. clandestina
L. 1767 *Indian Ocean and west Pacific including south Japan, Wake, Marshall, Gilbert, Cook and Lord Howe Islands and the Great Barrier Reef, 0.8in (20mm).*

White, covered on dorsum with three, very pale, broad bands of gray; dorsum is also banded with red-brown hairlines which need a magnifying glass to be seen properly; extremities have very pale pinky tinge; base and teeth are white.

Cypraea clandestina

C. lutea
Gmelin 1791 *South China Sea including the Philippines and Singapore; Sulu and Celebes Seas, west New Guinea and western Australia; 0.8in (20mm).*

Dorsum pale brown to green, sparsely dotted with small brown spots and having two, conspicuous, narrow, very pale blue-white bands. The base and margins are orange-red and profusely dotted with dark brown spots. The extremities are also dark brown.

C. saulae
Gaskoin 1843 *Philippines, Caroline Islands and Sulu Sea, and from the Torres Strait down the Great Barrier Reef to Brisbane, 1in (25mm).*

Cypraea lutea

This is a rare cowrie but I have included it as, to me, it is the most beautiful. There are three varieties and the illustration shows the variety *siasiensis* Cate 1960. It is a narrow shell with the dorsum somewhat inflated. It is white to light fawn, speckled with a few small chestnut spots which are larger on the margins and with a large almost square blotch on the dorsum. The extremities and teeth are orange-yellow or white.

C. coxeni

Cox 1873 *North New Guinea, New Britain and the Solomons, a small area and therefore not a common shell, 0.8in (20mm).*

It is long, narrow and cylindrical. Variety *hesperina* (not illustrated) Schilder and Summers 1963 is smaller with larger, darker dorsal markings. Pale fawn-cream; dorsum heavily mottled with a rich brown, leaving broad, unmarked margins and base.

Cypraea saulae var. siasiensis

C. punctata

L. 1771 *Indian Ocean, China Seas and central Pacific including south Japan, Marshalls, Tahiti, Cook Islands, New Caledonia, and northeast, north and northwest Australia, 0.6in (15mm).*

White, more or less heavily spotted on the dorsum and sides with dark chocolate brown; teeth often lined with brown.

Cypraea coxeni

C. walkeri

Sowerby 1832 *Seychelles and Maldive Islands, the south tip of Malaya and Singapore, the north coast of Sumatra, the Sulu Sea and the north coast of Australia, 1.2in (30mm).*

Found in two forms, one pyriform and inflated, the other, *surabajensis* Schilder 1937 from the Philippines, elongated and narrow. Fawn background is heavily mottled with purple-brown which forms a more solid band across the middle of the dorsum. Margins and extremities spotted with same color. In both forms the interstices of the teeth, and the labial side of the base are marked with purple.

Cypraea punctata

Cypraea walkeri

Cypraea walkeri form surabajensis

C. pyriformis

Gray 1824 *Singapore to the south Philippines then south to north Australia, 1.4in (35mm).*

Very pyriform and inflated. Blue-white heavily stippled with smudged, brown spots and three, interrupted bands of darker brown; base cream with quite long, dark brown teeth on the columella; labial teeth short and cream.

C. teres

Gmelin 1791 *Indo-Pacific from east Africa to the Galapagos, and from Japan to the northern half of Australia, 1.6in (40mm).*

Found in three main forms, one cylindrical and narrow, one cylindrical but more inflated and one altogether rounder. The labial margin has a more or less developed callus which does not show on the illustrated specimen. The dorsum is blue-gray heavily mottled with green-brown in dots and larger marks, the latter in three broken bands; base white; callus white with dark brown, rather smudged dots.

Cypraea pyriformis

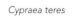

C. asellus

L. 1758 *Indo-west Pacific to Samoa, 0.8in (20mm).*

White with three broad bands of very dark brown-black edged with lighter brown.

C. quadrimaculata

Gray 1824 *Northern half of Australia, Indonesia, east Malay Peninsula, Singapore, Philippines and New Guinea, 1.2in (30mm).*

Cypraea teres

Rather square with strong teeth. White with a faint blue tinge; two, faint, narrow, darker bands on the dorsum and heavy stippling of light brown dots; two, large, dark brown spots at each end.

Cypraea asellus

C. pallidula

Gaskoin 1849 *Japan, Philippines, north Australia and east to Samoa, 0.8in (20mm).*

White or pale brown dorsum, more or less heavily speckled with green-brown dots and with four, equally spaced, narrow, blue-gray bands; base white. Closely related and very similar are *C. interrupta* Gray 1824 and *C. luchuana* Kuruda 1960.

Cypraea quadrimaculata   Cypraea pallidula

C. irrorata

Gray 1828 *Central Pacific, 0.6in (15mm).*
Blue-white dotted with red-brown; dots
darker on margins; may have a red-brown
blotch on columellar margin as illustrated.

C. fimbriata

Gmelin 1791 *Indo-Pacific to the Tuamotu
Islands and Tahiti, 0.8in (20mm).*
Blue-white with pale brown speckling and
interrupted bands; darker brown spots on the
labial margin; two purple-brown spots on the
anterior canal and one each on the spire and end
of the posterior projection of the labial margin.

Cypraea irrorata

   C. irrorata and *C. fimbriata* together with *C. gracilis* (see
page 98) are three of a complex of closely related and very
similar shells. Others in the group are *C. hammondae* Iredale
1939. *C. microdon* Gray 1828, *C. minoridens* Melville 1901,
and *C. serrulifera* Schilder and Schilder 1938. *C. raysummer-
si* Schilder 1960 is a synonym of *C. hammondae.*
All inhabit areas within the general limits of
north Australia, east Indonesia, the Philippines and eastward across the Pacific.

Cypraea fimbriata

97

Cypraea albuginosa

C. albuginosa

Gray 1825 *Gulf of California, the Bay of Panama, Ecuador and the Galapagos Islands, 0.8in (20mm).*
Pyriform with rather fine teeth. Pale lilac base color which forms a much darker line on the margins; dorsum is heavily ocellated with dark red-brown rings with white-lilac centers and also with small white-lilac spots; three faint bands show through; base is lilac at edges fading to white at aperture; teeth white.

C. poraria

L. 1758 *Indo-Pacific from east Africa to Tahiti including south Japan and northeast Australia, 0.6in (15mm).*
Somewhat similar to *C. albuginosa* but heavier and rounder, and extremities less produced. Background rich purple-lilac, darker than in *C. albuginosa*, with white spots and ocellations, but rings are purple instead of red-brown. The color tends to fade quickly after collection.

C. helvola

L. 1758 *Indo-Pacific from east Africa to Tahiti, including south Japan and the northern half of Australia, 0.8in (20mm).*
Beautifully colored when fresh – like *C. poraria* it fades rapidly. Dorsum has background color of pale blue heavily dotted with lighter spots, and is more or less sparsely blotched with large, dark red-brown spots which run together toward the margins to form solid uneven bands, one on each side, which do not join at the extremities. Margins, sharply divided from sides, are callous and a rich red spreading over the base and coarse teeth. Convex base bears darker red mark on center of columellar side. This very handsome shell varies somewhat over the vast area in which it occurs.

Cypraea poraria

C. gracilis

Gaskoin 1849 *Indian Ocean and west Pacific including south Japan, the Philippines, south coast of New Guinea, north Australia, the Great Barrier Reef and Fiji, 0.6in (15mm) to 1in (25mm).*
This shell has a number of races and varies considerably in size and depth of color.

Cypraea
gracilis
(Philippines)

Cypraea helvola

Cypraea
gracilis
(Singapore)

Background color blue-gray, more or less heavily stippled with brown and one or more irregular brown spots across the center of the dorsum; faintly banded; brown spots on margins tend to spread on to white base; two dark spots at each extremity which spread into the anterior and posterior canals.

C. spurca

L. 1758 *The only cowrie found throughout the Atlantic and Mediterranean area in which cowries occur, 1in (25mm).*
The Mediterranean shell is long and narrow with slightly swollen base and very open anterior canal. The extremities are produced, especially anteriorly. Its dorsum is light tan with darker heavy stippling and larger dark brown spots around the margins which are slightly callous; base cream to light tan.

Cypraea spurca

C. spurca acicularis

Gmelin 1791 *America, 0.8in (20mm).*
Smaller, squatter and rounder than *C. spurca*. Heavily callous margins. Dorsum spots are orange; base and margins are white; dark spots on margins are more discrete. I have a beautiful specimen taken from the digestive tract of the fish *Amphyethys cryptocentum*.

Cypraea spurca acicularis

C. boivinii

Kiener 1843 *South Japan, the Philippines, Malaya, Singapore and Sumatra, 1in (25mm).*
Narrow shell with quite strong teeth. Very pale, smoky, blue-gray with indistinct brown spots, and a conspicuous dorsal line edged in pale brown, running from a spire blotch to the edge of the anterior canal; extremities, margins and base white.

Cypraea boivinii

C. labrolineata

Gaskoin 1849 *central Indo-Pacific from Sumatra to Fiji and Hawaii including Okinawa and north and northeast Australia, 0.8in (20mm).*
Somewhat elongate; rather coarse teeth. Dark green dorsum, heavily spotted with white; line of dark spots, often joining up around the margins, especially on either side of anterior and posterior canals; extremities and base white.

Cypraea labrolineata

Cypraea eburnea   Cypraea miliaris   Cypraea lamarckii

C. eburnea

Barnes 1824 *West and south New Guinea, Queensland and the Solomons, to Fiji and the Cook Islands, 2in (50mm).*
Produced extremities; pitted labial margin; strong teeth. Pure white or with a very faint cream blush on the dorsum.

C. miliaris

Gmelin 1791 *North Australia, Philippines and Malay Peninsula to south Japan, 1.8in (45mm).*
Shaped like *C. eburnea,* above. Dorsum pale brown or green-brown with small white spots of varying size and usually a conspicuous dorsal line without spots; base and margins white.

C. lamarckii

Gray 1825 *West Indian Ocean to the Strait of Malacca and north to Karachi, 2in (50mm).*
Similar in shape to the two preceding shells and marked like *C. miliaris* but in addition some, at times many, of the dorsal spots are ocellated. It also has darker brown spots on the margins and axial lines of the same color at the extremities; base white.

C. erosa

L. 1758 *Indo-Pacific from east Africa to Tahiti including southeast Africa, Gulfs of Aden and Oman, Queensland, Japan and Hawaii, 2.2in (55mm).*
Variable within this large range but generally rather flattened with strongly callous and deeply pitted margins, and some-what produced extremities. Base convex with very strong teeth. Dorsum brown or brown-green with profuse small

Cypraea erosa   Cypraea nebrites

white dots, a few sometimes ocellated, and some larger brown spots; margins cream with some brown dots and dashes; usually a rather square, more or less colorful, purple-brown blotch halfway along each margin which may spread well on to the base.

C. nebrites
Melville 1888 *Red Sea and Gulf of Aden to Zanzibar, the Gulf of Oman and the Persian Gulf, 1.4in (35mm).*
Somewhat similar to *C. erosa* but more callous. The dorsum is darker as are the dots on the margin and the square blotches which do not spread on to the base; the latter has red-brown dots and dashes, especially on the outer ends of the labial teeth.

C. caputserpentis
L. 1758 *Indo-Pacific from east Africa to Tahiti, South Africa to Arabia and Japan, and from Queensland to Hawaii, 1.6in (40mm).*
Rather flattened with broad, angular margins and a humped dorsum. A broad, dark brown band covers the wide margins and part of the base, fading to a white aperture; pale pink to cream, squarish blotches divide the band at each end of the shell; dorsum is also brown with small, white spots of varying size; extremities have a purple tinge.

Cypraea
caputserpentis

101

C. caputdraconis

Melville 1888 *Easter Island, 1.2in (30mm).*
An uncommon shell because it is found only on Easter Island in the east Pacific, and is the only cowrie found there. Superficially it resembles the shell *C. caputserpentis*, but is less depressed, having a humped back and less expanded margins. Wide margins, base and interstices of teeth are very dark brown to black; spots on the lighter brown dorsum are smaller than in the average *C. caputserpentis* and are pale blue. Dorsal sulcus is red-brown.

Cypraea caputdraconis

C. sulcidentata

Gray 1824 *Hawaiian Islands, 1.8in (45mm).*
A broad, hump-backed shell with callous margins, a convex base, and very close-set, deeply cut teeth. The margins and base are dark brown when fresh but very rapidly fade to a fawn color (as illustrated), lightening to almost white at the teeth; dorsum has four, darker fawn bands against a blue-gray background.

C. schilderorum

Iredale 1939 *Central Pacific from Guam to Society Islands, and from Midway and Hawaii to Fiji and Tonga, 1.2in (30mm).*
Closely related to *C. sulcidentata* and *C. kuroharai* Hale 1961. It is smaller than *C. sulcidentata*, more depressed and has a pure white base and teeth, the latter being fine. The dorsal pattern and color are very similar, except for a red-brown line at the upper edge of the margins.

Cypraea sulcidentata

C. ventriculus

Lamarck 1810 *South Pacific from New Caledonia and Solomons to the Marquesas, 2in (50mm).*
It is a depressed, solid and heavy shell with large lateral calluses. The dorsum is banded as in the previous two

Cypraea schilderorum

Cypraea ventriculus

Cypraea
carneola

species, and is rich red-brown fading to a gray-brown margin and then to white at the lips; an uneven cream-tan band, showing the banding, runs axially across the dorsum.

Cypraea talpa

C. carneola

L. 1758 *Throughout the Indian Ocean and west and central Pacific Ocean, 2in (50mm).*
Pale pink-brown with four darker bands; teeth bright purple. Very large specimens up to 4in (100mm) may be a separate species *C. laviathan* Schilder and Schilder 1937, which has a smaller range-north Australia and central Pacific.

C. talpa

L. 1758 *Throughout the Indian and west and central Pacific Oceans, 2.2in (55mm).*
A beautiful cowrie, its base, margins and extremities are very dark brown to black; dorsum banded with shades of golden brown on a creamy background. A very similar cowrie, *C. exusta* Sowerby 1832, is found in the Gulf of Aden; it has finer teeth and is more pyriform.

C. cribraria

L. 1758 *East Africa to the central Pacific, Japan to northern half of Australia, 1in (25mm).*
The most common of a number of related and somewhat similar looking cowries including *C. cribellum* Gaskoin 1849, Mauritius and Reunion; *C. esontropia* Duclos 1833, Mauritius; *C. catholicorum* Schilder and Schilder 1938, New Britain and New Caledonia; *C. cumingii* Sowerby 1822, east Polynesia; and *C. haddnightae* Trenberth 1973, south Australia. It varies over its wide range and is divided into a number of races differing mainly in depth of color and callosity of the margins. The base and margins are white and the dorsum red-brown, and well-covered with largish, almost circular, white spots.

Cypraea cribraria

103

The *C. arabica* complex

The shells in this complex have long caused problems for the conchologist as they all have somewhat similar characteristics. However, it seems generally accepted today that there are seven species. While a typical specimen of one of the species is easy to classify, as in all species there occur atypical specimens in which one or more characteristics may resemble those of another species. Classification may then be very difficult even with a large series of shells for comparison.

Cypraea arabica

C. arabica

L. 1758 *Indo-Pacific from east Africa to Tahiti and from Japan to north Australia, 3in (80mm).*
Subcylindrical with strong callus on the margins. White, cream or pale brown; dorsum with overlay of fine, generally axial, brown lines interrupted by gaps or reticulations where the base color shows through; callus is spotted with darker brown; the base white, cream or pale brown; no dark blotch on the columella; teeth, often longer in the middle of the columella, pale or dark brown.

C. eglantina

Duclos 1833 *Central Indo-Pacific from Malay Peninsula to Samoa, including the northern half of Australia, Taiwan and the Marshalls, 2.8in (70mm).*

Cypraea eglantina

Cylindrical and elongate with a relatively straight aperture and poorly developed callus on the margins. Convex base. Short teeth. The reticulations on the dorsum are smaller and more even than on *C. arabica*. There is usually a small dark blotch on the spire.

C. histrio

Gmelin 1791 *Indian Ocean from east Africa across to Western Australia, 2.8in (70mm).*
Inclined to be rather humpbacked. Strong marginal callus. Moderately strong teeth. Convex base. Base color white or very pale blue-white; reticulations on dorsum large and clear-cut with the

Cypraea histrio

brown lines confluent and indistinct; large purple-brown spots on the callus and one on the spire; base white; teeth red-brown.

C. maculifera

Schilder 1932 *Central Pacific from Fiji and Tonga to Tahiti and northward to Hawaii and Midway, 3.5in (90mm).*
The largest of the complex. Strong marginal callus. The brown lines on the dorsum are replaced by solid brown color, even more than in *C. histrio;* quite large reticulations. Its most distinguishing feature is a dark brown blotch on the columella.

Cypraea maculifera

C. grayana

Schilder 1930 *Red Sea, Gulfs of Aden and Oman and the Persian Gulf, 2.6in (65mm).*
Convex base. Dorsum humped posteriorly; markings on it are between those of *C. arabica* and *C. histrio.* Seldom has a blotch on the spire. The faint bands which can be seen across the dorsum on most of the *C. arabica* complex are strongest in this species.

Cypraea grayana

C. scurra

Gmelin 1791 *Indo-Pacific from east Africa to Clipperton Island and Tahiti, 2in (50mm).*
Cylindrical and elongate. Very round base. Large dorsal reticulations; marginal spots purple to purple-brown; no blotch on spire; teeth red-brown.

C. depressa

Gray 1824 *Indian Ocean from east Africa to Java, and also the central Pacific from the Marshalls, to Clipperton Island and from New Caledonia to Tahiti, but has not been found in the Borneo, Philippines, New Guinea and Australian area, 2.2in (55mm).*
Heavily callous and expanded margins give the shell a depressed look and a round outline. Very convex base. Teeth relatively coarse and large. The reticulations are small and clear cut, white against a red-brown background; margins with strong, brown spots and purple-brown clouding which tend to run over on to the white base; teeth red-brown.

Cypraea scurra

Cypraea depressa

C. tigris

L. 1758 *Indian, west and central Pacific Oceans, 4in (100mm).*
Probably the best known of all the cowries and the most
variable in size, shape and color. It is one of the largest
cowries, up to 5in (130mm), the largest specimens being
found in Hawaii. Its base is white and the dorsum usually
cream-white with purple-black spots, sometimes so sparse
as to give the shell an almost albino appearance and sometimes so heavy as to make it look black. It is the only cowrie
which I have ever found blatantly exposed on a reef during
the day. All the others have been fairly well hidden in or
under coral and rock or marine growths.

Cypraea tigris

C. pantherina

Lightfoot 1786 *Red Sea and Gulf of Aden, 2.6in (65mm).*
Anterior end of aperture widens out markedly. This shell
varies little in shape but considerably in color. Base white;
dorsum can be from white with smallish dark purple-brown
spots and faint pale blue clouding, to darkish purple-brown
heavily mottled with deeper color; dorsal line is markedly
conspicuous and contrasting.

Vermetus pantherina

C. camelopardalis
Perry 1811 *Red Sea and Gulf of Aden, but not at the northern end of the former, 2in (50mm).*
Similar in shape to *C. pantherina*, but is much rarer and does not vary in color to any extent. Base, margins and extremities are a white or pale flesh color and the dorsum a pink-fawn with discrete white to pale blue spots; columellar sulcus is a rich purple with flesh-colored teeth.

C. vitellus
L. 1758 *Indian Ocean, west and central Pacific to Tahiti, 2in (50mm).*
This cowrie varies considerably in size but is similar in shape and markings to *C. camelopardalis* except that its dorsum is a light brown and the spots white. It has no coloring on the columella sulcus. It is also a much more common shell.

Closely related to *C. vitellus* are two rare cowries, neither of which are illustrated:

Cypraea camelopardalis

C. nivosa (not illustrated)
Broderip 1827 *From the central Indian Ocean northeast to Thailand, 2.4in (60mm).*
The spotting on the dorsum is not white, as with *C. vitellus*, but a paler brown than the surrounding color. Near the margin some of the spots are white and the base is pink-brown. The extremities are pale brown instead of cream or white.

C. broderipii (not illustrated)
Sowerby 1832 *East South Africa, 3.5in (90mm).*
One of the rarest of cowries, with fewer than ten specimens being known. It is white with an orange-red reticulated dorsum.

Cypraea vitellus

The three species of cowries on this page are very similar, and all are from tropical America, two from the Atlantic side and one from the Pacific. One, *C. cervus*, can grow to a greater length than any other cowrie, although *C. tigris* may be of greater volume.

Cypraea cervus

C. cervus

L. 1771 *Florida, the Bahamas and Mexico, 5in (130mm).*
It is somewhat inflated with a convex base and only a little callous on the labial margin. Its underlying color is blue-gray, and the dorsum and sometimes the columellar side of the base is heavily clouded with brown, the gray showing through as profuse, indiscrete spots except on the base itself. Three pale bands, also indiscrete, cross the dorsum. The teeth are a rich dark brown and the interior blue. Some of the spots on the sides may be faintly ocellated.

Cypraea cervinetta

C. cervinetta
Kiener 1843 *Southern end of the Gulf of California, northwest coast of South America and the Galapagos Islands, 4in (100mm).*
Despite living on the other side of the continent it is very similar to the cowrie *C. cervus.* It is, however, smaller and more cylindrical. It is not as inflated as its neighbor, and its extremities are more produced. Its teeth are more sharply defined and the banding on the dorsum is more distinct, as also are the ocellations of the marginal spots. Spots on the dorsum are also frequently ocellated. Its general color, however, is the same.

C. zebra
L. 1758 *Caribbean and down the east coast of South America to south Brazil, 3.5in (90mm).*
Not as inflated as *C. cervus* though often more so than *C. cervinetta.* Colors are generally rather lighter than in either of the others, and the interior is a paler blue. The spots on the margins are much more strongly ocellated. A variety from northern South America which is smaller and darker has been named *C.z. dissimilis* Schilder 1924.

Cypraea zebra

109

C. mappa

L. 1758 *Indian Ocean, west and central Pacific but excluding north and west Australia, south Indonesia and the Hawaiian Islands, 2.9in (75mm).*

It varies considerably in size, shape and color, but is invariably handsome. It has a most unusual dorsal sulcus from which it gets its name, and can be heavily inflated or subcylindrical. The color of the base can be white or a rich pink; teeth white or orange; dorsum white or more usually brown with a darker reticulated pattern, and unreticulated spots; slightly callous margins are fawn with darker, indiscrete spots.

Cypraea mappa

C. stercoraria

L. 1758 *West Africa from Cape Verde Islands to Luanda, 3.3in (85mm).*

A somewhat gross shell, very variable in size. It is inflated with the lateral calluses extended at both the extremities, which are markedly produced. Its teeth are coarse, crossing the columellar sulcus and the conspicuous columellar fossula, and reaching to the margins of the extensions at the anterior end of the aperture. Teeth white with black interstices; base white or fawn; margins blue-gray and spotted with brown and with dark clouding at the upper edge; dorsum fawn to blue mottled with brown; small spire blotch. Dwarf specimens are found in the islands in the Bight of Benin.

Cypraea stercoraria

Cypraea stercoraria

C. turdus

Lamarck 1810 *Red Sea, Gulf of Aden and Oman, the east African coast to Mozambique and Madagascar, 1.8in (45mm).* Variable in shape and size but usually depressed, with callous margins. White with small olive brown spots profusely covering the dorsum which give way to larger purple spots on the sides and margins; base white.

Cypraea turdus

C. lynx

L. 1758 *Indian, west and central Pacific Oceans, 1.2in (30mm)*.
It varies in size and shape over its vast range, where it is
common, but is easily recognizable. It has a ridge on
each side of the base running the length of the shell.
The dorsal sulcus is conspicuous. Creamy dorsum is
covered with small, purple spots and blotches, and
a few larger spots of the same color; base white
and interstices of orange teeth.

C. mauritiana

L. 1758 *Indian, west and central Pacific Oceans
but not in north and west Australia nor in most
of the China Seas, 2.6in (65mm)*.
Often found where rough water is common. It is a
very heavy, solid shell with strongly callous margins
and a humped back. Base and sides almost black
and teeth dark brown with white interstices; dorsum
dark brown, reticulated with pink-brown and a deep
mahogany, dorsal line.

Cypraea lynx

Cypraea mauritiana

111

C. testudinaria

L. 1758 *Central Indian and Pacific Oceans from Mombasa and Madagascar to Tahiti including Sri Lanka, Malaysia, the north Indonesian Islands, the Philippines and north New Guinea, 4.1in (105mm).*

It is the third largest of the cowries. Cylindrical and heavy. Base fawn, light at aperture and teeth; dorsum also fawn with dark brown spots, irregular light and dark brown blotches covering much of the area especially at the extremities. All but the area adjoining the aperture is profusely covered with minute, white spots which often barely show unless they are examined very closely or with a magnifying glass. They appear to be in the glaze and look as if they are imperfections in the specimen being examined.

Cypraea testudinaria

Cypraea aurantium

C. aurantium

Gmelin 1791 *Central Pacific including the Society, Ellice, Gilbert, Marshall, Caroline, Guam, New Caledonia and Fiji Islands; it has also been found in the Philippines; 3in (80mm).*
Though a comparatively rare shell it is includ-ed here as it is among the cowries much as *Conus gloriamaris* is among the cones – not by any means the rarest, but probably the most sought after. Inflated and heavy. Dorsum rich peach orange; base and extremities white with orange teeth.

C. argus

L. 1758 *Indian, north, west and central Pacific Oceans, 3.5in (90mm).*
Another very beautiful cowrie which varies considerably in size. Cylindrical with only slightly callous margins. Base fawn with two, dark brown blotches on either side of aperture, those on the right (outer lip) side being sometimes absent or nearly so; teeth edged with brown; dorsum lighter fawn with four, darker bands, darkest at top of shell. Whole of dorsum down to callus profusely covered with dark red-brown rings of varying thickness – the 'Argus' Eyes' or 'Pheasant's Eyes' from which it takes its name.

Cypraea argus

Cypraea limacina

C. limacina

Lamarck 1810 *Indo-west Pacific to Samoa and from northern Australia to Japan, 1.4in (35mm).* A fully adult shell has very fine nodules on the dorsum, stronger on the sides, unless inhabiting quiet water when, like a juvenile, it is smooth. When fresh it is a rich, deep, red-brown to black which soon fades to a fawn-gray; dorsum is covered with small, white spots again absent in the juvenile; callous labial margin is pitted and white; base white; long, strong teeth and extremities red-brown.

C. staphylaea

L. 1758 *Location as C. limacina above, 1in (25mm).*
Similar to *C. limacina,* but rounder, more inflated and has tiny nodules generally white and more profuse. It is also dark-colored when taken alive soon fading through gray to almost white. The main distinguishing feature is the teeth which cross the base to both margins. The extremities are also red-brown.

Cypraea staphylaea

C. nucleus

L. 1758 *Indo-Pacific to Tahiti but not north and northeast Australia nor Papua New Guinea and Solomon Islands area, 1.2in (30mm).*
The dorsum of *C. nucleus* is covered with small pustules and fine ridges. The latter seem to be extensions of the teeth which completely cover the base and the slightly callous margins; they do not, however, cross the dorsal sulcus. Convex base. Pale brown to off-white, bright and shiny.

C. granulata

Pease 1862 *Hawaiian Islands, 1.6in (40mm).*
The only cowrie not shiny as an adult, although the juvenile is. Rounder in outline than *C. nucleus,* its dorsal pustules are fewer and higher, as are the teeth and their extensions as dorsal ridges. The latter give the margins a strong, toothed effect. Every second or third ridge is much bigger than the intervening ones. Brown-gray to white; teeth edged and pustules ringed red-brown.

Cypraea nucleus

C. bistrinotata

Schilder & Schilder 1937 *Indo-Pacific to Tahiti, bar southeast Africa and Hawaii, 0.8in (20mm).*
Adults have a pustulate dorsum with a callus posteriorly and three dark brown blotches each divided by the dorsal sulcus. Juveniles smooth. It has four dark brown spots, one at each corner of the base. Teeth are prominent and cross most of the base; anteriorly on the columella they cross the margin on to the edge of the dorsum. One of a complex of five or six species having many similar characteristics. All are small, globose with produced extremities and generally pale brown or tan.

C. cicercula

L.1758 *Indian Ocean and the Pacific to*

Cypraea granulata

Tahiti, including Hawaii, 0.9in (24mm).
Dorsum similarly pustulate but without callus. Instead there is a groove in which is a small dark spot on the spire. No spots on the base. Long teeth. Generally a lighter color than *C. bistrinotata. C. margarita* (not illustrated) Dillwyn 1817 which is smooth on top of the dorsum and has shorter teeth may be a variety of *C. cicercula* or a separate species.

C. globulus

Cypraea bistrinotata

L. 1758 *Indo-Pacific to Tahiti, bar the Arabian Sea and northwest Australia, 0.9in (24mm).*
Smooth dorsum. May have four, dark spots on the base. The anterior teeth on the columella do not cross the margin on to the dorsum. The latter often has small, brown dots, especially on the sides. Like *C. bistrinotata* it has a callus posteriorly on the dorsum.

Cypraea cicercula

The following shells are also in this complex but not illustrated.

Cypraea globulus

C. dillwyni (not illustrated)

Schilder 1922 *central Pacific, 0.6in (15mm).*
Elongate; light brown; white base; small and very small white spots on the dorsum and a brown blotch at each end.

C. mariae (not illustrated)

Schilder & Schilder 1927 *Philippines and central Pacific including the Solomons, Tonga, Hawaii and the Tuamotu Archipelago, 0.8in (20mm).*
Extremities hardly produced. White with small and very small brown rings on the dorsum and sides.

Cypraea kieneri

C. kieneri

Hidalgo 1906 *Indo-west Pacific to Fiji, 0.9in (22mm).*
With the two following species, this forms another group of small, very similar cowries. Somewhat inflated, more so posteriorly; a little rostrate anteriorly. Very little marginal callus except on those from Australia. Teeth moderate but very short on the anterior of the columella (chief difference from *C. hirundo* below). Cream or white; dorsum largely clouded with blue and divided in three parts by two, uneven, wavy bands. Degree of marking variable. Margins have more cream than blue area and are speckled red-brown. Two, dark brown spots at each end, others forming a more or less broken band on dorsum which is also minutely speckled with brown; base white.

Cypraea hirundo   *Cypraea ursellus*

C. hirundo

L. 1758 *Area as for C. kieneri but not southeast Africa or north Pacific east of Japan and the Philippines, 0.9in (22mm).*
Similar to *C. kieneri* except that the teeth are fine and cross most of the base.

C. ursellus

Gmelin 1791 *West Pacific in the triangle south Japan, Tonga and the Great Barrier Reef, 0.5in (12mm).*
Like *C. hirundo* but smaller and more inflated; teeth crossing almost the entire base. It is extremely difficult always to distinguish a *C. ursellus* shell from a small *C. hirundo*.

Cypraea stolida

C. stolida

L. 1758 *Indo-Pacific to Samoa, 1.4in (35mm).*
Very variable in size, shape and color but always a beautiful shell. Many of the varieties have been given names. May be subcylindrical and elongate or almost rectangular in shape. Moderate callus; strongish teeth except in the variety *breventata* Sowerby 1870, where the columellar teeth are short. Base white or cream; dorsum pale blue to pale blue-green; there is usually a rather square, dark brown blotch on the dorsum which is often more or less joined to other rectangular blotches at each corner; the latter lighter in their centers and on the margin of the shell. Small brown dots more or less profuse over the light-colored areas and especially on the margins and on each side of the shell's extremities.

C. cylindrica

Born 1778 *North Australia, South China Sea to Guam, the New Hebrides and New Caledonia, 1.6in (40mm).*
Usually elongate and cylindrical, but northwest Australian specimens may be rather inflated. Teeth variable, from very short and small to longer and strong. Blue or pale green-blue with irregular, more or less dark, brown blotches or

Cypraea cylindrica

blotch on the dorsum; basic darker banding is often inconspicuous; profuse, tiny, brown dots; two, larger spots on each side at both extremities; base white.

C. caurica
L. 1758 *Indo-Pacific to Samoa, and from Japan to north Australia, 2.2in (55mm).* Elongate and usually a little inflated. Labial teeth very strong; has a more or less developed callus. Cream shell with three, blue-brown dorsal bands; the whole dorsum heavily stippled with tiny, brown dots, thickest and confluent on the center; large and small, brown spots on the yellow-tinged margin; base pale fawn to off-white; teeth lighter.

C. xanthodon
Sowerby 1832 *East Australia from Sydney and northward, 1.4in (35mm).*
Pyriform; moderately callous margins. Dorsum blue-green; profuse, brown speckles; three, indistinct, dark bands. Dark brown spots on margin, one on the spire and one each side anteriorly. Those on the margin are smudged toward, and sometimes on to base. Margin, base cream; teeth darker.

C. subviridis
Reeve 1835 From *northern Australia, New Caledonia and Fiji, 1.6in (40mm).*
Variable; pyriform and inflated from Western Australia, smaller and more cylindrical from the east of its range. Pale blue-cream speckled brown; an irregular blotch of darker brown on dorsum; indistinct purple-brown band; extremities may be tinged pale purple or brown; base white or cream.

Cypraea caurica

Cypraea xanthodon

Cypraea subviridis

The south Australian Cowrie Complex

There are a number of cowries from south Australia which raise considerable difficulties in classification. Much work has already been done on these, but much more is necessary. I have followed C. M. Burgess who, in his leading work *The Living Cowries* (see Bibliography), has dealt with this complex in detail. The problems arise through many specific and subspecific names having been given because individual characteristics of specimens of the same species vary considerably. It has been noted that some characteristics vary a great deal with the age or state of development of an individual, and also with the depth of water which it inhabits. Characteristics of the animal itself have not yet provided means of specific identification.

C. angustata

Gmelin 1791 From *southeast Australia and north and east Tasmania, 1.4in (35mm).*
Somewhat inflated. Deep water varieties *emblema* and *molleri* both Iredale 1931, are more inflated, thinner and lighter colored. Dorsum usually not banded; pale pink-brown; the margins with discrete, brown spots often extending well up the sides and on to the base.

C. declivis

Sowerby 1870 *South Australia from Cape Howe, south of Sydney westward across the*

Cypraea angustata
var. *molleri*

Cypraea angustata
var. *mayi*

Great Australian Bight and north Tasmania, 1.1in (28mm). From dark brown to cream or rose and always with pale to dark brown speckling on the dorsum and margins; base usually white.

C. comptonii

Gray 1847 *South Australia, not quite reaching Sydney or Perth.*
The most variable, especially in color. Pink-brown, quite dark (var. *trenberthae* Trenberth 1961) through cream (*C. angustata* var. *mayi* Beddome 1897) to pure white (*C. angustata* var. *albata* Beddome 1897). Usually with brown or gray-brown spotting on the margins and sometimes a little brown on the dorsum. Two narrow bands close together across the middle of the dorsum are, however, characteristic except in the pure white variety.

Cypraea declivis

Cypraea comptonii

There may be a third near the spire and occasionally a fourth anteriorly. In the variety *wilkinsi* Griffiths 1959 the spotting and banding is faint or absent, and in *C. angustata* var. *subcarnea* Beddome is a pale flesh color.

C. piperata

Gray 1825 *Same area as C. comptonii but including Perth, Western Australia, 1in (25mm).*
Cream to white, spotted and/or reticulated with pale brown. Three, broad bands of irregular, broken, darker brown spots; fine light or dark spots on the margin, sides and outer edge of the base; latter white. It is probably as well known by the name *C. bicolor* Gaskoin 1849.

C. pulicaria (not illustrated)

Reeve 1846 *Southwest Australia only, from the Swan River to Cape Leeuwin, 0.8in (20mm).*
Cylindrical. Cream or white with four, narrow, broken, brown bands on the dorsum and brown, spotted margins. The columellar teeth appear to be relatively longer than in the other species in the complex. The main characteristic which distinguishes it is a strongly concave fossula which projects into the aperture.

Cypraea piperata

C. errones

L.1758 *East Indian Ocean and west Pacific from the Strait of Malacca to Samoa, and from Japan to the northern half of Australia, 1.6in (40mm).*
Very variable in size, shape and color. Pyriform to cylindrical, more or less inflated and callous with sunken spire. Aperture wider anteriorly. Generally pale green or blue-green dorsum with three or four, rather faint, bluer bands; heavily speckled with green or green-brown, and often with a dark brown, irregular blotch in the middle of the dorsum and a spot on each side anteriorly.

Cypraea errones

C. ovum

Gmelin 1791 *Area as for C. errones but not quite as far east, 1.6in (40mm).*
Very similar to *C. errones* but with yellow or orange between the teeth, the color being strong or weak. Generally more pyriform than *C. errones*.

Cypraea ovum

119

Cypraea moneta

Cypraea annulus

Cypraea
felina
var. fabula

C. moneta

L. 1758 The Money Cowrie Indo-Pacific from east Africa to the Galapagos Islands, 1.6in (40mm).
Very variable, usually rather flattened and angular; heavily callous sides. Dorsum rich or pale yellow, sometimes a fine and very bright ring like C. annulus; sides and margins paler; base white; three, more or less conspicuous, narrow, dorsal bands. Illustrated specimen has the uncommon ring and its sides are unusually white. Teeth less coarse than in C. annulus but sometimes cover much of base as low, blunt ridges.

C. annulus

L. 1758 Indian, west and south Pacific Oceans, 1.2in (30mm).
Variable, generally oval with a somewhat humped dorsum. Smoothly rounded margins, lacking any keel. Dorsum yellow-green or blue-green, faintly banded; it is separated from the callous sides by a narrow ring of bright yellow-orange; flesh-colored below the ring, becoming paler toward the teeth.

C. obvelata

Lamarck 1810 East central Pacific Ocean, including the Society Islands, Tahiti, the Marquesas and Jarvis Islands, 1in (25mm).
Somewhat similar to C. annulus but with a very strong, lateral callus which is so heavy that it forms a groove separating it from the dorsum. Teeth coarse and long. Dorsum pale to very pale blue, narrow banding faint or absent; usually with a thin yellow ring. Callus and base very pale pink, sometimes white.

Cypraea
obvelata

C. felina

Gmelin 1791 Indo-Pacific from east Africa to Samoa, and from Japan to the northern half of Australia, 1in (25mm).
Another extremely variable species with named varieties, especially four described below. All have very dark, almost black, discrete spots on their margins. The largest, C. felina, is from east Africa, from Zanzibar southward. Ovate; callous margins. Dorsum cream to pale green with four, blue bands and speckled with tiny, brown dots; margin pale tan with large black spots especially on each side of the two ends; base also pale tan. C. fabula Kiener 1843 from the Gulfs of Aden and Oman is much rounder in outline; dorsal markings are darker; its margins have more, bigger and

Cypraea
felina
var. listeri

sometimes confluent spots; base lighter or white. *C. listeri* Gray 1825 from Mauritius and the Seychelles, is more cylindrical; dorsum blue-white; the blue banding is more conspicuous; marginal spotting less heavy; base white with the banding showing on the left side. *C. melvilli* Hidalgo 1906 is from Japan to north Australia; close to *C. listeri* but more cylindrical and generally more green than blue.

C. arabicula

Lamarck 1810 *West Central America from the southern half of the Gulf of California and Lower California to Peru and the Galapagos Islands, 1.2in (30mm).*
High dorsum hump posteriorly; callous, rather sharp margins. Convex base with fine, sharply cut teeth and a deep fossula. Dorsum pale mauve reticulated with dark green-brown; margins broad centrally, pale mauve with smudged dark mauve to black spots which are sometimes profuse and cover the outer third of the base. There is a small, creamy white spot from the spire to the posterior canal.

Cypraea arabicula

Cypraea robertsi

C. robertsi

Hidalgo 1906 *Areas as C. arabicula, 1.2in (30mm).*
Pyriform with callous margins and convex base. Much coarser teeth than *C. arabicula*. Dorsum very pale mauve to white or blue-white with heavy, fine, dark green-brown reticulations. Wide margins are smoky brown with mauve spots which may spill over on to the white base; canals with a dark purple-brown spot on either side and a creamy white spot between.

C. spadicea

Swainson 1823 *South California from Monterey Bay to San Benito Island, 2.4in (60mm).*
Elongate and produced anteriorly. Dorsum is rich brown fairly sharply but unevenly edged with darker brown; margins wide and gray-pink or gray-cream; very faint, smudged spots can sometimes be seen under the callus; base white.

Cypraea spadicea

Cypraea edentula

Cypraea capensis

C. edentula

Gray 1825 *South Africa from Cape Town to north of East London, 1in (25mm).*

One of a group of endemic South African cowries, few if any of which have been taken live. Almost all specimens of this cowrie are toothless. It is hump-backed and its outer lip is callous and extended posteriorly. Its spire is sunken. Base white and dorsum pale brown with darker brown spots.

C. capensis

Gray 1828 Found *South Africa from Cape Town to East London, 1in (25mm).*

Another of the group of South African cowries which includes also *C. algoensis* Gray 1825, *C. fuscorubra* Shaw 1909, the rare *C. fultoni* Sowerby 1903, and very rare *C. broderipii* Sowerby 1832 (see page 106). *C. capensis* is a little more cylindrical than *C. edentula* but has the same extended outer lip posteriorly and sunken spire. Fine ridges run around the shell – except across the dorsal sulcus-giving the impression of a thumb print. This impression is heightened by the decidedly flesh color with a few brown marks and faint banding. There is also a brown spot on the spire.

C. friendii

Gray 1831 *South and west Australia from Spencer's Gulf to Shark Bay, 2.8in (70mm).*

This species, which is now thought to include *C. thersites* Gaskoin 1849, is very variable in shape and color. *C. friendii* is found at the northeastern end of the range, at shallower depths, and is narrower than *C. thersites*. The margins project anteriorly and posteriorly to form a flange, larger on the outer lip, at each end of the shell. Base and margins are

Cypraea friendii

Cypraea thersites
(See *C. friendii*)

mostly dark brown; teeth white; columellar groove white with brown markings. *C. thersites,* found at the eastern end of the range and in deep water, is more inflated. Base white around the aperture – the dark brown of the margins spreading on to the outer edge of the base. Cream background of dorsum is almost completely covered by a very deep brown.

C. decipiens
Smith 1880 *Northwest Australia, 2in (50mm).*
Pyriform, and margins only slightly callous. Both the spire and outer lip project posteriorly. Base and teeth brown; dorsum white; almost obscured by a network of light and dark brown markings.

C. hesitata
Iredale 1916 *Southeast Australia from the Bass Strait to Sydney, in deep water, 3.75in (95mm).*
This once rare shell is found in three forms, the normal *C. hesitata,* the dwarf form *beddomei* Schilder 1930 (which may be the female) and the albino variety *howelli* Iredale 1931. The shell is very pyriform with the anterior extremity produced and the posterior sharply turned through 45° toward the left or columellar side. Deeply sunken spire. White, profusely marked on dorsum with light brown blotches and darker spots, the latter becoming more discrete on the margins; extremities are also light brown. *C. beddomei,* 2in (50mm), is similarly colored.

Cypraea decipiens

Cypraea hesitata

The false cowries are related to the true cowries. They include the families Ovulidae or Amphiperatidae, Eratoidae and Lamellariidae.

FAMILY: OVULIDAE

Ovula ovum
L. 1758 *Indo-west Pacific, 4.75in (120mm)*.
Smooth with no spire but extended posterior canal and coarsely ridged lip. Pure shiny white; chocolate or red-brown interior. Found on coral reefs. Used a great deal in the South Seas as jewelry and charms, and for canoe decoration.

O. costellata
Lamarck 1810 *Indo-Pacific, 2in (50mm)*.
Similar to above, but posterior canal is somewhat notched on body side, and interior is rose pink.

Calpurnus verrucosus
L. 1758 *Indo-west Pacific, 1.4in (35mm)*.
Cowrielike bar two ribs crossing dorsum giving it an angular shape, and tubercle at each end of dorsum. Outline of base rather angular, with very fine, spiral striae. Toothed lip is coarsely ribbed. White; pink-white at extremities.

Ovula ovum

Volva brevirostris
L. 1758 *South China Sea, 1.6in (40mm)*.
Long, thin, spindle shape. Narrow aperture except near siphonal canal where lip expands a little. Lip thickened and smooth like columella. Faint, spiral lirae at extremities. Flesh, red or yellow-pink, depending on color of gorgonian (coral) on which it lives.

Volva sowerbyana

Calpurnus verrucosus

Ovula costellata

Volva brevirostris

Cyphoma gibbosa

V. volva
L. 1758 *Central Indo-Pacific, 5in (130mm).*
Rounded body whorl with fine, axial grooves; expanded, thickened lip; very long, slightly curved, obliquely ridged canals; smooth columella. Flesh-pink or brown-pink; lip white or paler pink; extremities of canals with brown tinge.

Volva volva

V. sowerbyana
Weinkauff 1881 *Indian Ocean and west Pacific, 1.2in (30mm).*
Slightly inflated body, with fine, axial striae. Short and obliquely striate canals. Thickened lip has furrow behind. Columella with about twenty, oblique, incised striae anteriorly; thick, broad rib posteriorly. Body dark flesh-pink, faintly banded centrally with cream; lip white; extremities may be orange in color.

Cyphoma gibbosa
L. 1758 *The Flamingo Tongue, southeast USA and West Indies, 1.2in (30mm).*
Chunky, callous shell with heavy, encircling ridge. Obsoletely toothed lip and smooth columella. Apricot-cream; long, rather narrow oblong of white on dorsum; callus paler; base almost white. Lives on gorgonian (coral).

Jenneria pustulata
Lightfoot 1786 *West Central America, 1in (25mm).*
Depressed; pustulate dorsum. Base has coarse ribs from aperture to margin, fifteen per side and most with a short, small rib between. Blue-white; pustules bright orange ringed with dark brown; base blue-white overlaid with dark brown; ribs white ending at margin with orange, and each joining a pustule.

FAMILY: ERATOIDAE

Trivia sanguinea
Sowerby 1822
Lower California, 0.5in (14mm).
Inflated; high dorsum with a small crease along the midline. Raised, coarse, radial, white riblets, about twenty-three a side, extending across base into aperture; slightly expanded margins. Color purple-brown; darker blotch centrally on dorsum; inside of columella, lip white.

Trivia sanguinea

T. monacha
da Costa 1778 *Mediterranean to British Isles, 0.6in (15mm).*
Chubby little shell with fairly high dorsum. Encircled by about twenty-five, coarse riblets. Thickened lip backed by shallow channel. Flesh; purple spots, one at each end and one in middle of dorsum; base white. *T. arctica* (not illustrated) Montagu 1803, from the same area, is similar but lacks the purple spots.

Jenneria pustulata

Trivia monacha

SUPERFAMILY: TONNACEA

FAMILY: CASSIDAE

The helmet shells are solid with large body whorls and short spires, usually with blunt knobs, varices, and a thickened, toothed outer lip. There is usually a broad shield beside the plicated columella or over the parietal area. They have thin, horny opercula. The animals live in sandy areas in the tropics and temperate zones, in shallow and deep water. They prey on sea urchins and other echinoids. There are about sixty species.

Cassis cornuta

L. 1758 *Indo-Pacific, up to 14in (350mm).*
Very solid and heavy with a short spire of about seven whorls. Pitted all over with mostly rather long, narrow pits between small, spiral ridges. Angular shoulder has five to seven, flat, protruding knobs or blunt spines. The suture generally outlines these knobs on the earlier whorls. Body whorl with two medium and one small smooth band with lumps or very blunt knobs. The posterior ends of earlier lips show as varices on earlier whorls – one about every two-thirds of a whorl. Outer lip thickened, widened, and the

Cassis cornuta

edge recurved. Siphonal canal twisted and turned up vertically. Narrowly umbilicate. Large parietal shield almost obscures the body whorl when looked at from below. Outer lip with up to twelve, blunt teeth. Columella has up to fifteen plaits on the lower two-thirds. Sculpture and color show through the parietal shield at the posterior end of the columella. Anterior end, columella and surrounding part of the shield are indented. White with light brown shading and sparse brown spots; purple-brown marks on the smooth bands; outer lip has about seven, brown 'squares'; teeth and outer lip white; interstices of teeth, the interior, columella and inner area of shield orange-brown; rest of shield pinky-white. The males tend to be abit smaller than the females with a slightly less expanded shield.

Cassis flammea

C. flammea

L. 1758 *Caribbean, 5in (125mm)*.
It has a low spire, about seven whorls and is axially ribbed. A row of blunt knobs on the shoulder and one of smaller knobs a little below it, one or both of which may show on earlier whorls. A row of nodules immediately below suture and another between this and the shoulder. Earlier varices about every two-thirds of a whorl. Thickened, callous lip is dentate – about ten teeth. Columella with about twenty, long, raised plicae. Short siphonal canal is twisted vertically. Color shows through much of the parietal shield. White with brown mottling and darker brown, axial, zigzag markings; outer lip has about six, dark brown spots, two or three of which show on early varices.

C. tuberosa

L. 1758 *Caribbean to Brazil, 9in (230mm)*.
Very low spire. Covered with very small, axial riblets. A row of blunt knobs on the shoulder, and two others with much smaller knobs or bumps. Early varices. Thickened, callous outer lip with about eleven teeth. Short, upturned siphonal canal. Coarsely and strongly lirate columella. Parietal callus is triangular in shape. White to blue-gray with axial, dark purple-brown, zigzag lines. About seven, rather obscure, brown spiral lines which end in dark brown, rectangular blotches on the outer lip; the interior and teeth dirty white; brown in the interstices; columella and inner area of shield dark brown; lirae white; part of parietal shield a metallic brown-pink. The illustration is of a rather young shell on which the color is particularly strong.

Cassis tuberosa

C. tessellata

Gmelin 1791 *West Africa, 10.25in (260mm)*.

Rather light and fragile for its size. Low spire and about seven whorls. Former varices about every two-thirds of a whorl. Body inflated with three rows of small knobs, the ones on the shoulder row being relatively sharp. It has one other row of very small knobs a little above the first large row, and another of small riblets immediately below the suture. It is otherwise smooth apart from axial growth lines. Inside lip turned in and back on itself; nine teeth, the center one rather elongate. Columella with eight, long, thin folds, the largest in the middle. Four teeth at the bottom of the parietal shield. The callus on the parietal wall is thin and may be pustulate from covering grains of sand or other foreign matter. Siphonal canal twisted vertically. Narrowly umbilicate. Light brown; knobs with darker brown or white blotches and other spiral rows of brown and white, alternate marks lower on the body whorl; outer lip, interior and columella white; parietal shield white but with much of the underlying color pattern showing through.

Cassis tessellata

C. nana

Tenison-Woods 1879 *3ast Australia, 2.4in (60mm)*
The smallest of the Cassidae. Very low spire with a short,
pointed apex. About five or six whorls with two, spiral rows
of small, sharp knobs on and below the shoulder; sometimes
up to three other rows with blunt nodules lower on the body
whorl. Early varices show and there are fine growth lines.
Outer lip inverted and toothed, the teeth and columella with
fine folds. Thin parietal wall, channeled toward the anterior
end and lirate below the channel. Anterior end of columella
has a shelf within the aperture. Gray-white with light brown,
axial flame marks on the spire, and three rows of white
and orange-brown spots on the body whorl, coinciding
with the rows of nodules. Outer lip white with brown tinge at
each end; columella white; parietal shield is brown with
markings behind it.

Cassis nana

C. madagascariensis

Lamarck 1822 *Caribbean, Bermuda and southeast USA,
up to 14in (350mm).*
Very short spire of about ten whorls, and inflated body,
especially ventrally. Spiral cords and ridges, the largest
below the shoulder on the body whorl which carries six,
blunt spines. There is a second row of small knobs and may
be another ridge with 'bumps'.
Suture roughly follows the
shoulder on earlier whorls;
varices about every two-
thirds of a whorl. Outer lip is
turned in then back on
itself and has about
eleven, blunt teeth.
Upturned siphonal
canal. Columella has
many strong ribs
and folds extend-
ing into the pari-
etal wall. Parietal
shield rather pear-
shaped; underlying
knobs show through
as they do also within
the aperture. Creamy
white with pale brown
clouding, especially on the
spire; outer lip and parietal
shield pink; columella and adjacent
area of parietal shield dark brown; lirae
white; interstices of teeth and outer lip
brown. *C. madaga iensis* and *C. tuberosa* are very
similar but can easily be distinguished by the shape of
the parietal shield, which in the former is somewhat
pear-shaped with a rounded outer edge, while in the
latter is triangular with a straight edge.

*Cassis
madagascariensis*

Cypraecassis rufa

L. 1758 *Indo-west Pacific, 7in (180mm).*

Solid with low spire, a sharp apex and angulate shoulders. Body whorl has three or four rows of blunt knobs, posterior row biggest, decreasing anteriorly. Spiral cords and bands, some with small knobs and some, near anterior, with axial ribs; overall fine axial cords. Thickened, broad, recurved lip, with twenty-two elongated teeth. Heavily lirate columella is toothed; large parietal shield. Siphonal canal is turned up vertically. Red-brown; pale orange-brown bands; columella red; teeth white; interstices dark brown; parietal shield pink-brown with vague darker bands.

Cypraecassis rufa

C. testiculus

L. 1758 *Tropical east and west Atlantic, 3in (80mm).*

Solid with short spire and deep suture, having small nodules below it. Body whorl has axial riblets and very fine spiral striae at each end, smooth centrally. A row of nine, small, blunt nodules on shoulder and one row a little below it. Lip is thickened, callous, backed by a deep, narrow channel, and has twenty-five teeth, large and small mostly alternating. Columella has twenty-four long ribs; heavily callous parietal shield; siphonal canal turned up vertically. Pale brown with darker brown spots; lip, interior and columella white with metallic brown nacreous overlay; outer edge of lip has seven pairs of dark brown spots.

Cypraecassis testiculus

Phalium glaucum

L. 1758 *Indo-west Pacific, 4.75in (120mm).*
Early whorls roundly shouldered with fine, spiral and axial cords; last three angular and crenulate; usually one or more varices. Expanded, rotund, smooth or malleate body whorl. Narrow ridge below suture; shoulder crenulations becoming weak nodules. Thickened lip, backed by deep channel, with three or four, strong, sharp spikes anteriorly; inside lip are up to twenty-five teeth. Columella has wide shield at anterior end and is weakly spirally wrinkled. Narrow, deep umbilicus; siphonal canal turned up vertically. Gray; lip orange; the columella and shield creamy pink to white; interior rich dark purple-brown; umbilical area white.

P. strigatum

Gmelin 1791 *North China Seas and Japan, 4.3in (110mm).*
Solid with moderate, concave spire. Varices every two-thirds of a whorl; spiral cords on earlier whorls; axial riblets becoming obsolete on penultimate whorl. Body whorl with cords and

grooves below suture, covered with incised, spiral grooves, deeper nearer anterior end but barely visible on upper body whorl. Lip is thickened, recurved, backed by deep narrow channel, and has twenty teeth. Columella has shield at anterior end; upper part of parietal shield and columella with incised, spiral striae, lower half with coarse, irregular folds. White; brown axial streaks; lip with six, pale brown blotches; interior tan.

P. decussatum
L. 1758 *From Indonesia and southeast Asia to Taiwan, 2.8in (70mm).*
Moderate spire; six or seven former varices; finely cancellate including upper part of parietal shield. Thickened, recurved lip backed by deep, narrow channel, has twenty teeth. Lower half of columella and shield with irregular, coarse, spiral ridges; upper half with four small teeth over cancelations. Posterior end of lip has two small ribs showing on later varices. Two color forms; one with spots like *P. areola*, one (illustrated) with stripes like *P. strigatum*, color blue-gray; stripes or spots dark brown; anterior part of columella and shield white; interior brown; lip, later varices white with brown squares.

Phalium glaucum

P. areola
L. 1758 *East Africa and central Indo-Pacific, 2.8in (70mm).*
Shaped like *P. decussatum* above. Spire and shoulder of penultimate whorl cancellate. Body whorl has fine, incised, spiral lines visible below suture and near base, but barely so centrally. Lip, columella and parietal area as *P. decussatum*. Blue-white with rows of brown, square-shaped spots, their axial sides curved toward the lip; lip and outer edge of shield with a pink-brown tinge.

Phalium strigatum   *Phalium decussatum*   *Phalium areola*

Phalium pyrum   Phalium labiatum iheringi   Phalium labiatum iredalei

P. pyrum
Lamarck 1822 *New Zealand, Tasmania, south Australia and South Africa, 3.5in (90mm).*
Variable with many named forms. Generally moderate spire; usually globose but sometimes elongate. Early whorls have spiral cords, sometimes cancellate. Shoulder develops small nodules on penultimate whorl, becoming blunt, low, axial knobs on body whorl, but may be smooth. An incised spiral line below suture develops on last two or three whorls. Three or four weak striae near base of body whorl. Lip recurved, denticulate or almost smooth. Lower columella and shield have four folds; upper parietal wall has smooth white callus. Dull brown-gray; red-brown areas; four bands of arrow-shaped brown marks; lip, end of canal with purple marks; interior brown.

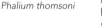

Phalium thomsoni

P. labiatum
Perry 1811 *2.9in (75mm).*
Three subspecies; from Australia and New Zealand *P.l. labiatum* Perry 1811; *P.l. iredalei*; and *P.l. iheringi*.

P. labiatum iheringi
Carcelles 1953 *South America.*
Seven or eight whorls; rather elongate with incised spiral striae on early whorls disappearing on later whorls which are roundly shouldered. Body whorl has seven, faint, blunt nodules on shoulder. Recurved, bluntly denticulate lip; columella and shield have four small and one large plait at base; thin parietal shield. Gray-cream; brown marks below suture and three rows of brown, arrow-shaped marks, backed by lighter area; aperture white; lip with brown marks.

P. labiatum iredalei
Bayer 1935 *Natal to the Cape of Good Hope, 2.8in (70mm).*
Variable from smooth-shouldered (illustrated), to knobbed, larger-shouldered form *zeylanica* Lamarck. Rather dark in

color; columella smooth with fold at bottom. Illustrated specimen has round shoulders of *iredalei,* and blue-white arrow-head spots on dorsum usually found on *zeylanica.*

P. thomsoni

Brazier 1875 *Southeast Australia, to north New Zealand, 3.5in (90mm).*
Rather light; spire usually shorter than illustrated. Early whorls cancellate; later whorls angulate, up to three spiral cords on shoulders, sometimes nodulose. Spiral incised striae on base of body whorl. Recurved lip is generally smooth, but may have very weak teeth. Posterior end of columella has a few weak folds; outer edge of columellar shield arched; lower columella folded; shield with many weak folds oblique to columellar folds. Dull white; four rows of square brown spots on body whorl, two on earlier whorls; five dark brown marks on lip.

Phalium bisulcatum

Phalium glabratum angasi

P. glabratum

Dunker 1852 *2.4in (60mm).*
Three subspecies: *P.g. glabratum* Dunker 1852, Philippines, Indonesia; *P.g. angasi; P.g. bulla* Habe 1961, China, Japan, Hawaii.

P. glabratum angasi

Iredale 1927 *East Australia.*
Thin, elongate with moderate spire; early whorls with finely beaded, spiral cords; round shoulders. Body whorl has faint spiral striae and five, incised spiral lines at base. Lip thickened and dentate, more strongly anteriorly. Columella has faint plaits at top and strong folds on lower half and shield; latter with deep indentation over umbilicus. Tan or white; dorsum side has faint brown tinge.

Phalium bisulcatum form diuturnum

P. bisulcatum

Schubert & Wagner 1829 *Indo-west Pacific, 2.8in (70mm).*
Very variable with many named forms. Heavy or light; spire moderate but variable; globose or narrow; spirally striate, smooth or striate below suture and at base. Lip with strong or weak, small teeth; columellar shield somewhat rugose. White or cream, may have blue-gray tinge; may have five rows of more or less prominent, squarish, light brown spots; lip with or without five groups of dark or light brown marks; columella and shield white; interior white or purple-brown. Illustrated are; spirally striate form with pale or absent markings, *diuturnum* Iredale 1927; one described by Schubert and Wagner; and *sophia* Brazier 1872 from east Australia with sharply angled shoulders and generally smooth, the brown squares tending to turn into axial streaks.

Phalium bisulcatum form sophia

Phalium bandatum

Perry 1811 *Japan, Philippines, Indonesia and north Australia, 4.75in (120mm).*

High concave spire. Early whorls with beaded spiral cords disappearing on last two whorls leaving faint striae; small knobs develop on antepenultimate whorl. May have nil to three former varices. Thickened, recurved lip has twenty elongate teeth, largest centrally. Columella with five small folds anteriorly. Columellar shield strongly folded with raised lirae. White; five spiral bands of pale brown; axial flame marks; darker brown squares at intersections; lip with six purple-brown spots, three short spikes posteriorly. Subspecies *P.b. exaratum* Reeve 1848, Indian Ocean islands, has spiral grooves, less shouldered whorls and reduced or absent spines on lip.

P. granulatum

Born 1778.

Three main subspecies: *P.g. granulatum* Born 1718, Caribbean; *P.g. centriquadratum* Valenciennes 1832, west Central America; *P.g. undulatum*.

Phalium bandatum

P.g. undulatum

Gmelin 1791 *Mediterranean and east Atlantic Islands, 4.3in (110mm).*

High spire; slightly angular shoulders. Strong spiral cords, beaded on early whorls and posterior of body whorl; axial riblets near lip. Thick, wide lip has seventeen teeth. Columella smooth posteriorly, pustulate or granulate anteriorly and on shield. Callous pad where lip joins body. Creamy brown; brown, axial flame marks; interstices of cords dark brown; outer lip with broad and narrow brown bands; inside lip, columella, shield, pad white. *P.g. granulatum* has shorter spire, more spiral cords, no flame marks or spiral lines. *P.g. centriquadratum* is much like *P.g. granulatum* but sometimes with knobbed shoulders and rather low spire.

Casmaria erinaceus

L. 1758.

Synonym *C. vibex* L. 1758. Three main subspecies: *C.e. erinaceus*; *C.e. kalosmodix* Melville 1883, east central Pacific; and *C.e. vibexmexicana* Stearns 1894, west Central America.

Phalium granulatum undulatum

C.e. erinaceus

L. 1758 *Africa eastward to west Pacific, 2.8in (70mm).*

Two forms, the typical having nodulose shoulders, and the large smooth-shouldered form, *vibex*. Moderate spire, rounded shoulders, faint axial striae, and axial folds near lip. Thickened, recurved lip is smooth bar five or six, small, sharp spines anteriorly. Smooth columella, two folds anteriorly; shield with spiral ridges. Cream-brown; purple tinges; aperture white; purple tip to up-turned siphonal canal; purple-brown blotches on outer lip; body whorl has faint yellow-brown squares and axial flares, yellow-brown marks below suture; growth striae have some minute brown specks on the inner side. Occasionally has a former varix (as illustrated). This specimen also has a pustulate columella and callous parietal shield.

Casmaria erinaceus erinaceus

Casmaria erinaceus erinaceus form *vibex*

C. ponderosa
Gmelin 1791 *Indo-Pacific, 2in (50mm).*
Varieties at extremes of its range have subspecific names. Stubbier than *C. erinaceus.* Moderate spire; sometimes nodulose shoulder; thickened, recurved lip with small, sharp teeth. Cream; two, pale brown, spiral bands; dark brown marks below suture and anteriorly on body whorl (*C. erinaceus* lacks specks); early whorls blue-white; up-turned siphonal canal has purple-brown spot; dark brown oblong marks on outer lip.

Casmaria ponderosa

Form *turgida* Reeve 1848 (illustrated) is rather large, lighter weight and smooth with teeth only on anterior two-thirds of lip, and axial red-brown flames.

Galeodea echinophora
L. 1787 *Mediterranean Sea, 4.3in (110mm).*
Medium spire. Five spiral ridges, two posterior rows bluntly nodulose, fainter on next two; blunt nodulose ridge on shoulder of penultimate whorl; spiral cords between suture and shoulders and anteriorly; smooth between body whorl ridges. Lip a little thickened, flared, obsoletely toothed within. Columella has smooth bar ridges, smooth shield and thinly callous parietal wall. Gray-brown; nodules white, brown between; aperture white.

Casmaria ponderosa form *turgida*

Galeodea echinophora

Morum oniscus

Morum grande

Morum macandrewi

Morum ponderosum

GENUS: MORUM

Shells in this genus of the Cassidae are solid, coarsely-sculptured and lack the turned-up siphonal canal of the preceding genera.

Morum oniscus

L. 1758 *Caribbean, 1in (25mm)*.
Flat spire; spiral cords and axial ribs on body whorl. Three adjacent cords below suture are raised – axial ribs giving a tubercled effect – two cords in middle of whorl, and one anteriorly. Thickened lip has about fifteen teeth. Columella, parietal shield callous, strongly rugose or pustulate. White speckled with brown; apex, interior white.

M. grande

A. Adams 1855 *South Japan, 2.8in (70mm)*.
Solid, rather elongate with moderate spire. Coarse, spiral cords becoming lamellated on later whorls; coarse axial ribs; pointed tubercles forming at their intersections. Lip is expanded, thickened, not recurved, has many folds and teeth. Columellar shield and parietal callus rather thin, pustulate and rugose. Short, slightly recurved siphonal canal. Dirty white; four, faint, interrupted, brown bands showing most clearly on lip edge; inside lip, interior, columella, shield, parietal callus white.

M. macandrewi

Sowerby 1889 *South Japan and China, 2in (50mm)*.
Moderately low spire and inflated at shoulder narrowing sharply anteriorly. Spiral cords, axial ribs and lamellated, axial growth lines. Ribs and cords form sharp points at their intersections. Thickened, wide lip, with about twelve large teeth, more small ones between. Narrow columella shield, parietal wall with thin callus; both pustulate and rugose as is columella. White; dark gray-brown bands and mottling; lip with ten, short, black streaks; inside lip, teeth, columella and shield white; brown bands showing through parietal callus.

M. ponderosum

Hanley 1888 *Indo-Pacific, 1.6in (40mm)*.
Solid, heavy with low spire; fine spiral cords; and nodulose shoulders. Body whorl has ten, broad, spiral ridges with small cords between; faint lamellate growth lines. Thickened lip has about fifteen, small teeth becoming obsolete at ends. Columella with fine, raised lirae and smooth, callous parietal wall. White; four, obscure, red-brown bands; sparse, small spots; lip white with small, brown spots; interior, lirae white.

M. tuberculosum

Reeve 1842 *Lower California to Peru, 0.7in (17mm)*.
Similar to *M. oniscus* L. 1758 of Atlantic coast of Central America. Flat spire and pointed apex. Cancellate, finely on spire; spiral cords. Five, spiral rows of heavy, blunt knobs –

about six per row – absent on the parietal wall. Narrow aperture. Lip turned in with some eighteen teeth. Smooth columella, narrow thin callus. Dark brown, almost black; white or yellow dots; lip edge, interior white or yellow.

M. cancellatum
Sowerby 1824 *South Japan, China, 1.8in (45mm).*
Similar in sculpture to M. macandrewi but smaller and more delicate. White or cream; about four, more or less indistinct, brown spiral bands; interior white.

Morum cancellatum

Morum tuberculosum

FAMILY: FICIDAE
A small family (one genus) of tropical shells. They are fig-shaped, thin and low-spired with a large, long body whorl, long, wide aperture and siphonal canal. They live on sand usually in fairly deep water.

Ficus gracilis
Sowerby *South Japan, 6in (150mm).*
Small spire with spiral cords and smaller axial cords. Light brown; many, axial, darker brown, wavy lines; interior rich chestnut brown; lip pale blue-gray.

F. ficoides
Lamarck 1822 *Indo-Pacific, 4in (100mm).*
Almost flat spire. Siphonal canal relatively shorter than the above species. Cancellate with fine spiral and smaller axial cords. Pink-fawn; about five, narrow, pale or white bands; dark brown spots and blotches especially on the pale bands; interior white with a violet tinge becoming brown toward the interior.

Ficus gracilis

Ficus ficoides

Tonna variegata

Tonna tessellata

FAMILY: TONNIDAE

The Tonnidae are not a large family. They have thin, rather fragile shells, some of which are large, with short spires and highly inflated body whorls. The shells are sculptured with spiral cords or ridges. The animals live mostly in the tropics, on sandy areas beyond the reefs. They are carnivorous, living mainly on a diet of echinoderms and crustaceans.

Tonna variegata
Lamarck 1822
Indo-Pacific, 6.25in (160mm).
Globose, low-spired with seven whorls and deep suture. Body has about sixteen, prominent, broad ribs, five showing on the penultimate whorl. Interstices channeled, posterior ones having faint cords. Deeply and narrowly umbilicate. Crenulated lip. Small columellar shield and thinly callous parietal area. Creamy white to oat-meal with pale cream-pink or fulvous red staining and indistinct axial streaks; a few ribs spotted with red-brown especially near the suture – seen very faint in the illustrated specimen; inside lip white; orange interior

T. tessellata
Lamarck 1816 *West Pacific to South China Sea, 3in (80mm).*
Moderately high spire; about seven whorls and deep sutures. Body whorl has about fourteen, rather narrow, rounded ribs, four on penultimate whorl. Wide, smooth interstices, which sometimes have a single thread. Lip fluted with about ten pairs of teeth on the inner edge. A small parietal shield. Body whorl an opaque white; ribs white with brown spots; penultimate whorl with pink tinge; earlier whorls with dark pink spiral band to the apex.

T. cepa
Röding 1798 *Indo-Pacific, 5in (130mm).*
Ovate with moderately high spire; about seven whorls and with deeply channeled sutures. Spiral cords on early whorls, becoming obsolete on the penultimate

whorl. About sixteen, broad, flat ribs on body whorl divided by narrow grooves. Rounded and malleate shoulders. Narrowly umbilicate. Unevenly marked shell with light browns, purple-brown, and creamy white, spiral smears, seen especially on the shoulders; inside lip, small columellar shield and thin parietal callus white; interior brown.

T. luteostoma
Küster 1857 *West Pacific, Japan to New Zealand, 8in (200mm).* Globose and low-spired; about seven whorls and deep suture. Broad, rather flattened, rounded ribs, about seventeen on the body whorl and five showing on the penultimate whorl; rather narrow, excavated channels between some posterior ones with a single cord. Crenulate lip; small columellar shield over, but not closing, the rather deep umbilicus; thin parietal callus. White or light tan with alternating white and red-brown axial stripes across the ribs with color gradations between them; some ribs have long streaks of browns without white; very shiny; lip and columella white; parietal callus clear and faintly white; interior brown. This shell is rather variable in its coloring.

Tonna cepa

T. dolium (not illustrated)
L. 1758 *Indian Ocean, west Pacific Ocean, 6in (150mm).* Very variable. It is generally globose and has from ten to twenty, broad, flat, spiral ribs which may or may not have intermediate threads between them on the posterior half of the whorls; two to four of the ribs show on the penultimate whorl. Deep sutures, fluted outer lip and umbilicus is open and deep; no parietal shield. White to fawn, with rectangular orange-brown spots on the ribs; apex brown; and brown interior.

Tonna luteostoma

139

T. allium

Dillwyn 1817 *Indo-Pacific, up to 3.5in (90mm).*

Rather high spire for a *Tonna* giving an ovate, rather than globose, outline. Rather widely-spaced ribs, about fourteen on the body whorl and three showing on the penultimate. Ribs widest apart at the posterior and closest at the anterior end. Interstices mainly concave and smooth except for fine growth striae. Deep suture. Crenulated lip may have up to twelve pairs of teeth. Small, thin columella and parietal shield. Narrowly umbilicate. Shell opaque white and may have a brown tinge on the ribs; apex and lower half of early whorls purple.

Tonna allium

T. sulcosa

Born 1778 *Indo-west Pacific, 4.75in (120mm).*

Moderate spire; seven whorls. Flat ribs, about twenty on the body whorl and four on the penultimate whorl; ribs are of varying width as are the shallow channels that separate them. Moderately deep suture. Lip thickened and a little expanded, with about twenty teeth, some paired. Small, thin columellar shield over a very narrow umbilicus; quite thin parietal callus. White with three or four brown bands covering about two ribs each; apex dark purple.

Tonna sulcosa

T. perdix

L. 1758 *The Partridge Tun, Indo-Pacific, 8in (200mm).*

Narrow, high-spired and rather thin with rounded shoulders and not very deep sutures. There are narrow, shallow grooves between flat ribs, about twenty on body whorl and eight on penultimate. Slightly thickened lip; thin, small parietal callus; deeply umbilicate; siphonal canal twisted toward aperture. Brown with dark brown and white smears on ribs, especially near suture, base and lip; the white marks are to the right of the brown ones. In some specimens, as illustrated, the brown and white marks cover almost the whole shell. Columella, callus white; interior brown.

T. maculosa (not illustrated)

Dillwyn 1817 T*he Atlantic Partridge Tun, eastern tropical America, 5in (130mm).*

It is very similar to the above, but the spire is lower and has more spiral ribs. The rectangles of color are more blurred.

Tonna perdix

140

T. galea

L. 1758 *Tropical Indo-Pacific ocean, west Atlantic ocean, Mediterranean, 8in (200mm).*
Globose and low-spired with about seven whorls. Body whorl has some fifteen to twenty, broad, flat ribs; on the upper half up to three smaller ribs between, and up to five between the top two ribs. Deep suture; two or three cords at the top of the whorl within the sutural channel; about three main ribs show on the penultimate whorl. Fluted outer lip is slightly expanded and obsoletely toothed. Narrow umbilicus almost closed by small columellar shield; thin parietal callus. Light milk-chocolate brown, axially streaked with lighter brown, also light at the suture; apex dark purple; interior and columellar shield white; brown marks on inside of lip and edge of siphonal canal.

T. tetracotula

(not illustrated)
Hedley 1919 *East Australia and New Zealand, 8in (200mm).*
Similar to *T. sulcosa*, of which it may be a sub-species from temperate water. Globose, it has about twenty, flattened ribs which become smaller toward the anterior end of the whorl. Between the ribs are threads varying from four at the posterior end to one or none at the anterior end. Deep suture; lip finely denticulate within, denticles in pairs; deep and narrow umbilicus. White, it may or may not have brown spiral bands and these may not completely encircle the body whorl; part of the body whorl may be pale cream-brown; area round siphonal notch may be gray-brown; inside of lip white; interior tan; columella and thin parietal callus white.

Tonna galea

T. olearium

L. 1758 *South Japan and South China Sea to the Philippines, Indonesia and Malaysia, 8in (200mm).* Very similar to *T. galea* but with a higher spire. About seventeen main ribs on the body whorl which are narrower and slightly more rounded and may have threads or small cords between all the main ribs. The shoulders are more rounded; the siphonal canal is longer. It is a darker brown; the lip is edged with dark brown; the early whorls are lighter.

T. cerevisina (not illustrated)

Hedley 1919 *Southwest Pacific ocean, up to 9.5in (240mm).*
Shape similar to *T. galea.* About twenty rather flat ribs on body whorl with shallow channels between some of the anterior channels which have small intermediate threads, as also have the five or six ribs showing on the earlier whorls. Coarse growth lines near the aperture. Crenulate lip. Columella with small parietal shield partly covering deep umbilicus; parietal wall glazed. Color is variable from dark brown with light spots and streaks, to off-white with about five, brown, spiral bands and brown spots on the white areas between; sometimes off-white with rather sparse brown spotting.

Tonna olearium

Malea ringens

Swainson 1822 *The Grinning Tun, west tropical America, can grow to 9.5in (240mm), but usually about 4in (100mm).*
Solid and heavy with low spire. About seven whorls with eighteen flat ribs on the body

Malea ringens

whorl, three showing on the penultimate. Shallow sutures and rounded shoulders. Outer lip strongly constricted before flaring out and flattening; outer edge fluted; inner edge with about seventeen long teeth, opposite the outside constriction. Columella with a triple-ridged boss in the middle and five, high, narrow, folds, the first two and last two joined. This sculpturing gives the shell its apt common name. Columellar shield is rather uneven and faintly rugose, almost sealing the umbilicus. Broad parietal callus and reverted siphonal canal. Putty colored; paler on inside of outer lip, columella, callus and early whorls; interior pale brown.

M. pomum

L. 1758 *The Pacific Grinning Tun, Indo-Pacific ocean, 2.9in (75mm)*.
Solid, with a low spire, about seven whorls and sutures a little indented. Body whorl with about twelve, smoothly rounded ribs and shallow interstices; three ribs show on the penultimate whorl. Restricted before the outer lip which is fluted, thickened and somewhat flattened, and shows coarse growth lines. Inside lip has ten or eleven, strong, toothlike, folds. Columella and parietal area callous, underlying channels showing through at the top of the columella. Lower end with about four folds and one large rib above the siphonal notch.
The umbilicus is covered by the parietal callus. Cream-fawn with white squares and oblongs on the ribs and a few darker fawn markings; outer area of lip white becoming orange-brown within the aperture; columella and callus white.

Malea pomum

Malea ringens

Family: Cymatiidae

Rather solid shells, angulate with spiral ribs and cords, knobs, tubercles and varices. They are operculate and the siphonal canal is often long. They live in sandy and rocky areas in deep and shallow water in the tropics worldwide. The periostracum is sometimes very thick and hairy and the operculum is horny. They are carnivorous, living on the echinoderms and mollusks. They have a long veliger or free-swimming stage, after they are hatched and before developing into the final form. This is likely to account for some species being found in the Atlantic and Mediterranean as well as in the Indo-Pacific oceans – e.g., *Ranella olearium L.*

Genus: Charonia

There are about a dozen species of tritons. They have high spires and large apertures. Some grow to a large size, all are tropical or subtropical.

Charonia tritonis

L. 1758 *Triton's Trumpet, Indo-Pacific, 15in (400mm).* Sometimes used, particularly in the Pacific, as a horn. High, pointed spire; coarse, spiral cords and axial ribs on early whorls. Spiral ribs below suture – two on earlier whorls, three on the body whorl being beaded – are broad and flat with a small, narrow rib between. Outer lip flares to form large aperture and expands to form a low ridge

Charonia tritonis

before the lip which recurves. These axial ridges and lips show as varices on earlier whorls, one every two-thirds of a whorl, and therefore line up axially on every alternate whorl. Scalloped lip has about fifteen, spiral ribs running into the interior, posterior ones forming pairs of denticles on the lip. Concave columella is strongly and coarsely lirate. Narrowly umbilicate. Short siphonal canal. Creamy white; purple and brown, rounded, scalelike markings on spiral ribs; lip pinky-white; interior of aperture and inner ribs orange; denticles white; columella orange-pink, purple-brown between the lirae.

C. variegata
Lamarck 1816 T*he Atlantic Triton, Florida to Brazil, 380mm.*
Similar to the above but squatter. The whorls are sometimes unevenly swollen and occasionally bulge over the suture which descends in an uneven spiral thereafter. Outer edge of lip is scalloped but less projected, and toothed with riblike teeth which are mostly in pairs, about ten pairs in all. Coloration similar to *C. tritonis* except that the teeth on the lip are white and each pair is in a rich brown blotch; inside of aperture orange-pink; interior white.

Charonia variegata

C. lampas
L. 1758 *Mediterranean, up to 12in (300mm).*
Spirally corded; two rows of blunt nodules per whorl, lower row sometimes hidden in places beneath suture. Varices about every two-thirds of a whorl. Body whorl with two, broad, flat ridges on which the cords show and earlier nodules almost disappear, and with other lesser bands. Expanded, thickened, scalloped lip with about twelve, blunt, riblike denticles. Columella with one large and one smaller fold posteriorly; three or four, oblique, large ones anteriorly; many, fine, obsolete ones between. Umbilicus sealed by parietal shield. Siphonal canal larger than in preceding species. White; broken, brown bands axially and spirally on body whorl; teeth on lip brown; brown blotch at base of columella.

Charonia lampas

Cymatium gutturnium

Röding 1798 *Indo-Pacific, 3.5in (90mm)*.
About six whorls with spiral cords and axial riblets or folds, and larger ribs, about eight on the body whorl, carrying pointed nodules where they are crossed by the spiral cords. Slightly constricted suture. Former varices every 240°. Outer lip thickened and callous with seven strong teeth. Columella and parietal wall heavily callous, three or four folds at the top; one strong rib near the lower end; about three smaller ones at the top of the long, angular siphonal canal. White with brown axial marks along the large axial ribs; inside lip, columella, callus, and interior of siphonal canal, orange-red, or may be white or yellow.

*Cymatium
gutturnium*

C. (Ranularia) pyrum

L. 1758 *Indo-Pacific, 3in (80mm)*.
Solid and heavy. Sculptured with beaded spiral cords. Ribs have pointed nodules where they intersect on angular shoulders and below; about eight on the body whorl each with some four to six nodes – two or three showing on earlier whorls. Outer lip with thick, heavy varix; strongly toothed internally – about seven teeth – with much smaller teeth – about eight pairs – just within lip. Heavily plicate columella and parietal callus; long, contorted siphonal canal. Red-brown; varices with darker and lighter markings; inside lip, interior white with pink areas round the teeth; columella orange-red with white plicae. Coarse, heavy periostracum.

*Cymatium
lotorium*

*Cymatium
pyrum*

C. lotorium

L. 1758 *Indo-Pacific, 4in (100mm)*.
Solid, heavy and rugged. Smooth suture, high spire and body whorl just over half the length of the shell. Heavy varix every 240°. Spiral cords; fine threads. Shoulders angulate with heavy knobs, each carrying about three cords, three or four between each varix. Outer lip has about seven teeth. Columella with heavy, callous rib at posterior end, a small one at top of long siphonal canal, and lirate between. Narrow columellar shield, lirate at edge where it crosses the fasciole. Yellow-brown; varices dark brown and

white; inside lip and interior white; edge of columellar callus stained with dark brown and columella with pale brown marks.

C. (Monoplex) parthenopeum
Von Salis 1793 *Worldwide in warm waters, 6in (150mm)*.
Solid, fairly high spire. Irregular, weak former varices. Whorls angulate with fine spiral threads, nodulose ribs, and fine axial growth striae and folds. Outer lip with heavy varix; interior callous with six plicae of long, thin teeth. Columella with narrow parietal shield and lirate with a tooth posteriorly. Short, slightly recurved siphonal canal. Dark brown with lighter areas; varices white and very dark brown; inside lip pink with white denticles on a dark brown base; columella dark brown with white lirae and tooth; interior white.

C. (Septa) pileare
L. 1758 *Indo-Pacific, 4in (100mm)*.
High-spired and elongate with varices about every 240°. Spirally beaded ridges of varying size and intermediate threads. Two ridges on the shoulder bear small blunt nodes. Outer lip with heavy varix and about eight pairs of long teeth. Columella heavily lirate. Shades of light and dark tan; varices darker brown and white; inside of lip, interior and columella deep rich red or may be pale orange. Extremely hairy periostracum.

Cymatium lotorium
juvenile

Cymatium pileare

Cymatium parthenopeum

147

Cymatium
hepaticum

Cymatium
nicobaricum

Cymatium
clandestinum

C. (Septa) hepaticum

Röding 1798 *Pacific and Indonesia, 2in (50mm).*
Broad ribs, wide interstices and axial riblets. 'Lump' on shoulder in middle of dorsum. Lip has thick varix and nine teeth; lirate columella; spirally channeled interior. Cords red or orange-brown; interstices mostly black; varices white, black and red; lip edge pink; interior white; columella red, lirae white.

C. (Turritriton) gibbosum

Broderip 1833 *Found west Central America, 1.6in (40mm).*
Constricted at suture and then expanded at shoulder also with expanded varices. Fine, beaded spiral cords and axial riblets. Shoulder with one large and three small knobs, lower cords having two or three small nodules. Lip with large varix has four weak teeth. Columella obsoletely plicate with small tooth, and callous over lower end of penultimate varix and much of dorsum. Red-brown;

Cymatium
gibbosum

five, indistinct, purple-brown, spiral bands; early whorls gray-purple; varices with white area on aperture side, edged with brown; nuclear whorls obvious, smooth, white with dark brown line below suture.

C. (Cymatriton) nicobaricum

Röding 1798 *Indo-Pacific, 2in (50mm).*
Spiral nodulose cords and fine threads. Three to five large knobs on shoulder between each pair of varices; latter every 240°. Lip with heavy varix and seven to fourteen long teeth; columella lirate. Gray, red stains, sometimes indistinct cream band; varix dark gray and white; lip, teeth, lirae white; interior, columella yellow or orange-yellow.

C. (Gelagna) clandestinum

Lamarck 1816 *Indo-Pacific, 1.8in (45mm).*
Light, no varices and six inflated whorls with twenty spiral cords, seven on penultimate whorl, and smooth wide channels between. Faint axial ribs which disappear on body whorl. Interior channeled; lip expanded, not thickened; columella smooth. Pale brown; cords red, inside of lip, interior, lower columella white.

C. (Mayena) australasia

Perry 1811 *South Australia and New Zealand, 3.5in (90mm).*
Very fine spiral threads; blunt nodules on shoulders, twelve on the body whorl; oblique varices every 200°. Lip heavily dentate; columella with one fold; bottom of earlier varix protrudes into top of aperture behind columella. Dark brown; varices brown, white; inside lip, columella, interior white.

Cymatium
labiosum

Cymatium australasia

C. labiosum

Wood 1828 *Indo-Pacific and Caribbean, 1.2in (30mm).*
Fine, beaded spiral threads and six spiral cords;
four axial ribs between varices, forming blunt
nodules where cords cross. Lip with well-
developed varix; aperture with six blunt teeth;
columella with blunt tooth posteriorly and
anteriorly; columellar shield edge faintly plicate.
Red-brown; aperture, inside lip, columella white.

C. (Argobuccinum) argus

Gmelin 1791 *South Africa in deep water, 2.4in (60mm).*
Spiral threads; five rows of small nodules on body,
two on earlier whorls. Varices every 200°. Lip thickened
to weak varix with eight pairs of teeth. Columella with three
plicae posteriorly; outer edge of parietal callus plicate
anteriorly. Light brown; dark brown stripes across the light
brown nodules, one above and two below without nodules
and with dark brown lines between stripes; inside lip,
columella, interior white. Spire and nodules often worn to
white, as illustrated.

Cymatium argus

C. (Cabestana) dolarium

L. 1758 *South Africa, 1.6in (40mm).*
Angulate with spiral ridges carrying fine incised line centrally;
a small cord between ribs; axial ribs, ten on body, becoming
blunt nodules where ridges cross; two ridges show on the
penultimate whorl. Flared, crenulate outer lip, with seven
teeth, some bifurcated. Smooth columella. Brown or off-
white; inside lip, aperture, columella white.

Cymatium dolarium

C. (Cabestana) spengleri

Perry 1811 *East Australia, New Zealand, 4.75in (120mm)*.
Spiral ribs and cords of different widths, all closely beaded. Close axial riblets; spiral, raised lines; fine threads. Angular shoulders have six, small knobs. Varices every 240°. Lip with thick varix, denticulate, seven pairs of teeth. The Weakly furrowed columella has bifurcated tooth posteriorly. Narrow parietal shield, pustulate anteriorly; open canal. Creamy tan; black in some interstices; inside of lip, interior, columella white.

C. muricinum

Röding 1798 *Indo-Pacific and Caribbean, 3in (80mm)*.

Solid; long siphonal canal; coarse spiral and axial cords and threads, jumbled below suture. Varices every 240°. Seven, main cords on body whorl, three on penultimate. Axial ribs nodulose where cords cross. Lip with strong varix, heavily callous inside, as is parietal shield. Canal angled at about 45°. White; gray and brown mottling, basically in spiral bands; inside of lip, columella, parietal callus all cream; interior purple-brown.

Cymatium spengleri

Cymatium muricinum

C. (Fusitriton) laudandus

Finlay 1927 *South New Zealand, 4.3in (110mm)*.
Deep water. Round shoulders; fine, spiral cords, axial ribs, and nodules at intersections. Former varices are indistinct; lip with small varix. Columella has a large, callous tooth posteriorly; extended siphonal canal. Cream; cords chestnut; interior, columella white, sometimes has a pink or purple tinge; gray-brown periostracum (illustrated).

C. (Ranella) olearium

L.1758 *Mediterranean to South Africa, 8.25in (210mm)*.
Varices every 200°. Fine spiral threads and low ridges, six showing on upper whorls. Axial, fine, close striae. Twenty ribs on upper whorls, ten ribs indistinct on last three whorls. Upper whorls have small, sharp nodules where ridges and ribs intersect; on last three whorls, especially centrally, pointed nodules on some ridges become larger and coarser. Lip with edge flattened, slightly expanded behind varix, seventeen teeth. One, strong, columellar tooth posteriorly; small parietal callus. Siphonal canal moderate, a little curved. White; light brown stains; interior, columella white. Was believed to be confined to Mediterranean and Lusitanian areas, but the illustrated specimen was trawled off south Zululand, South Africa.

Cymatium laudandus

C. africanum

A. Adams 1855 *South Africa, 2.4in (60mm)*.
Elongate or stubby. Spiral ridges on upper whorl, obsolete and noduled on shoulder of last few. Six nodules on body; varices every 200°. Lip with heavy varix, seven teeth. Columellar tooth posteriorly; umbilicate. Red-brown; lip, interior, columella white.

Gyrineum gyrinum

L. 1758 *Indo-Pacific, 2in (50mm)*.
Compressed. Spiral threads; larger cords, seven on body whorl, three on earlier; axial threads; ribs, twelve on body whorl; cords and ribs form small nodules at intersections. Varices every 200°. Lip has seven denticles, some bifurcated. Columella has tooth posteriorly, weak plicae. Dark brown; white band on dorsum; nodules with red tinge; varices orange-brown and white; lip, columella white; interior dark brown, white spiral band; nuclear whorls dark, conspicuous.

G. natator

Röding 1798 *Indo-west Pacific, 1.6in (40mm)*.
Dorso-ventrally compressed; varices almost aligned each side. Ten, spiral cords on body, four on early whorls. Fine raised threads; axial ribs, fifteen per whorl; rounded shiny nodules at intersections. Lip with strong varix, seven teeth. Columella with posterior tooth, obsolete plicae. Gray-tan; dark brown bands and nodules; varices brown and white; inside lip, columella and interior white.

Cymatium olearium

Biplex bitubercularis

Lamarck 1816 *Indo-west Pacific, 1.6in (40mm)*.
Slightly inflated. Varices every 180°. Fine spiral and axial threads. Spiral ridges, ten on body whorl; axial ridges, five between each varix on upper whorls, two or three on last two whorls. Nodules where ridges and ribs cross, larger on two or three ridges in middle of whorl. Lip with nine teeth; columella plicate at top and bottom, rugose centrally; twisted siphonal canal. Pale fawn; varices cream; larger nodules red; aperture white.

Gyrineum gyrinum   *Gyrineum natator*   *Biplex bitubercularis*   *Cymatium africanum*

Biplex jucundum

B. jucundum

A. Adams 1854 *North Australia, Indonesia, Malaya, 1in (25mm)*.
Better known as *B. pulchella* Forbes 1852. Very flattened
dorso-ventrally. Varices every 180°, thin, expanded, running
together. Spiral, alternately wide and narrow cords, five on
body whorl, with deep narrow interstices; broader cords end
in points on varices. Whorls have axial riblets, twenty-five on
body whorl, forming nodules at intersections with spiral
cords. Lip, columella smooth; slender, moderately long
siphonal canal. Cream or gray-brown.

Biplex perca

B. perca

Perry 1811 *Central Indo-west Pacific, 3in (80mm)*.
Flattened dorso-ventrally. Expanded, flattened varices every
180°. Spiral threads and ridges, seven on body whorl,
ending in blunt points on varices; axial ribs, twenty on
body whorl. Blunt nodules where ridges and ribs
cross. Rugose or obsoletely toothed lip; columella
with double tooth posteriorly, obsoletely plicate;
extended, slightly curved siphonal canal. Pale
gray-brown, stained brown on the larger whorls;
nodules cream; aperture white.

Distorsio anus

L. 1758 *Indo-Pacific on reefs, 3in (80mm)*.
Pointed spire. Irregularly inflated whorls giving
distorted shape. Nodulose, spiral ridges; axial
riblets. Crenulate lip with row of seven teeth
near edge pointing outward, a second row of
bigger teeth pointing inward; a channel between
rows. Heavily rugose parietal shield fluted round
edge. Very large columella has deep wide notch cen-

Distorsio anus

trally. Siphonal canal ridged along both sides, sharply recurved. White; brown spiral bands and blotches; aperture, shield shiny white with pink and brown areas.

D. reticulata
Röding 1798 *Indo-Pacific, deep water, 2.2in (55mm).*
Similar to above but less extreme. Spiral cords; axial ribs; sharp nodules at intersections. Flattened lip; ten, very small, outer teeth; inner teeth at end of ridges crossing lip. Thinly callous pareital area. Columella with long tooth at top; large, rectangular notch centrally; lower area strongly plicate. Cream; teeth, interior white.

Distorsio reticulata   Distorsio clathrata

D. clathrata
Lamarck 1816 *Caribbean and west Africa, found in deep water, 2.4in (60mm).*
Similar to *D. reticulata* but sculpturing much coarser, and nodules become blunt spines on middle of whorls. Narrower lip, ten outer and inner teeth, that opposite columellar notch being much bigger than the others. Columellar sculpturing very similar, but with ridges instead of rows of small nodules across parietal area. Cream with brown clouding; interior and columella white; parietal callus shiny brown.

FAMILY: COLUBRARIIDAE
False tritons. Long, narrow, with varices, short siphonal canal and horny operculum. Not well studied and may be more correctly placed among the Buccinidae.

Colubraria obscura
Reeve 1844 *Indian and tropical Atlantic, 2.4in (60mm).*
Narrow, high-spired, solid and rather flat. Varices every 240°. Spiral rows of granules, twenty rows on body whorl; axial growth lines. Short siphonal canal. Lip with heavy varix and about thirteen teeth. One columellar tooth posteriorly. Cream; pale brown marks on varices and some nodules.

Colubraria obscura

153

Bursa caelata

FAMILY: BURSIDAE

The frog shells are close relatives of the Cymatiidae. They live mainly in tropical areas among rock and coral in shallow water. Most are nodulose, have coarse heavy varices and strong anterior and posterior canals.

Bursa caelata

Broderip 1833 *California to Peru, 2in (50mm)*.

Rectangular and flattened; moderate straight-sided spire; and five whorls. Fine, spiral, faintly beaded ridges; six larger rows of nodules, that on broadest part of the body whorl largest, and, like the next anteriorly, a double row. Lip fluted and strongly toothed. Columella and parietal area lirate and pustulate. Short, deep siphonal canal; deep, open, curved anterior canal; weak fasciole. Dark red-brown; nodules shiny; interior, columella white, pale chestnut clouding.

B. rosa

Perry 1811 *Indo-west Pacific, 1.6in (40mm)*.

Bursa rosa

Squat, solid, moderate spire, two varices per whorl and fine spiral cords. Three, uneven spiral ridges, two posterior ones coalescing to form two or three blunt knobs between varices. Narrow, nodulose lip with nine, small, strong teeth. Columella with three, strong teeth anteriorly, lirate behind. Long, extended, almost tubular posterior canal; deep, curved anterior canal. Creamy white; red-brown broken lines on ridges; lip, narrow parietal area creamy yellow; teeth white; interior mauve.

B. bufonia

Gmelin 1791 *Indo-west Pacific, 3in (80mm)*.

Solid, heavy, fairly high spire, two varices per whorl. Coarse, granular spiral ridges with three, coarse, blunt knobs on shoulders between varices. Expanded, fluted lip, with nine teeth on inner and outer edge. Coarsely lirate columella. Deep, extended, tubular siphonal canal; deep, sharply curved, almost closed anterior canal. Coarse, strong fasciole. Creamy white; brown markings; lip, parietal area cream; interior white.

Bursa bufonia

B. granularis

Röding 1798 *Indo-west Pacific, 2.4in (60mm)*.

Slightly flattened; high spire; suture a little constricted. Spiral rows of corded nodules, fine striae between. Lip has fourteen strong teeth. Lirate columella. Short, deep posterior canal; deep, curved, open anterior canal; weak fasciole. Shades of red-brown; white beading on varices; lip, columella creamy white; interior white.

B. bubo

L. 1758 *Indo-Pacific, 10.25in (260mm)*.

Solid, heavy, coarsely sculptured with fairly high spire. Large, rough spiral cords and knobs at shoulder, five between varices. Slightly constricted suture and circular aperture.

Bursa granularis

Flaring, toothed lip with internal denticle bordering posterior canal. Concave, plicate columella with tooth posteriorly. Short, deep, open posterior canal; short, deep, nearly closed, twisted anterior canal; wide, callous parietal shield. Creamy white; light brown flecks and splashes; aperture cream to straw.

B. rubeta
L. 1758 *Indo-Pacific, 10in (250mm)*.
Similar to *B. bubo* except spire is slightly higher. Outer edge of lip denticulate, fourteen teeth on inner edge, coarsely lirate within. Columella profusely plicate, plicae stronger anteriorly and covering most of the expanded parietal shield. Creamy white with brown markings; aperture red or orange-red; teeth, plicae white or pale yellow.

B. foliata
Broderip 1825 *Indian Ocean, 3.5in (90mm)*.
Solid, moderate spire, two flattened varices per whorl forming a flange on each side. Fine, nodulose spiral cords and three rows of axially flattened spines, posterior row largest; four spines between varices; rows end with short spines on varices. Oval aperture; expanded, flattened, fluted, denticulate lip; columella profusely plicate; short, deep, open posterior canal; short, recurved anterior canal. Cream or pale tan with darker brown shading; spines with dark brown and white rectangular spots; aperture white with orange-red on lip and columellar shield; interior gray-brown.

Bursa bubo

Bursa rubeta

Bursa foliata

SUPERFAMILY: MURICACEA

FAMILY: MURICIDAE

The murex live among rock and coral, mostly in shallow water, in the tropics. They are carnivorous, preying on other mollusks by boring a hole through their shells and eating the contents. They are usually highly sculptured with spines or fronds on early varices. A number of genera and many species.

Murex troscheli

Lischke 1873 *North Australia through Philippines to Japan, 5.5in (140mm)*.
Moderate spire; deep suture; three varices per whorl. Narrow spiral cords with small threads between; about twelve threads on body whorl; small ridges becoming obsolete toward aperture. Lip is backed by solid varix on which the cords end in long, sharp spines, longer ones more or less at 90° to shell surface, smaller ones pointing more toward aperture. Very long, almost sealed siphonal canal bearing similar spines. Lip has blunt tooth anteriorly; smooth columella has small shield. Cream white; cords light brown; aperture white.

Murex troscheli

M. pecten

Solander 1786 *The Venus Comb Murex, Indo-west Pacific, 5in (125mm)*.
Synonym *M. triremis* Perry 1811. Moderate spire and deep sutures; spiral cords, large and small alternately. Axial ribs and small lamellae, nodulose at intersections. Three varices per whorl with about sixteen long spines and a number of short ones at an angle to the others; spines on shoulder of body whorl and on spire point posteriorly. Long, straight, almost sealed siphonal canal; finely toothed lip with large tooth anteriorly, and backed by small varix; smooth columella. Creamy white, biggest spines a little darker; lip edge has tiny brown marks which show on earlier varices; aperture white.

Murex mindanoensis

Murex pecten

M. mindanoensis
Sowerby 1814 *Philippines, 63mm.*
High spire and strong spiral ridges, some with a
weak cord between. Three varices per whorl
and three strong axial ribs between varices:
latter with short, sharp, hollow spines. Finely
dentate lip; columella has three pleats anteriorly;
long, recurved siphonal canal. Light tan-yellow
to brown; canal darker; aperture white.

M. nigrispinosus
Reeve 1845 *Indo-west Pacific, 3.5in (90mm).*
Moderate spire; fine spiral striae and microscopic
lamellae. About six, large spiral ridges on body whorl;
four or five axial ribs between varices, nodulose at
intersections; three varices per whorl having strong, rather
straight spines, those on shoulder largest. Lip has strong
varix, with three large and about six intervening small teeth;
dentate inside lip, sometimes with larger internal tooth.
Siphonal canal long. White; ends of spines dark gray;
aperture white.

Murex nigrispinosus

M. trapa
Röding 1798 *Central Indo-Pacific, 4.3in (110mm).*
Moderate spire; strong spiral ridges and axial ribs on early
whorls, ribs becoming obsolete on body whorl; uneven axial
striae. Three varices per whorl with larger and
shorter spines, some curving
posteriorly. Dentate lip
with not very strong
varix, and a large,
prominent and flat-
tened tooth poste-
riorly. Long, straight
siphonal canal. Blue-
gray, tinged brown
on early whorls;
aperture white; dark
gray spots at base of
interior of large spines;
interior brown with blue-
gray spiral streaks.

M. tribulus
L. 1758 *Indo-Pacific, 4.75in (120mm).*
Moderately high spire; spiral cords
and axial ribs, nodulose at intersections. Three varices per whorl; varices
spinous, those on shoulders longest.
Lip with weak varix; dentate inside lip
has large tooth anteriorly. Long, almost
straight siphonal canal. Light tan; aper-
Murex ture white; lip edge with tiny brown
trapa marks which show less on earlier whorls.

*Murex
trapa*

*Murex
tribulus*

Haustellum haustellum

L. 1758 *Indo-Pacific, 4.3in (110mm)*.
Solid body; low spire; long, slender and almost closed siphonal canal. Axially ribbed; three varices per whorl, three axial ribs between varices, or four on body whorl. Blunt spines where ribs cross sharply angled shoulders. Spiral, raised threads which also cover most of the canal, and three or four, spiral rows of nodules on ribs on the anterior half of the body whorl. Wide aperture; finely dentate lip, lirate within; concave columella, rugose anteriorly.

Haustellum tweedianum

Bolinus cornutus

Haustellum haustellum

Cream with dark brown blotches; threads red-brown; aperture pink, interior white.

H. tweedianum

Macpherson 1962 *East Australia, 2.6in (65mm)*.
Similar to the above but smaller with a relatively shorter siphonal canal which has short spines. The spiral threads are wider apart and finely beaded. White with brown clouding and touches of mustard yellow on the varices and threads.

Bolinus cornutus

L. 1758 *West Africa, 6in (150mm)*.
Solid, strong body with long, almost closed siphonal canal; short spire; angular shoulders; slightly constricted suture; fine, spiral ridges and axial striae. About seven varices per whorl which are not very raised except between shoulder and

Bolinus brandaris

158

suture; the posterior ends of earlier lips show as low, wavy ridges on the spire. Each varix carries a strong, more or less hollow spine on the shoulder, a second on the center of the body whorl, and two or three short ones on the siphonal canal. Wide aperture; coarsely dentate lip, ridged internally; concave, smooth columella. Strongly developed parietal shield. Cream to white with brown, generally spiral clouding; parietal area, outer edge of shield and between teeth on lip tan.

B. brandaris
L. 1758 *Mediterranean, Portugal and west Africa, 3.5in (90mm)*.
Similar to, though smaller than, the above. Spines much shorter and less pointed; base sculpturing relatively coarser. Tan; aperture slightly darker tan. It was from this animal that the Romans produced the Royal Purple dye.

Murex bellegladensis
Vokes 1963 *Florida and the Caribbean, 2.8in (70mm)*.
Moderate spire and extended siphonal canal; spirally ridged. Three varices per whorl each with three or four, long, sharp spines; one to three, axial ribs between varices. Slender and delicate siphonal canal with three rows of spines. Off-white, sometimes with a pink tinge between varices.

Murex bellegladensis

M. kiiensis
Kira 1962 *Japan, 2in (50mm)*
Moderately high spire; constricted suture; straight, slender siphonal canal. Three varices per whorl bearing short, strong spines; two or three, axial ribs between varices. Fine, sharply raised, spiral threads overall. Very finely dentate lip; almost closed siphonal canal with a very few, small spines posteriorly. White with a very pale, rather indistinct, brown band on the body whorl and on the canal; raised threads are mostly red-brown on the last three whorls; aperture white.

Murex kiiensis

Siratus pliciferoides
Kuroda 1942 *Japan, 4.3in (110mm)*.
Moderately high spire; constricted suture. Three small varices per whorl bearing short, strong spines, the largest on the shoulder. Finely spirally striate; two axially elongate knobs on the shoulder between each pair of varices. Dentate lip; smooth columella, almost closed, spinous and somewhat recurved siphonal canal is extended, but not comparably with the other species on this page. White with some light brown shading; aperture white.

Siratus pliciferoides

Chicoreus brevifrons

Lamarck 1822 *Caribbean and south Florida, 6in (150mm).*
Moderate spire; three varices per whorl; fine spiral cords; two nodulose axial ribs between varices. Solid varices covered with fairly long, foliate spines from largest on shoulder to end of moderate, recurved siphonal canal. Dentate lip; columella has spiral ridge posteriorly. Shades of light brown.

C. ramosus

L. 1758 *Indo-Pacific, 12in (300mm).*
Largest Indo-Pacific murex. Rather short spire; angular and inflated whorls with three varices per whorl; fine spiral striae. One or two small knobbed axial ribs between varices, latter with recurved, frondlike spines, ten from shoulder to end of recurved siphonal canal, which is quite long for the genus. Dentate lip with large tooth anteriorly. White; aperture tinged pink.

Chicoreus brevifrons

Chicoreus ramosus

Chicoreus cornucervi

C. cornucervi

Röding 1798 *Northwest Australia, 4.3in (110mm).*
Synonym *M. monodon* Sowerby 1825. Reasonably high spire; roundly angled shoulders deep sutures; fine, spiral ribs; and finer, uneven, axial riblets. Three varices per whorl; varices very weak with frondlike recurving spines, three of those on lip narrower and longer; one or two obsolete ribs between varices. Lip has spines growing directly out of edge and one large tooth anteriorly. Smooth columella has small, blunt, posterior tooth; fairly long, somewhat recurved siphonal canal. Usually brown; dark brown spines; uncommonly white as illustrated; aperture white; columellar edge pink.

C. palmarosae

Lamarck 1822 *Indo-Pacific, 4in (100mm)*.
Rather elongate; high spire. Three varices per whorl
and strong, spiral, beaded cords. Strong varices
have frondlike spines down to base of quite long
siphonal canal those on shoulders much bigger
and more fronded; two axial ribs between varices.
Lip has ten, small denticles, backed by channel
and row of blunt, rounded teeth. Smooth columella
has short, oblique plicae on outer edge. Deep,
almost closed, recurved siphonal canal. Pale brown;
darker cords; ends of fronds white, sometimes pink;
aperture and columellar plicae white.

Chicoreus palmarosae

C. axicornis

Lamarck 1822 *Indo-Pacific, 2.8in (70mm)*.
Moderate spire; very large solid varices, three per whorl.
Fine, spiral, minutely beaded threads and obsolete axial
riblets. Two coarse ribs between varices; latter with one,
long, hollow, blunt spine, very slightly foliate, on shoulder,
one shorter lower down, remainder smaller to long, slightly
recurved siphonal canal. Finely dentate lip with large
tooth posteriorly, inside edge lirate; smooth columella.
Cream, clouded or faintly banded with light brown;
aperture white.

C. saulii

Sowerby 1841 *Indo-Pacific, 5in (125mm)*.
Solid and rather elongate with high spire and fine, minutely beaded spiral cords. Three varices per whorl, having eight,
moderately long, foliated spines, smaller ones between
each pointing slightly forward; a large and small axial ridge
between varices. Dentate lip; smooth columella, spiral ridge
posteriorly; deep, long, recurved siphonal canal. Pale yellow-
brown; cords usually stained dark brown; interior white.

Chicoreus axicornis

C. clausii

Dunker 1879 *West Africa, Brazil, 2.2in (55mm)*.
Squat, angulate; fine, beaded, spiral cords and ridges. Three
varices per whorl; one, large, coarse, slightly lop-sided, axial
ridge between varices. Lip
and varices have hollow,
nonfoliate spines, those on
shoulder long and recurved,
two others of moderate length
and two very small. Dentate
lip; columella has two spiral
ridges posteriorly; deep
siphonal canal of moderate
length and rather open.
Cream; brown clouding; dark
brown apex; white band near
base, taking in second largest
of the spines.

Chicoreus clausii

Chicoreus saulii

161

Chicoreus rubiginosus

C. rubiginosus
Reeve 1845 *Australia, 3.5in (90mm)*.
High spire. Fine, spiral, granulose cords; three varices per whorl; fairly long, straight, frondose spines with smaller ones between. Edge of lip dentate. Columella has one spiral ridge posteriorly and faint plications; deep, recurved, open siphonal canal. Rusty brown; darker spiral ribs and fronds; sometimes cream, or orange-red; aperture white; edge of columella pink. This may be a variety of *C. torrefactus* Sowerby 1841 (see below), but the latter usually has shorter, less frondose spines and the shell is more elongate.

C. territus
Reeve 1845 *Queensland, Australia, 2.8in (70mm)*.
Sculptured with finely beaded, spiral ridges, each with a beaded thread on either side, and pustulate channel between; ridges end in spines on varices, three to each whorl; one nodulose rib between varices and sometimes a much smaller one as well. Spines are open and joined together to form a frilly curtain from suture to top of quite long, almost straight siphonal canal. Dentate lip; columella with posterior tooth. Normally white, cream, gray or brown, with white aperture. However, I have a specimen the color of cream toffee, inside and out, which is illustrated here. A more typical specimen is illustrated on page 175.

Chicoreus territus

C. torrefactus
Sowerby 1841 *Indo-Pacific, 4in (100mm)*.
High spire; many, close-set, granulose, spiral cords and small ridges ending in fronds on varices; three varices per whorl. Very small, axial ridges one large, one smaller, and sometimes a third and/or a fourth. Solid varices; very short, frondose spines. Dentate lip, Columella with one posterior ridge and a notch anteriorly. Deep, recurved and almost closed siphonal canal. Brown-gray; spiral ribs, spines darker; interior white; columella pink or orange, darker at the edge.

Chicoreus torrefactus

C. damicornis
Hedley 1903 *Southeast Australia, 2.4in (60mm)*.
Thin with high spire; constricted at suture. Rather shouldered with fine, spiral, granulose threads and cords. Three varices per whorl; one to three axial ridges between each; strong varices with long, hollow spine bifurcated at tip, on the shoulder, and a number of shorter webbed spines below,

some very small. Finely dentate lip; smooth columella; short, well-developed anal canal; short, recurved posterior canal. Cream, occasionally stained with brown.

Chicoreus
damicornis

Chicoreus
capucinus

C. capucinus
Röding 1798 *Southwest Pacific, Samoa to Malay Peninsula, 2.6in (65mm).*
High spire and six whorls with three varices per whorl. Strong, spiral ridges and may have two, weak, flat, broad, axial ribs between varices; varices have no spines. Bluntly dentate lip; columella with one small posterior denticle; moderate siphonal canal. Dark brown; aperture gray-brown; interior white.

Chicoreus brunneus

Chicoreus brunneus

Chicoreus brunneus

C. brunneus
Link 1807 *Indo-Pacific, 2.9in (75mm).*
Solid and heavy with many, close-set, finely beaded, spiral cords. Three varices per whorl. Very thickly foliate, foliations wide but not long. One, large, blunt knob on shoulder between varices. Finely dentate lip; columella with blunt tooth posteriorly; short, closed siphonal canal. Dark gray-brown or brown-black; aperture white, edged with orange. *C. brunneus* is, however, variable and a form often found in Singapore is much less heavy and coarse. The foliations are fewer, less frondose and usually longer, and the knob between the varices is smaller. The aperture and columella are dark purple-blue. Illustrated bottom left.

Chicoreus laciniatus

Chicoreus laciniatus

Sowerby 1841 *Philippines, 2.4in (60mm).*
Rather elongate, though with moderately short spire; constricted suture. Three varices per whorl only slightly frondose; two, axial ribs between varices; spiral lamellate ridges and threads. Finely crenulate lip; 0.smooth columella; broad, open siphonal canal, recurved at tip. White; mauve tinge and very pale brown clouding; darker brown on the short fronds; columella, inside of canal mauve; rest of aperture white.

Hexaplex stainforthi

Reeve 1843 *Northwest Australia, 2.6in (65mm).*
Solid, chubby, with moderate spire and slightly constricted suture. Eight varices per whorl with short, frondose spines; spiral ridges and fine threads. Dentate lip; smooth columella; broad, short siphonal canal, almost completely closed and recurved at the tip. White with a yellow, pink or orange flush between the dark brown varices; aperture may also be yellow, pink or orange.

Hexaplex stainforthi

H. cichoreum

Gmelin 1791 *Indo-Pacific, 2.9in (75mm).*
Moderate spire with slightly constricted suture. Six, weak varices per whorl with separate, open, more-or-less foliate spines. Spiral ridges on which spines develop; fine, intermediate threads. Crenulate lip; smooth columella; broad, narrowly open siphonal canal. Narrow, deep posterior canal near end of lip. Deeply umbilicate. White with dark brown banding so that spines alternate

Hexaplex cichoreum

brown and white; those on shoulder, the largest, brown as those on canal; aperture white. An all-white form of this shell occurs.

H. rosarium
Röding 1798 *West Africa, 8in (200mm).*
Moderately high spire; suture becomes increasingly constricted anteriorly. Six to seven varices per whorl, bearing short, strong, slightly foliate spines. Spiral ridges and threads. Dentate lip; smooth columella; broad, open, recurved siphonal canal. Deep umbilicus. Light brown with darker brown on most spines; lip white with some rose pink marks; columella rose pink with some white; interior white.

H. regius
Swainson 1821 *Tropical west America, 6in (150mm).*
Globose with rather short spire and slightly constricted suture. Eight varices per whorl with strong, open spines – those on the shoulder are the largest and all but those in one other row are double, one behind the other. Surface rough with fine, spiral threads. Crenulate lip; smooth columella; broad, strong, open and recurved siphonal canal; well-developed anterior canal. May be deeply umbilical. White, some pale brown areas and a band of brown marks, mostly on the varices, on the body whorl and another just posterior to the siphonal canal; aperture pink with a broad, dark brown swathe on the outer edge of the parietal area which shows above the suture on earlier whorls; lip with a few brown marks; aperture side of siphonal canal is dark brown with a pale blue-white overlay.

Hexaplex rosarium

Hexaplex regius

Phyllonotus pomum
Gmelin 1791 *Southeast USA and Caribbean, 4.3in (110mm).*
Solid with moderate spire and slightly constricted suture. Three varices per whorl with blunt knobs where crossed by obsoletely beaded, low, spiral ridges and fine threads; one, short, axial rib between varices, highest at periphery. Crenulate lip; broad, rough-surfaced, open, slightly recurved siphonal canal. Dark or light brown; some off-white and darker brown marks on the varices; shiny aperture from white to orange or yellow; dark brown marks on lip, and one at end of parietal area where it is joined by lip; may be pale brown marks on columella and anterior end of parietal area; interior paler.

Phyllonotus pomum

Hexaplex brassica

Lamarck 1822 *West Central America, Mexico to Peru, 8in (200mm).*
Low spire and seven angular whorls with about six varices per whorl. Fine, uneven spiral threads. Each varix has a strong, blunt spine on the shoulder – showing on early whorls just above the suture – two or three small spines, and then, on the base of the body whorl and slightly recurved siphonal canal, about six, hollow, sharp spines of varying lengths. Edge of lip and edges of varices with some fifteen small points. Columella with posterior tooth, otherwise smooth. Siphonal canal and end of each varix builds up like a fan. White with three brown bands and other brown shaded areas; aperture white with salmon pink only on the outer lip and parietal wall.

Hexaplex brassica

H. kusterianus

Tapparone-Canefri 1875 *Persian Gulf, 2.8in (70mm).*
Squat and heavy with about five whorls and six varices per whorl. Spirally sculptured with fine threads over unevenly-sized, rounded ridges. Coarse, hollow spines on the shoulder of the varices and nodules below, and one row of larger spines near the anterior end. Indented lip; smooth columella has one posterior tooth. Putty-colored with pink on the columellar edge.

H. erythrostoma

Swainson 1831 *Gulf of California to Peru, 4in (100mm).*
Moderate spire and about eight whorls. Fine spiral threads and finely lamellated growth lines. About six varices per whorl with some eight, hollow spines on ridge of earlier, frilled lip; a short ridge with three spines (not hollow) in the middle of the body whorl between each varix. Columella with posterior tooth and expanded, plicate parietal shield. Long, deep, recurved siphonal canal is slightly open. White, sometimes with pink tinges; aperture bright shiny pink.

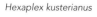
Hexaplex kusterianus

Muricanthus nigritus

Philippi 1845 *Gulf of California, 6in (150mm).*
Moderate spire; about seven whorls; about eight varices per whorl; spirally finely threaded. Varices with hollow spines, largest on the angular shoulder, one smaller and two very

Hexaplex
erythrostoma

Muricanthus nigritus

small above it, and about twelve of varying size –
three quite big – below. Indented lip; siphonal canal
is open and built up fanlike with each new growth
period; smooth columella. White; spines and end of
siphonal canal very dark brown, almost black; spiral
brown streaks behind the spines; aperture white.

M. radix

Gmelin 1791 *Panama to south Ecuador, 4in (100mm).*
Solid and pyriform, like a small edition of its northern
neighbor *M. nigritus,* but relatively more solid and more
spinous and the spines more gemmate. Columella has
posterior tooth. White; spines, areas behind them and
siphonal canal very dark brown to black; aperture white.

Muricanthus radix

M. callidinus

Berry 1958 *East Central America
from Guatemala to Costa Rica, up
to 4in (100mm).*
About nine varices per whorl, all
with long thin frondlike spines,
longest on the shoulder. Columella
has posterior tooth. White; dark
brown spines and siphonal canal;
brown spiral stripes of varying
width; aperture white. Some
authors consider this to be a variant
of *M. radix* Gmelin 1791.

Muricanthus
callidinus

Ceratostoma nuttalli

Conrad 1857 *California, 2.2in (55mm).*
Solid with moderate to short spire. Three varices per whorl and a nodulose axial rib between; spiral ridges and cords; varices solid but with sharp edges. Edge of lip finely denticulate with one, long, pointed tooth near the anterior end; inside lip has about five, blunt teeth. Columella smooth with one blunt tooth posteriorly. Deep, sealed and short siphonal canal. Cream, brown, or banded cream and brown; aperture white.

Ceratostoma nuttalli

C. foliatus

Gmelin 1791 *Alaska to California, 3in (80mm).*
High spire and about seven whorls constricted at the suture. Strong, well-separated spiral ridges, two large ones on the shoulder. One larger and some lesser axial ribs between varices which are broadly frilled, the frills lamellated on the aperture side. Outer lip with rough edge and one, large, pointed tooth near the posterior end. Smooth columella and short siphonal canal, sealed and sharply turned to the right at the tip. White with light or dark brown banding; the two larger ridges on the shoulder and the area between white; aperture white.

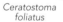

Ceratostoma foliatus

Pteropurpura trialatus

Sowerby 1834 *California, 3in (80mm).*
High spire and seven whorls, three varices per whorl. Fine spiral cords and about six, low, blunt ridges on the body whorl and a blunt knob on the shoulder between varices; the latter frilled and foliate, and the frond on the shoulder pointed up, out and

Pteropurpura trialatus

Pteropurpura erinaceoides

slightly backward. Dentate lip and smooth columella.
Siphonal canal is long, deep, sealed and slightly curved.
Flesh-colored with dark brown clouding especially between
the ridges; aperture white.

P. erinaceoides
Valenciennes 1832 *South and Lower California and
northwest Mexico, 2in (50mm).*
Moderate spire; about six whorls, three varices per whorl
and a large, knobbed, axial ridge between each whorl.
About six spiral ridges on body whorl, ending in sharply
recurved spines on the varices. Fine spiral cords and very
fine lamellae overall. Finely dentate outer lip edge, smooth
columella and moderate siphonal canal, sealed and slightly
recurved. Shades of red-brown, darker on the knobs and
spines; aperture white.

*Pterynotus
vespertilio*

Pterynotus vespertilio
Kira 1955 *South Japan, 1.8in (45mm).*
Delicate and elongate with about six whorls, three varices
per whorl. Spirally corded and varices unevenly frilled. Light
brown with darker brown spots.

P. bednalli
Brazier 1878 *Northwest
Australia, 3.3in (85mm).*
One of the most beautiful of
the murex, it is delicate and
elongate. High spire; about
seven whorls; somewhat
constricted suture; three
varices per whorl and
spiral well-separated ridges.
Varices have large, thin,
rather smooth-edged and
slightly fluted projections, flaring
at the shoulders but running
together with earlier varices. Outer
lip is faintly ridged; smooth columella;
siphonal canal moderate, deep, slightly
open and recurved at the tip. Glossy cream with
pink tinge; pale brown spots and lines on the
varices; aperture white.

*Pterynotus
bednalli*

P. tripterus
Born 1778 *Indo-west Pacific, 2.4in (60mm).*
Moderate spire with about seven whorls, three varices per
whorl. Granulose with spiral cords. Varices have fine frilly
projection, lamellate on the aperture side; one knob on the
shoulder between varices. Outer lip denticulate and about
seven teeth within. Columella has seven to ten teeth.
Siphonal canal is deep, narrow and recurved at the tip.
White or cream; aperture white with a touch of pale yellow-
green on the outer edge of the columella.

Pterynotus tripterus

Siratus motacilla

Siratus motacilla

Gmelin 1791 *Lesser Antilles, but Reeve records it as being Senegal in west Africa, 2.4in (60mm).*
Solid except for the delicate canal. Moderate spire; seven whorls with three varices per whorl; spirally ridged and roughly axially striate; two nodulose ribs between varices have a short, sharp spine on the shoulder of each and another where they join the siphonal canal. Bluntly dentate lip is plicate within and has about three small teeth posteriorly. Smooth columella; plicate edge to narrow parietal shield. Long siphonal canal is straight but angled upward from its base and nearly closed. Cream-white with pale pink-brown bands and blotches.

S. perelegans

Vokes 1965 *Caribbean and Florida, 2.4in (60mm).*
Very similar to its neighbor *S. motacilla*. Solid with long, straight, upturned siphonal canal, but the spines on the shoulder are lacking or minute, and the ridges and ribs are finer; spire slightly lower.

Siratus perelegans

Pterynotus pinnatus

Swainson 1822 *East Asia, 2.8in (70mm).*
Elongate with high spire. About eight whorls and three varices per whorl. Fine, spiral ridges; one rib between varices which have a thin, delicate, continuous, fanlike projection from suture to end of long, curved, rather open siphonal canal. Lip finely dentate on the edge and toothed within; smooth columella. White; rather translucent.

P. elongatus

Lightfoot 1786 *Indo-Pacific, 4in (100mm).*
Synonym *M. clavus* Kiener 1842. Graceful and a collectors' item. Elongate with about seven whorls; fine, spiral, minutely beaded cords. Three varices per whorl, with a blunt low ridge between each and with frilly, fanlike projections, slightly pointed at the shoulder and running down to the end of the long, almost sealed siphonal canal; the latter is recurved at the tip. Finely dentate lip. White or creamy white; parietal wall with faint pink tinge.

Pterynotus pinnatus

P. bipinnatus

Reeve 1845 *Indo-Pacific, 1.8in (45mm).*
Elongate and narrow with rather towerlike spire. About seven whorls; spirally and axially finely ridged; the upper whorls have blunt knobs, about seven per whorl. Body whorl has three varices, those two nearest the aperture carrying delicate wavy fins. Lip edge with tiny, sharp teeth, and plicated within, as is the lower half of the columella. Siphonal canal almost as long as the spire and slightly open. White; aperture pale rose.

Pterynotus bipinnatus

Ceratostoma fournieri

Crosse 1861 *Japan, 2in (50mm).*
Rather low spire. About six whorls with three varices each. Malleate surface with low, blunt, spiral ridges. One large knob between varices which carry a wavy frilly fin. Uneven lip with a projecting tooth near the anterior end. Moderately long siphonal canal is deep, curved and sealed. White, profusely clouded with dark tan.

Pterynotus elongatus

Pteropurpura plorator

A. Adams & Reeve 1849 *south Japan and Korea, 1.6in (40mm).*
Moderate spire. About six whorls with three varices per whorl, a blunt knob on the shoulder between each. Faint spiral ridges and axial striae. Varices with wavy, winged projections, pointing up and outward at the shoulders. Bluntly dentate lip; smooth columella; sealed siphonal canal. White with spiral tan lines and rows of wavy axial flames; aperture white.

Ceratostoma fournieri

Eupleura muriciformis

Broderip 1833 *Gulf of California to Ecuador, 1.6in (40mm).*
About six angular whorls with a varix about every three-quarters of a whorl. Spirally ridged, with about four knobs on the shoulder between varices, which are more or less strongly developed. Denticulate lip; smooth columella; extended, recurved, open siphonal canal. White to dark gray-brown; varices with large blotch of dark brown; interior purple-brown.

Eupleura muriciformis

Pteropurpura plorator

171

Homalocantha scorpio
L. 1758 *Philippines and east Indonesia, 2.4in (60mm).*
Low spire and about four whorls with about seven varices per whorl. Very deep, wide sutures crossed by the varices; spirally corded; angular shoulders. Early varices with short, hollow spines which increase in length up to the body whorl; the last two varices have long, rather triangular, hollow projections, the apex being at the varix and the flat 'base' being furthest from the body whorl; they are joined at the lip edge by a small, continuous frill. Finely dentate lip; smooth columella; long, straight siphonal canal. Dark brown to black; light gray or white in places; aperture with purple tinge.

Homalocantha scorpio

H. zamboi
Burch 1960 *Philippines, 2.2in (55mm).*
Short spire and about five whorls. Deep, wide sutures crossed by varices of which there are about five per whorl. Malleate surface. Last four varices have four, hollow projections, widening toward the tip where they flatten out and may become slightly palmate; at their base they have short blunt 'fingers' pointing toward the finely dentate lip. Smooth inside lip and columella. Long, almost sealed siphonal canal is recurved at the tip. White; aperture pink to pale brown.

Homalocantha zamboi

Trunculariopsis trunculus
L. 1758 *Mediterranean and adjacent west Atlantic, 4in (100mm).*
Moderate to high spire and about seven, angular whorls. Very close, finely lamellate, spiral cords. About five, low, spiral ridges, the one on the shoulder with six to twelve,

more or less pointed spines. About six varices per whorl on which are the longest of the spines. Between varices from none to four, low, axial ribs on which there are low, blunt knobs where they cross the ridges. Varices little more than the edge of earlier lips, which are faintly denticulate. Smooth columella with tooth at posterior end. Deep, heavy, open and curved siphonal canal. White with three broad bands of brown or purple-brown; columella white or stained with purple; banding showing through the outer lip into the interior. A very variable shell in sculpture and coloring, but always easily distinguished. Two varieties are illustrated.

Trunculariopsis trunculus

Naquetia triqueter

Born 1778 *Philippines, 2.2in (55mm).*
Solid but elongate and six whorls with three varices per whorl. Spirally ridged; three, axial ribs between varices; latter small, those on body whorl with frilly, fanlike projection, narrow posteriorly, getting wider anteriorly and on the straight, almost completely sealed siphonal canal. Lip dentate within; smooth columella. Cream; banded and spotted with brown; aperture white, but with the brown bands showing through.

Naquetia triqueter

M. uncinarius

Lamarck 1822 *East South Africa,*
0.8in (20mm).
About five whorls; three varices per
whorl. A large knob on the shoulder
between varices; the latter with short,
blunt spines; the largest on the shoulder being hook-shaped. Smooth lip and
columella; sealed siphonal canal. Pale
brown; aperture white.

Murex
uncinarius

M. nodulifera

Sowerby 1841 *Philippines, 0.9in (23mm).*
Moderate spire; sculptured with spiral
ridges and axial ribs, nodulose where
they intersect. Lip dentate within;
columella with two, blunt teeth at the
base. Cream, spotted with dark brown;
aperture pale yellow.

Murex
nodulifera

Pteropurpura festiva

Hinds 1844 *Gulf of California, 2in (50mm).*
High spire; about six whorls; three varices per whorl; rough,
axial growth lines. A rib with a large, blunt knob on the shoulder
between varices. The latter with a fanlike projection folded
backward and lamellate on the aperture side; lip finely dentate
at the edge and within; smooth columella; deep, sealed, rather
short, and recurved siphonal canal. Light brown with fine, spiral,
dark brown lines; aperture blue-white.

Pteropurpura festiva

Ocenebra erinaceus

L. 1758 *Mediterranean and west*
Europe, 2.4in (60mm).
About six angular whorls. Sculptured with large, rounded,
spiral, lamellated ribs, smaller
ones between, and chan-
neled between them. Irregular varices, somewhat ridged
between. Dentate lip; smooth
columella; deep and sealed
siphonal canal. Gray-brown;
aperture white.

Ocenebra erinaceus

Vitularia miliaris

Gmelin 1791 *East Indian Ocean to*
Pacific, 2in (50mm).
Moderate spire; about six whorls;
deeply indented suture; oblique,
axial uneven ribs between irregular,
very small varices. The shoulder
of the body whorl has a shallow

Ocenebra
erinaceus

channel, which is almost overhung on the upper side. The
whole surface granulose. Lip edge rough, slightly expanded,

especially anteriorly, four teeth within; smooth columella; short, rather straight, and sealed siphonal canal. Yellow-brown with a row of brown spots on varices; aperture white.

Maxwellia gemma
Sowerby 1879 *California, 1.2in (30mm).*
Stubby; short spire. About five whorls; sutures deep but crossed by oblique varices, about six per whorl; low, spiral ridges; finely dentate lip; smooth columella; short and sealed siphonal canal. White with dark brown on the ridges.

Vitularia miliaris

Maxwellia gemma

Chicoreus territus
Reeve 1845
See page 162.

Chicoreus territus

Murex recurvirostris rubidus

Favartia tetragona

Murex recurvirostris rubidus
F. C. Baker 1897 *Florida and the Bahamas, 2in (50mm).*
About six whorls; moderate spire; three varices per whorl, which may have a spine on the shoulder; two, large, and one, small, axial rib between varices; spirally ridged with a cord between; lip faintly dentate and ridged within; plicate columella; noticeably long, open siphonal canal. Color variable from cream to red.

Favartia tetragona
Broderip 1833 *Australia to Fiji, 1.4in (35mm).*
Squat and solid; about four whorls; four, solid, oblique varices per whorl; coarse, spiral ridges; finely dentate lip; smooth columella; short, sealed and sharply recurved siphonal canal. White; aperture lavender.

Murex spec.
See page 4.

Murex spec.

FAMILY: THAIDIDAE

Rather solid, medium-sized shells, having wide apertures, low spires and no varices. They live in shallow water and are carnivorous, living on other mollusks, especially mussels.

Neorapana muricata

Broderip 1832 *West Central America, 4in (100mm).*
Sharply angled shoulder, flat from shoulder to suture, and axially lamellate overall. Smooth spiral cords, five large, bluntly knobbed ridges, plus a small wavy one at suture; largest one at shoulder, three on body whorl. Lip spirally ridged within, a tooth posteriorly. Smooth columella, blunt denticle posteriorly. Narrow columellar shield; strong fasciole; short, open siphonal canal. Cream-gray, possibly sometimes pink; aperture white, faint tinge of pink.

Neorapana muricata

Thais haemastoma

L. 1758 *Mediterranean, northwest Africa, 3in (80mm).*
Medium, conical spire; fine, spiral, granulose cords; and shoulder more or less angled. Four spiral rows of knobs; largest on shoulder, next largest below, two small ones below that; row on shoulder has about ten knobs which may have heavy, blunt or obsolescent spines. Lip ridged within; smooth columella with blunt tooth posteriorly; narrow columellar shield; well-developed fasciole; short siphonal canal. Light tan-gray to dark red-brown; lip edge usually dark brown between ridges; aperture and columella pink, orange or red, paler within; parietal wall with blotch of pale yellow and dark brown spiral lines.

Haustrum haustorium

Gmelin 1791 *New Zealand, 2.6in (65mm).*
Low spire and very inflated body whorl; constricted at suture. Coarse, flat spiral ridges; irregular, axial growth lines; very wide, long aperture. Lip runs to bottom of extended siphonal canal, ridged within for a short way. Smooth columella; large parietal shield, lower end level with fasciole. Brown-gray; edge of lip straw with dark purple-brown marking; interior blue-white; columella, shield white, latter with straw and purple-brown clouding posteriorly.

Thais haemastoma

Mancinella bufo

Lamarck 1822 *Pacific, 2.4in (60mm).*
Solid, heavy, with low spire and slightly shouldered. Flat spiral cords of varying widths and four spiral ridges, more

Haustrum
haustorium

Mancinella
bufo

or less knobbed, lower two almost obsolete. Beveled, dentate lip; smooth columella; well-developed but short anal and siphonal canals; moderate fasciole. Callous knob above columella forms one side of anal canal. Brown; interstices of cords cream; cream on ridges between knobs; columella apricot; aperture cream, paler within and dark brown between teeth.

Purpura persica
L. 1758 *Indo-west Pacific, 4in (100mm).*
Low spire; close-set, flat spiral cords; seven, larger, more or less knobbed, narrow spiral ridges. Slightly constricted below suture. Wide aperture with lip to end of extended siphonal canal. Dentate lip; smooth columella with small callous lump posteriorly; callous parietal wall; and narrow fasciole. Gray-brown; ridges darker; some cords with dark brown and white dashes; inside of lip with broad, dark purple-brown band; interior pale blue stripes on darker background; columella orange-pink; parietal wall dark brown, yellow and cream.

Purpura persica

P. columellaris
Lamarck 1822 *West Central and South America, 2.4in (60mm).*
Solid, heavy, with short spire. Broad, elevated, obsoletely knobbed, spiral ridges, about ten on body whorl; smaller ridges and cords between. Crenulate lip has eight, strong, blunt teeth running as ridges into aperture. Columella with low tooth centrally, callous lump posteriorly. Anal and siphonal canals not well-developed. Parietal wall with two or three faint obsolete folds. Gray-brown; lip orange-tan; interior cream; teeth and columella white; parietal wall red near columella, otherwise cream-tan with some purple marking.

Purpura columellaris

Purpura patula   *Thais carinifera*   *Purpura coronata*

Purpura patula

L. 1762 *Caribbean and south Florida, 4in (100mm)*.
Uneven, flat spiral ribs; axial threads; striations and growth lines. Six spiral rows of blunt knobs, becoming obsolete anteriorly. Wide, dentate lip, smooth columella, shallow recurved siphonal canal and weak fasciole. Dull brown-gray; inside lip edged dark purple-black; interior pale blue-gray; columella orange-pink; parietal wall straw, purple-black, and green-brown.

Thais carinifera

Lamarck 1816 *East Africa, 2in (50mm)*.
Inflated; very deep suture; close-set, finely beaded spiral cords. Widest part of whorls bear short, wide, flat, blunt projections, sometimes running together, forming uneven keel on last whorl; latter develops deeper suture and begins to drop away from penultimate whorl; it also develops spiral ridge on shoulder and a smaller one below. Dentate lip; columellar shield partly covers narrow, deep umbilicus; strong fasciole. Dirty gray-brown; aperture cream to orange; purple stains deep inside.

Purpura coronata

Lamarck 1816 *West Africa, 1.8in (45mm)*.
Solid; globose; low spire; spiral, uneven, beaded cords. Four rows of blunt, rounded knobs, those on two posterior rows larger. Below suture, very coarse lamellations develop from penultimate whorl, which become large and 'wart'-like near aperture. Lip dentate within; smooth columella; short, deep siphonal and anal canals; strongly developed fasciole. Crystalline white, usually with spiral brown lines; aperture cream.

Thais melones

Thais melones

Duclos 1832 *Tropical west America and Galapagos, 2in (50mm)*.
Solid, smooth, globose, with short spire and fine, incised, spiral striae. Finely dentate lip is plicate within and slightly concave posteriorly. Smooth columella, heavy callosity posteriorly; short siphonal canal; small fasciole. Brown; white

flashes on shoulder and anteriorly; inside of lip and siphonal canal pale primrose; columella white, bounded by broad purple-brown streak; callosity orange.

Neothais orbita

Gmelin 1791 *East Australia and New Zealand, 3in (80mm).*
Solid, not heavy, with moderate spire. Broad, high spiral ridges with deep, wide channels between; fine spiral threads between and on ridges and fine axial lamellae in channels. Coarse sculpture; dentate lip; smooth interior and columella; shallow, short siphonal canal; no umbilicus. Dirty white or cream; aperture edge straw-colored; interior pink-white; columella white.

Neothais orbita

Thais kiosquiformis

Duclos 1832 *Tropical west America, 1.8in (45mm).*
Very similar to *T. carinifera.* Inflated whorls; deep suture; flat points on shoulders, ten on body whorl. Spiral cords, lamellate below suture; three cords bigger than others, showing obsolete points. Dentate lip; straight, smooth columella; short siphonal canal; developed fasciole; narrowly umbilicate. Brown-gray; white spiral line on shoulder; aperture and interior white; lip edge brown-gray.

Thais armigera

T. armigera

Link 1807 *Indo-west Pacific, 3in (80mm).*
High spire; three rows of blunt spines on body whorl, shoulder row large and solid, one showing on the earlier whorl; spirally corded. Finely dentate lip, plicate within; columella with three pleats anteriorly, obsolete tooth posteriorly; moderate siphonal canal; fasciole. White; brown spiral bands between rows of spines; inside lip edge light brown, pale yellow within this; interior with pink tinge; columella white; parietal area pale yellow, brown edge.

Thais kiosquiformis

Mancinella mancinella

L. 1758 *Indo-Pacific, 2in (50mm).*
Solid, globose and spirally corded. Six rows of small strong spines on body whorl. Finely dentate lip; spirally corded interior; smooth columella, blunt posterior tooth; obsolete anal canal; short siphonal canal; fasciole. White or light gray, brown banding; aperture orange-yellow; interior dull orange.

Mancinella mancinella

179

Morulina fusca

Küster *Japan to Singapore, 1in (25mm).*
Four rows of blunt knobs with spiral cords between rows. Dentate lip, four teeth within. Smooth columella; obsolete plicae on parietal wall; short siphonal canal. White; posterior row of knobs red, then rows alternating black and red; lip straw-colored with purple blotches; teeth white; columella and interior blue-white; parietal wall purple at top and bottom.

Morulina fusca

Morula squamosa

Pease 1867 *Indo-Pacific, 1.2in (30mm).*
Low spire. Small spines below suture, two larger rows on shoulder and below, then two smaller rows; two incised lines between rows. Finely dentate lip; smooth columella; open siphonal canal. Gray-brown; coarse oblique white stripes; lip with broad purple band; interior blue-white; columella pinky white; parietal wall blue-white with purple-brown marks on edge and around siphonal canal.

Morula squamosa

M. margariticola

Broderip 1832 *Pacific and East Indies, 1.6in (40mm).*
Angular shoulders and spirally beaded ridges, two larger. Broad axial ribs, rather pointed on the shoulder. Dentate lip, six teeth within; columella with two or three plicae; short siphonal canal. Dark brown, lighter between ridges; aperture blue-white or mauve-purple; sometimes dark blotch on parietal wall.

Morula margariticola

M. spinosa

H. & A. Adams 1853
Indo-Pacific, 1.4in (35mm).
High spire. Finely spirally ridged; three rows of spines; often long and sharp. Dentate lip, five teeth within; columella with four obsolete teeth; narrow aperture; long siphonal canal. White or gray; spines dark brown; aperture rich violet.

Morula spinosa

Thais tuberosa

Röding 1798 *Indo-Pacific, 2in (50mm).*
Short spire. Spirally ridged; two rows of strong blunt spines on shoulder, and one thick ridge below. Dentate lip, spiral lirae within; columella with three short plicae; blunt tooth bordering obsolete anal canal; short siphonal canal. White; two broad uneven dark brown bands; lip with four brown marks; aperture cream; lirae pale orange; columella cream, large chestnut area posteriorly and small one below.

T. bitubercularis

Lamarck 1822 *Malaya, Indonesia and Philippines, 2in (50mm).*
Spirally ridged; two rows of solid, quite sharp, spines on shoulder; two, uneven, thick, nodulose ridges below. Dentate lip, two small and two obsolete teeth within. Columella has a faint plica; narrow shield. Creamy white; dark brown-gray axial stripes; lip cream with dark brown markings; interior and inner side of columella white; parietal wall cream.

T. lamellosa

Gmelin 1790 *west coast of North America, 5in (125mm).*
Very variable; high or low spire, angular or rounded shoulders. Beveled, dentate lip, three to six teeth within. Smooth columella; a blunt tooth low on parietal wall. Cream-gray to dark brown, sometimes banded; aperture white with clouding on lip.

Thais tuberosa

T. hippocastanum

L. 1758 *Indo-Pacific, 2.4in (60mm).*
Spirally ridged; four rows of blunt spines; oblique axial ribs. Dentate lip, four teeth within. Columella with central ridge and one short plica. Cream and purple-brown; white streaks between ribs; aperture blue-white; dark purple-brown band or splashes inside lip, and spiral streaks; columella brown; ridge blue-white; sometimes pale primrose on parietal wall or anteriorly on lip.

Thais bitubercularis

Thais lamellosa

Thais hippocastanum

Drupella ochrostoma

Blainville 1832 *Indo-Pacific, 1.4in (35mm).*
Four rows of rounded nodules set on twelve axial ribs; two cords between rows. Lip with five or six teeth; columella with two to four. Creamy white with pale yellow areas; nodules dark red-brown; aperture orange or pink.

Drupella ochrostoma

181

Concholepas peruvianus

Lamarck *Peru and Chile, 5in (130mm) wide.*
Like the Haliotidae, this animal lives attached to rock by its strong foot It has a very expanded aperture and looks a little like one valve of a bivalve. The shell expands in increasing concentric growth from the apex, narrowly on one side and widely on the other, so that the apex overhangs the narrow side. The growth lines cross small, uneven ridges radiating from the apex. Dirty white-gray; interior cream with pale brown clouding and a few blue spots and flecks.

Concholepas peruvianus

Drupa rubusidaea

Drupa rubusidaea juvenile

Drupa rubusidaea

Röding 1798 *Indo-Pacific, 2.2in (55mm).*
Solid and rather globose with almost flat spire. Spiral, fine, scaly ridges and five rows of strong spines, longest nearest the aperture and also posteriorly, except the row immediately below the suture where they are smaller; the spines are on low axial ribs, about eight on the body whorl. Lip with about ten teeth; columella with two plicae anteriorly. Callous parietal wall has narrow shield anteriorly. Fasciole has strong spines; no umbilicus. White-gray; points of spines black in illustrated juvenile specimen; outer edge of aperture pale lemon yellow area of teeth and columella rich pink; interior and band in middle of columella white. Adult and juvenile illustrated.

D. ricina

L. 1758 *Indo-Pacific, east Africa to Clifton Island and the Galapagos, 1.2in (30mm).*
Low spire. Slightly scabrous, spiral ridges. Five rows of spines, longest on the shoulder and nearest the aperture, and more or less joined spirally by a low rib. Lip finely

dentate between spines; two double teeth within posteriorly and two single ones anteriorly. Columella has three plaits anteriorly – middle one may be bifid – and one plait posteriorly. Dirty white; spines purple-black; spiral ribs white; aperture white and may have a broken ring of pale yellow round the outside. A subspecies *D.r. hadari* Emerson and Cernohorsky 1973, found in the Red Sea, is larger, up to 38mm, heavier and with a more developed parietal wall.

D. lobata
Blainville 1832 *Red Sea and Indian Ocean to South China Sea and Western Australia, 32mm.*
Rather flattened ventro-dorsally. Low spire and apex at an angle of about 30° to the columella. Sculptured with large and small, lamellate spiral ridges, the former ending in four frondlike projections on the lip. There is also a longer, spatulate projection on the lip at the shoulder along which runs the extension of the deep anal canal. Lip with about eight teeth. Coarse fold at bottom of parietal wall. Short, deep, open siphonal canal. Dirty white-brown; interior yellow; edge of lip, outer columella and parietal wall rich chocolate.

Drupa ricina

Drupa lobata   *Drupa morum*   *Drupa grossularia*

D. morum
Röding 1798 *Indo-Pacific to Clifton Island and Easter Island, 2in (50mm).*
Solid, slightly flattened, with very low spire. Four rows of blunt nodules on body whorl, striate between. Narrow aperture; lip unevenly thickened internally and with about eight denticles in groups, about four anteriorly, then two or three, then one or two. Columella with three or four plaits anteriorly, from the parietal wall to the interior. Deep anal and siphonal canals. Dirty white-gray; nodules dark brown; aperture rich purple; cream on parietal wall and edge of lip.

D. grossularia
Röding 1798 *Cocos and Keeling Islands eastward to the Pacific, 1.2in (30mm).*
Similar in shape and sculpture to *D. lobata* above, but with a golden yellow instead of brown aperture. The two species overlap only in the Cocos-Keeling, Western Australia areas.

Nassa francolina

Nassa francolina

Bruguière 1789 *Indian Ocean, 2.8in (70mm).*
Moderate spire; very fine, close, spiral striae. Slightly shouldered and inflated body whorl. Growth lines. Smooth lip has denticle posteriorly opposite a spiral rib on the otherwise smooth columella, which together form anal canal. Short, deep, open siphonal canal; small fasciole. Light red-brown; row of irregular light blotches on shoulder, partly showing at suture; may be some small, light patches further forward on body whorl; lip edge brown; interior cream; columella white backed with brown streak and then pale yellow.

N. serta

Bruguière 1789 *East Australia and west Pacific, 2.8in (70mm).*
Pacific counterpart of the above. Similar except more solid, much coarser, spiral sculpturing, dentate inside lip, and light blotches bigger and running together.

Acanthina imbricatum

Lamarck *West South America, 2.2in (55mm)*
Rather low spire; spiral ridges; channels strongly imbricately scaled. Finely denticulate lip; large, thornlike tooth – typical of genus – anteriorly. Smooth columella; short siphonal canal; small fasciole. Brick red to brown; lip edge brown; interior brown or white; columella white bordered brown.

Nassa serta

Nucella lapillus

L. 1758 *Atlantic, 2.6in (65mm).*
Moderate spire and spirally corded. Dentate lip is ridged within; smooth columella; short, deep siphonal and anal canals. White, yellow or brown; sometimes banded.

Rapana bezoar

L. 1758 *Japan, 2.4in (60mm).*
Short spire. Rounded, spiral, nodulose ridges; strong growth lines cause imbricated effect; shoulder with blunt, open spines. Three ridges and nodulose, axial folds between constricted suture and shoulder. Dentate lip, ridged within; smooth columella; deep, short, recurved canal; deep umbilicus; fasciole. Cream-fawn; interior white.

Nucella lapillus

R. rapiformis

Born 1778 *West Pacific, New Caledonia to Japan, 4in (100mm).*
Lighter than *R. bezoar.* Very low spire; expanded body whorl. Fine, incised, spiral lines; axial striae; three, low, slightly nodulose, spiral ridges. Shoulder with fifteen, open, more or less blunt spines, showing on earlier whorls above deep, channeled suture. Wide aperture; denticulate lip, ridged within; wide, shallow channel level with shoulder spines.

Acanthina imbricatum

Smooth columella; extended, open canal; wide, deep umbilicus; imbricately scaled fasciole. Pale brown to off-white; aperture very light brown to cream.

FAMILY: COLUMBARIIDAE

Columbarium pagoda
Lesson 1831 *Japan, 2.4in (60mm).*
Large nuclear apex and deep, constricted suture. Whorls sharply angled with about ten, flat, slightly upturned, triangular spines. Faint axial striae. Body whorl has strong cord below shoulder, hidden beneath suture on earlier whorls; cord has short, sharp spines near aperture. Very long, open, delicate siphonal canal. Shiny-fawn; siphonal canal darker; apex red-brown.

FAMILY: MAGILIDAE

Rapana bezoar

Rapa rapa
L. 1758 *Indo-Pacific, 3.3in (85mm).*
Fragile with flat or slightly sunken spire and very expanded body whorl. Fine, spiral lamellae overlap suture. Rounded, spiral ridges increase in size and distance apart toward anterior; fine threads between some posterior ridges replaced by fine, axial lamellae anteriorly. Thin lip, crenulated by ridge ends; callous columella; shield partly covers deep, wide, open umbilicus; strong fasciole. Opaque white or cream.

Coralliophila violacea
Kiener 1836 *Indo-Pacific, 1.6in (40mm).*
Solid; short spire. Uneven, fine, spiral, incised lines. Beveled lip is finely dentate, finely ridged within. Callous columella has lump posteriorly; strong parietal shield; fasciole; short, recurved, open canal. Off-white; aperture rich violet.

Rapana rapiformis

Rapa rapa

Coralliophila violacea

Columbarium pagoda

Latiaxis japonicus

Latiaxis japonicus
Dunker 1882 *Japan, 1.4in (35mm).*
Moderate spire; whorls with sharply angled shoulder. About eighteen, strong, spiral ridges carrying closely packed, small spines; a deep canal between ridges. Up and outward pointing frill on shoulder with triangular hollow spines – about twelve on body whorl – open toward aperture and having fine, beaded striae on their surface. Dentate lip; smooth columella; quite long siphonal canal; umbilicate; small fasciole with lamellated edge. White.

L. dunkeri
Kuroda & Habe 1961 *Japan and Taiwan, 1.6in (40mm).*
Solid with about six whorls and fine, rough spiral cords. Angular shoulders with triangular spines, about ten on body whorl. Finely dentate lip is strongly ridged within; about twelve spiral ridges. Smooth columella; long, open, recurved siphonal canal; umbilicate; strongly lamellate fasciole. White.

Latiaxis dunkeri

L. mawae
Griffith & Pidgeon 1834
Japan, 2.2in (55mm).
Sunken spire with sharp, pointed apex. Shoulder carries small frill with blunt, triangular spines; the area between it and suture slightly concave. Up to last whorl suture is formed with shoulder of previous whorls as its edge, but last whorl develops outward and downward, so that suture ceases to exist. Smooth lip; no columella in an adult shell; deep, quite long, curved siphonal canal. White.

Latiaxis mawae

L. pagodus
A. Adams 1853
Japan, 1.2in (30mm).
High spire; about six whorls with very deep suture. Convex above shoulder which bears long, pointed, triangular, hollow spines, open toward aperture; second row of smaller spines below; about four rough cords below that. Lip faintly plicate within; smooth columella; moderate, recurved siphonal canal; umbilicate fasciole with long spines – the ends of earlier canals. White or pale brown with purple stains in aperture; columella white.

Latiaxis pagodus

Latiaxis lischkeanus

Latiaxis pilsbryi

Latiaxis idoleum

Latiaxis kiranus

L. lischkeanus

Dunker 1882 *Japan, 1.6in (40mm)*.
Rather similar to *L. japonicus*, but more finely sculptured with spinous, spiral cords and curved, triangular spines on shoulders; about eighteen on body whorl, and with two rows of smaller spines near base of siphonal canal. Finely dentate lip; smooth columella; moderately long, open, curved siphonal canal; umbilicate; lamellate fasciole. White.

L. pilsbryi

Hirase 1908 *Japan, 0.9in (22mm)*.
Spire almost flat with sharp apex. Whorls with sharp shoulder carrying flat, slightly up-pointing, triangular spines. In adults last two whorls break away and suture ceases. Fine spiral threads. Smooth lip; rather short, curved siphonal canal; wide, deep umbilicus; spinous fasciole. White.

L. idoleum

Jonas 1847 *Japan and Taiwan, 1.6in (40mm)*.
Solid with about seven, rather inflated whorls, constricted at suture. Fine, distinct, slightly scabrous, spiral ridges; low, uneven, oblique axial ribs. Finely dentate lip; smooth columella; open siphonal canal is a little recurved; umbilicus may be very wide or narrow and rather shallow; very rough fasciole. White.

L. kiranus

Kuroda 1959 *Japan and Singapore, 1.2in (30mm)*.
Rather high spire and angular whorls. Spiral ridges with irregular, very small spines; larger, triangular spines on shoulders; a row of small ones on siphonal canal. Axially ribbed, about nine ribs on body whorl. Dentate lip ridged within; smooth columella; almost straight siphonal canal; narrow, shallow umbilicus; lamellate fasciole. Cream.

L. gyratus

Hinds 1844 *West Pacific, 1.8in (45mm)*.
High spire; inflated whorls; constricted sutures. Spiral cords close-set, finely beaded. Axially uneven rather than ribbed. Strong, beaded keel projects from shoulders of whorls Lirate inside lip; wide, rather shallow umbilicus; strong fasciole. White.

Latiaxis gyratus

SUPERFAMILY: BUCCINACEA

FAMILY: PYRENIDAE

The dove shells. Generally small and colorful. Live in coral or sand; tropical or semitropical. Most are carnivorous. Synonym Columbellidae.

Pyrene testudinaria

Link 1807 *Pacific, to Singapore, 1in (25mm).*
Solid, pyriform with deep suture. Corded spiral lines below shoulder, stronger toward base. Nine teeth on lip; four columellar teeth anteriorly. White; brown-black spots or streaks or brown with white spots or streaks; aperture blue-white.

Pyrene testudinaria

P. varians

Sowerby 1832 *Pacific, 0.4in (10mm).*
Short spire. Smooth, or strong axial ribs on early whorls and posterior of body whorl; spiral striae. Toothed lip; bifid columellar tooth, five teeth on edge. White, cream or brown; sometimes dark brown, wavy, axial lines and rows of V-shaped marks; aperture white or blue-white; purple marks on lip and canal.

P. rustica

L. 1758 *Mediterranean, west Atlantic, 1.2in (30mm).*
Variable. Moderate spire. Spiral striae, obsolete in middle of body whorl. Thickened, strongly toothed lip indented centrally; five columellar teeth anteriorly. White or blue-white, more or less mottled purple, purple-brown, or red.

Pyrene varians   *Pyrene rustica*

Pyrene flava

P. flava

Brugière 1789 *Indo-Pacific, 1in (25mm).*
Solid; deep suture. Ten, strong, spiral ridges anteriorly on body whorl and in short, slightly recurved siphonal canal. Beveled lip has axial rib with three, strong and two, weak teeth. Columella smooth but with obsolete nodules on edge of narrow columellar shield. Color variable, usually dark or pale brown; dark brown, zig-zag, axial lines or spiral bands cut by white spots on shoulder, or with irregular mottling; aperture white.

P. philippinarum

Recluz *Philippines, Malaysia, 1in (25mm).*
Concave spire. Angular shoulder, narrowing to slightly recurved and twisted siphonal canal. Beveled lip has twelve, weak teeth. Smooth columella. White or cream; strong, wavy, axial, red-brown or purple-black marks; aperture white.

P. ocellata

Link 1807 *Indo-Pacific, 0.8in (20mm).*
Solid; short spire; angled shoulder; narrowing to anterior. Spirally corded anteriorly. Lip turned in with nine internal teeth on axial ridge. Columella with row of small teeth near edge of narrow shield. Dark brown to black; white or yellowish spots or zigzag stripes; lip mauve; outer edge of columella brown.

*Pyrene
philippinarum*

P. splendidula

Sowerby *Indo-Pacific, 1.2in (30mm).*
Low spire. Inflated body whorl, narrowing anteriorly to short siphonal canal. Anterior with spiral ridges crossing columella. Large brown and white blotches; aperture white; thick periostracum (illustrated).

Strombina maculosa

Sowerby 1832 *North tropical west America, 1in (25mm).*
High spire; nodulose shoulder. Spiral ridges on lower body whorl. Thickened, beveled lip with six teeth. Smooth columella. White maculated with brown, white showing mainly as tent marks.

Pyrene ocellata

Pyrene splendidula   *Strombina maculosa*   *Microcithara harpiformis*

Microcithara harpiformis

Sowerby 1832 *Central America, 18mm.*
Solid; short spire. Axial ribs, fourteen on body whorl, form blunt points on angular shoulders. Narrow aperture. Finely dentate lip, thickened, especially on inside, extends out and up to deep, narrow posterior canal, and has sharp ridge on edge opposite columella; latter has obsolete fold. Dark chocolate; white spots; suture, knobs on spire, apex white; inside lip white, may have some brown dots; columella as body whorl.

FAMILY: NASSARIIDAE

Dog whelks or basket shells live mostly in tropical or semitropical shallows. Carnivorous, scavengers; active, especially at night.

Bullia grayi

Reeve 1846 *South Africa,*
2.9in (75mm).
Smooth; deep suture; strong, flattened ridge below, then incised line and short, sharp shoulder. Body whorl has nine, faint, incised lines; obsolete, axial striae. Livid; gray band on shoulder; early whorls blue-gray; columella white; interior brown.

Niotha gemmulata

Bullia grayi

Lamarck *Philippines,*
Japan, 1.2in (30mm).
Stubby; expanded body whorl; channeled suture; cancellate; nodulose. Dentate lip, ridged within; granulose columella and shield; short, recurved canal; fasciole. Cream; light brown and blue-gray clouding; aperture white; interior purple.

Niotha gemmulata

Zeuxis olivaceus

Bruguière 1789 *Pacific and China Seas, 1.8in (45mm).*
High spire. Early whorls obliquely ribbed, later smooth bar growth striae and ten ridges anteriorly on body whorl. Thickened, beveled lip, dentate within; shallow, well-developed siphonal canal; short anal canal; outer edge of columella with twelve blunt teeth. Dark brown sometimes with a yellow band; aperture purple-white; interior purple.

Zeuxis olivaceus

Plicarcularia pullus

L. 1758 *West Pacific, China Seas, 0.8in (20mm).*
Solid; short spire; humped dorsum. Axial ribs on columellar side, other smooth. Early whorls ribbed; incised line below suture. Heavily callous parietal shield forming flat 'pad' with lip; latter thickened, dentate. Prominent columellar tooth bordering short, deep anal canal, three or four teeth anteriorly; short, deep siphonal canal. Brown or green; usually yellow band above suture, dark spot on hump; columella, callus white; interior purple-brown.

Nassarius arcularius arcularius

L. 1758 *Central and west Pacific, 1.2in (30mm).*
Globose; short spire; flat shoulders. Prominent axial ribs, disappear on last third of body whorl, except on shoulder where ends remain as nodules. Lip ridged internally; posterior columellar tooth, two plicae anteriorly.

Plicarcularia pullus

Rugose with expanded callus over parietal area. White or cream; sometimes brown spots between nodules on shoulder of body whorl; aperture white.

N. arcularius plicatus
Röding 1798 *Indian Ocean, 1.2in (30mm).*
Differs from above in having spiral, incised lines overall.

Nassarius arcularius arcularius

Nassarius arcularius plicatus

Nassarius coronatus

N. coronatus
Bruguière 1789 *Indo-west Pacific, 1.2in (30mm).*
Moderate spire; sharply angled shoulders with blunt, heavy nodules, twelve on body whorl. Finely dentate lip, ridged within; columella has posterior ridge, four, small teeth anteriorly. Callous parietal shield; short siphonal and anal canals. White with brown band, or green-brown; knobs, lip, aperture, callus white.

Tarazeuxis reeveanus
Dunker 1847 *Indo-Pacific, 0.8in (20mm).*
Smooth; slightly expanded. Lip toothed within; columella with ridge posteriorly, rugose anteriorly; short, deep anal and siphonal canals. Opaque blue-white-green; white spots and dashes; central band of white and brown; ten, red-brown lines on body, a few on earlier whorls; aperture white; interior purple-brown, two white stripes.

Tarazeuxis reeveanus

Northia northiae

FAMILY: BUCCINIDAE

Found worldwide, these shells are carnivorous, living mostly on bivalves.

Northia northiae

Griffith & Pidgeon 1834 *Tropical west America, 2in (50mm).*
High spire; sharply angled shoulders. Early whorls with spiral cords and axial riblets, disappearing on penultimate whorl. Body whorl smooth bar fine growth lines and six, spiral ridges anteriorly. Slightly thickened lip with blunt knob on shoulder; finely dentate, ridged within. Columella with ridge posteriorly; short canal; broad fasciole. Olive brown; early whorls darker; lip, canal, edged inside red-brown; columellar shield flesh; interior white; ridges brown.

Hindsia magnifica

Lischke *Japan, 1.8in (45mm).*
High spire; slightly inflated; restricted suture; spiral ridges; axial ribs; may have earlier varices. Lip with swollen varix, ridged internally. Columella ridged posteriorly, pustulate anteriorly; recurved siphonal canal; weak fasciole. White; brown clouding, banding.

Hindsia magnifica   *Cantharus erythrostomus*   *Cantharus undosus*   *Cantharus fumosus*

Cantharus erythrostomus

Reeve 1846 *Indian Ocean, 2in (50mm).*
Moderate spire; angular whorls. Strong spiral ridges; axial ribs strong on shoulder, obsolete anteriorly. Crenulate lip, ridged within; ridges cross posterior of columella. Pale orange; darker ridges, shoulders; inside lip orange; columella paler; interior white.

C. undosus

L. 1758 *China Seas and Pacific, 1.6in (40mm).*
Solid; spiral ridges and axial ribs, obsolete on penultimate whorl, rounded and heavy on body whorl. Lip with varix, beveled ridges within; columella smooth on inner side,

unevenly plicate on outer; weak fasciole. White, blue-white or pale yellow; ridges dark brown or purple; aperture edge pale orange; thick periostracum.

C. fumosus
Dillwyn 1817.
As C. undosus but axial ribs overall. Cream or yellow-tan; ribs brown; pale band on body whorl; interior white.

C. elegans
Griffith & Pidgeon 1834 *Tropical west America, 1.8in (45mm).*
High spire and angular whorls. Well-separated, strong, spiral ridges; spiral threads and axial striae between; axial ribs on early whorls and upper half of body whorl, nodulose on intersections. Lip weakly ridged within; columella weakly plicate. Dark brown maculated with some white; interior blue-white.

Cantharus elegans

C. ringens
Reeve 1846 *Tropical west America, 1.2in (30mm).*
Solid; moderate, sharp spire; concave between suture and shoulder. Spiral ridges and cords, and axial ribs. Finely dentate lip, with strong varix, ridged within, indentation posteriorly. Well-developed anal and siphonal canals; columella ridged posteriorly, pustulate anteriorly. Dark brown; aperture blue-white, darker interior.

Cantharus ringens

Pisania pusio
L. 1758 *West Indies and south Florida, 1.8in (45mm).*
Smooth; slightly swollen; high spire. Weakly toothed lip is spirally ridged. Smooth columella, strong ridge posteriorly. Narrow, rugose parietal shield; moderate siphonal canal. Purple-brown; narrow, spiral, broken, dark brown bands; aperture edge orange-red.

Pisania pusio

Pisania ignea

P. ignea
Gmelin 1791 *Pacific and China Seas, 1.4in (35mm).*
High spire. Early whorls have axial riblets, later whorls smooth bar faint lines anteriorly. Lip a little expanded, obsoletely fluted, teeth anteriorly; smooth columella. Cream or pale orange; brown axial flames; band on body whorl; interior blue-white.

Buccinulum littorinoides
Reeve 1846 *New Zealand, 1.4in (35mm).*
High spire. Early whorls have obsolete axial ribs; fine growth lines. Beveled lip, ridged within; smooth columella. Gray; darker spiral lines; aperture white.

Buccinulum littorinoides

Phos senticosus
L. 1758 *Indo-Pacific, 1.6in (40mm)*.
High spire; early varices; square shoulders; constricted suture. Spiral ridges, threads between; axial ribs, short sharp riblets at intersections, axial striae between. Lip ridged within; irregularly plicate columella; strong fasciole. Cream or pink-brown; darker band on body whorl, suture; aperture white; interior white or violet.

P. veraguensis
Hinds 1843 *Tropical west America, 1in (25mm)*.
High spire and constricted suture. Spiral ridges, cords between; axial ribs, nodulose at intersections. Lip ridged within; columella has ridge anteriorly; small fasciole. Pale brown; darker brown bands; interior white-cream.

Phos senticosus

Phos veraguensis

Buccinum undatum
L. 1758 *North Atlantic and the Mediterranean, 6.25in (160mm)*.
The European Whelk has a shell which is very variable in shape, sculpture and color. More or less solid with usually moderate spire of about seven, slightly inflated whorls. Spirally ridged and with oblique axial ribs becoming obsolescent on the body whorl. Outer lip a little expanded and S-shaped; smooth columella; short siphonal canal; weak fasciole. Dirty white, gray or cream, sometimes with brown band at the suture and on the body whorl; interior cream or white.

Buccinum undatum

Siphonalis signum
Reeve 1846 *Japan, 2.4in (60mm)*.
Moderate or short spire; about six whorls. Spirally ridged; rather angular shoulders with flattened nodules, about twelve on body whorl and less on early whorls. Straight sides from shoulder to suture. Fluted lip is ridged within; very thin columellar wall, callous posteriorly; produced, recurved and open siphonal canal; strong fasciole. Color very variable; white or pale yellow to light or dark brown, with axial, dark brown flame markings, blotches and spiral lines; aperture edge white; interior gray-brown.

Siphonalis signum

Penion adustus
Philippi 1845 *North New Zealand, 5in (125mm)*.
Solid with moderate to high spire; about six whorls; spiral ridges and cords between. Weak axial ribs; nodulose at the angular shoulder. Outer lip slightly fluted and lirate within. Columella smooth, with a strong callus posteriorly;

Penion adustus

extended, open, slightly twisted and curved siphonal canal; a small fasciole. Light red-brown to gray; aperture white.

P. mandarinus
Duclos 1831 *South New Zealand and Cook Strait, 5in (125mm)*. Lacks the angular shoulders of its northern counterpart, *P. adustus*, the whorls being a little inflated. Spiral sculpturing very similar. Dirty gray-white to brown; aperture white.

Hemifusus ternatana
Gmelin 1798 *North China Seas, 8in (200mm)*. Long, rather slender, with a high spire of about seven, more or less angular whorls, slightly constricted at the suture. Spirally ridged and corded and axially finely striated. Also ribbed on early whorls with small nodules on the shoulders tending to become obsolete on later whorls, but growing stronger again on the last half of the body whorl. Weakly fluted and ridged lip, smooth within; columella smooth anteriorly, weakly callous posteriorly over the body sculpture; long, open and slightly twisted siphonal canal. White to cream; aperture flesh-cream. This shell has a thick, strong, dark brown periostracum, some of which is shown in the illustration, still adhering. The animal is used for food.

Hemifusus
ternatana

Penion
mandarinus

Babylonia lutosa

Babylonia lutosa

Lamarck 1822 *East Asia, 2.4in (60mm).*
Rather high spire and about six slightly inflated whorls and sharply rounded shoulders. Axial growth lines and microscopic axial and spiral striae. Smooth lip is a little expanded. Smooth columella, heavily callous, especially posteriorly. Rather weak anal canal; short, deep siphonal canal; strong fasciole; deep umbilicus. White with pale fawn clouding on broad spiral bands; aperture white.

B. japonica

Reeve 1842 *Japan and Taiwan, 2.9in (75mm).*
A shorter spire than *B. lutosa*, and not such a solid shell. More smoothly rounded shoulders and more moderate sculpturing. Smooth lip; less callous columella; shallower siphonal canal; smaller umbilicus; weaker fasciole. Creamy white with a row of V-shaped, liver-colored blotches below the suture and at the widest part of the body whorl, profusely spotted elsewhere with the same color; postnuclear whorls have a mauve tinge.

B. formosae

Sowerby 1866 *Taiwan, 2in (50mm).*
Moderate spire. slightly constricted at the suture. The whorls have a sharply angular shoulder and are flat from shoulder to suture. Smooth lip and columella, the latter heavily callous posteriorly. Deep, open umbilicus; strong fasciole; weakened anal canal and short, deep siphonal canal. Cream with a broad band of wide, <-shaped marks below the suture and two rows of squarish blotches below this, all of which are dark liver-brown. The aperture is white, with the brown showing through on the edge of the lip. The mail nuclear whorls have a noticeable mauve tinge.

Babylonia japonica

Babylonia formosae

B. zeylanica

Bruguière 1789 *India and Sri Lanka, 2.9in (75mm).*
Rather like B. japonica in shape but less robust with less inflated whorls. White with large brown blotches and spots generally smaller in center of the last whorl and above the suture. Inside edge of fasciole ridge, and apex purple.

B. areolata

Link 1807 *Southeast Asia, 2in (50mm).*
Rather similar in shape to *B. formosae*, but slightly shorter spire, shoulders a little more rounded, narrower umbilicus and weaker fasciole. Very smooth and shiny. White; a row of dark liver-colored oblongs below the suture, then a row of

rather square blotches followed by a row of more or less triangular blotches; blotches tend to have a golden lining; aperture white; postnuclear whorls mauve.

B. canaliculata

Schumacher 1817 *Arabian Sea, 2.6in (65mm).*
Solid, heavy, with short spire and channeled at suture. Whorls somewhat inflated; smooth except for some coarse growth lines. Smooth lip; heavily callous columella; weak anal canal; deep, short siphonal canal. Fasciole is broad and strong but shiny, and umbilicus is very narrow and shallow. White-cream with pale liver-colored blotches, streaks and spots, the blotches forming a discontinuous band low on the body whorl; aperture white.

Babylonia areolata

Babylonia zeylanica

B. spirata

L. 1758 *Indian Ocean, 2.9in (75mm).*
Also solid and heavy, but less coarse than *B. canaliculata* and with a high spire. The suture more deeply and widely channeled and the edge of the channel much sharper. Smooth lip and heavily callous columella. Anal canal is more developed than in others of the genus. Short, deep siphonal canal: wide fasciole; shallow umbilicus. White, heavily marked with light brown blotches, oblique streaks and spots; aperture white; fasciole mostly orange-brown; nuclear and postnuclear whorls purple, becoming lighter, and the brown growing stronger anteriorly.

Babylonia canaliculata

Babylonia spirata

Fasciolaria hunteria

FAMILY: FASCIOLARIIDAE

The tulip shells are found worldwide and, like Buccinidae, are carnivorous.

Fasciolaria hunteria

Perry 1811 *Southwest USA, 4in (100mm)*.
Inflated; smooth bar fine growth lines and weak ridges at base of body whorl and on canal. Smooth lip, columella. White; three, broken, spiral, green bands; five, purple, spiral lines on body whorl, two on early whorls; purple bands inside lip.

F. trapezium

L. 1758 *Indo-Pacific, 8in (200mm)*.
Solid; heavy; moderate spire; constricted suture. Shoulders with slightly pointed, strong knobs. Incised spiral lines, mainly paired; lip with seven pairs of teeth where lines meet edge; strong ridges internally. Columella smooth posteriorly, three plaits anteriorly; extended siphonal canal; weak fasciole. Flesh; incised lines, teeth, interior cords, fasciole, brown; columella pale coffee; dark periostracum.

F. filamentosa

Röding 1798 *Indo-Pacific, 6in (150mm)*.
High spire; round shoulders, low on whorls; constricted suture. Pairs of incised spiral lines with ridges between and obsolete axial ribs, ten on body whorl. Lip has pairs of small denticles at end of incised lines, spirally ridged within. Columella callous anteriorly and with three plaits; extended, open, slightly twisted siphonal canal; weak fasciole. Blue-white profusely clouded, especially on ribs, with red-brown; teeth brown; aperture flesh; internal ridges, columella red-brown.

F. salmo

Wood 1828 *Tropical west America, 5in (125mm)*.
Solid; heavy; short spire; fine spiral ridges. Angular shoulders have blunt knobs, nine on body whorl; deep suture. Finely denticulate lip, ridged within; columella has ridge edging anal canal, and two anterior plaits; long, open, slightly curved siphonal canal; fasciole. Yellow-flesh; columella, lip edge salmon pink; interior white; end of siphonal canal purple; strong, brown periostracum (illustrated).

Latirus polygonus

Gmelin 1791 *Indo-Pacific, 2.8in (70mm)*.
Fusiform; angulate; constricted suture; spiral ridges; axial ribs, seven on body whorl; nodulose at shoulder and lower on body whorl where one ridge is strong. Finely

Fasciolaria
trapezium

dentate lip is ridged within; columella has about four small plicae anteriorly; extended, open siphonal canal; weak fasciole. Cream to pale yellow-brown; axial, broken, dark brown stripes on ribs; aperture pale brown at edge; ridges, interior white.

Peristernia philberti
Recluz 1844 *South China Sea, 1.2in (30mm).*
Moderate spire; angular; constricted suture. Spiral ridges, channels between. Axial ribs, ten on body whorl, nodulose on shoulder. Finely dentate lip, ridged within, blunt tooth anteriorly. Smooth columella, posteriorly callous, narrowly umbilicate. Red-brown; ridges white; aperture violet; strong fasciole dark brown; interior white.

Fasciolaria salmo

Fasciolaria filamentosa

P. incarnata
Kiener 1840 *Indo-Pacific, 1.2in (30mm).*
Solid with moderate spire, channeled sutures and broad, flat, slightly oblique axial ribs, twelve on body whorl. Fine spiral cords. Finely dentate lip, ridged within, blunt tooth anteriorly. Columella has strong ridge posteriorly and large, flat, rectangular tooth anteriorly. Well-developed anal canal; short, deep, open siphonal canal. Ribs orange-red; interstices dark brown; aperture pinky mauve; fasciole flesh.

Peristernia philberti   *Peristernia incarnata*   *Opeatostoma pseudodon*

Opeatostoma pseudodon
Burrow 1815 *Tropical west America, 1.8in (45mm).*
Moderate spire and very angular, flattened shoulders. Strong, flat spiral ridges with weaker cords between. Lip has obsolete spiral ridges internally, long, strong, pointed spine anteriorly. Columella has ridge posteriorly and six plicae anteriorly. Short siphonal canal; fasciole. White; ridges dark brown-black, showing within lip; interior white; strong, brown periostracum (illustrated).

Latirus polygonus

199

Fusinus colus

Fusinus longicaudus

Genus: Fusinus

There are over fifty species of spindle shells. They are quite distinctive with a long spire and a long, generally straight siphonal canal and spiral ribbing. In the small subgenera *Aptyxis* and *Barborofusus*, however, the canal may be relatively short. The columella is smooth and most species are white, often with some brown marks or clouding. They are found in tropical and temperate waters worldwide. As the rest of the family, they are carnivorous. They live on sandy bottoms and are usually found in pairs.

Fusinus colus

L. 1758 *Indo-west Pacific, 8in (200mm)*.

Fusiform and rather angular with high spire. Spiral ridges and cords; fine axial striae; early whorls axially ribbed; on last two or three whorls these become obsolete and remain only as nodules on the shoulders. Finely dentate lip ridged within. Thinly callous columella, ridges showing through; long, slender and slightly wavy siphonal canal. White or cream with a few, axial, brown streaks; brown between the ribs and nodules, more conspicuous on earlier whorls; a few spots at the suture; siphonal canal brown growing dark toward the tip; aperture white, edged faintly with brown.

F. dupetitthouarsi

Kiener 1840 *Tropical west America, up to 10in (250mm)*.

Rather similar to F. colus but less slender, rounder shoulders, shorter, broader and more open siphonal canal, bigger aperture. White; faint brown marks.

F. longicaudus

Lamarck *Japan, 4in (100mm)*.

Narrow spire and long, narrow siphonal canal; spirally ridged and axially ribbed on early whorls. Fluted lip; columella smooth anteriorly but only thinly callous posteriorly where the ridges show. White with faint shading between ribs; darker between ribs on early whorls.

Family: Melongenidae

Genus: Busycon

The fulgur whelks are found off the east coast of North America. It seems, however, that one species is also found off the east African coast (see below). It includes in addition to those species illustrated and described below: *Busycon perversum* L. which may be sinistral or dextral; *B. carica* Gmelin; *B. spiratum* Lamarck; and *B. coarctatum* Sowerby The latter three species are all dextral.

Fusinus dupetitthouarsi

B. contrarium

Conrad *Southeast North America, up to 15in (400mm).*
Sinistral with low spire. Angular shoulder with more or
less developed, triangular knobs. Spirally striated,
except in middle of the body whorl where it is
almost smooth. Smooth lip and columella;
long and open siphonal canal. Gray with
irregular, axial, dark brown lines; two gray-
brown bands on body whorl; siphonal canal
gray-brown; aperture with brown staining;
columella thin, callous posteriorly allowing
shell color to show through, flesh-colored anteriorly. The illustration is of a juvenile.

A sinister busycon (probably also *B. contrarium*)
is found off east Africa, and a specimen 6.25in
(160mm) is illustrated. Its shape and sculpture are the
same, but it is colored pale yellow-brown with axial purple-brown lines strongest on the spire; aperture white.

Buscycon spec.

*Busycon contrarium
juvenile*

*Busycon
canaliculatum*

B. canaliculatum

L. 1758 *East North America, 7in (180mm).*
Rather short spire with angular shoulders and a deep, wide
channel at the suture. Fine, obsolete, spiral cords; strong
ridge at the shoulder which is nodulose on early whorls.
Smooth lip; columella only weakly callous; extended and
open siphonal canal. Light brown-gray; shoulder ridge
nodules cream-white, with brown interstices; inside edge of
lip light brown.

Melongena patula

Melongena patula

Broderip & Sowerby 1829 *West tropical America, 10in (250mm)*.
Short, sharp, concave spire; angular, nodulose shoulders; sometimes spinous, sometimes almost smooth on body whorl. Spirally corded above the shoulder and at base of body whorl. Smooth lip; callous, smooth columella; extended siphonal canal; weak fasciole. Chestnut brown banded with yellow, white or tan; lip edged interiorly with browns merging into white then blue-white; columella cream-peach; fasciole dark brown; and tip of siphonal canal purple.

M. melongena

L. 1758 *Caribbean, 4in (100mm)*.
Solid, heavy, with short spire and channeled suture. Axial growth striae; two spiral rows of short sharp spines in the widest part of the rather inflated body whorl, and one near the base. Uneven lip; heavily callous columella; strong fasciole; short, open siphonal and anal canals. Dark chocolate brown; canals and suture white; more or less narrow white bands below the two upper rows of spines; white axial hairlines and tips to spines; aperture and fasciole white.

Melongena melongena

Melongena corona

Melongena morio

M. corona

Gmelin 1791 *Southeast America, Mexico, 4in (100mm)*.
Variable. Generally with a moderate spire and angular whorls. Spirally corded and axially ribbed, ribs becoming obsolete on body whorl. One or two rows of spines on shoulder, hollow, more or less numerous, and vertical to horizontal, sometimes a row at base of body whorl. Smooth columella; strong fasciole; short, open siphonal canal. White; spiral bands of purple-brown or blue-black; spines white; lip stained brown internally; interior, columella white.

M. morio
L. 1758 *West Africa, Brazil, West Indies, 6.9in (175mm).*
Rather elongate; angular shoulders; spiral ridges. Early
whorls ribbed, ribs becoming obsolete on later whorls
but shoulders more or less nodulose. Lip ridged
internally; columella weakly callous anteriorly
and barely at all posteriorly. Long, open
siphonal canal; weak fasciole. Chocolate
brown; one moderately broad yellow-
white band and a number of narrow
ones; aperture brown; columella
dirty white.

*Melongena
galeodes*

M. galeodes
Lamarck *Red Sea, Indian Ocean
to China, Philippines, 2.6in (65mm).*
Short sharp spire; about six
whorls with short frilly spines at the
suture. Spirally corded; a row of
about eight, heavy, sharp spines at
the shoulder of the body whorl, and
may have two other rows of spines on
body whorl, center one usually small, one
nearer base larger. Finely dentate lip; callous, smooth columella; narrowly umbilicate; strong fasciole; moderate siphonal
canal; short, fairly deep anal canal. Gray or
pale brown, ridges darker; inside of lip
white with purple-brown banding, deeper
within; columella cream.

*Volema
cochlidium*

Volema cochlidium
L. 1758 *Indian Ocean, South China Sea, 6in (150mm).*
Solid; heavy; angular whorls; concave from suture to
shoulder. Spirally corded; early whorls axially
ribbed; body and sometimes penultimate whorls
with about eight, strong, heavy, flattened spines. Lip
weakly ridged within; smooth columella; moderately
short, open siphonal canal; very narrow, shallow umbilicus; short, strong fasciole. Red-brown; aperture peach
with brown edging. It has a thick periostracum (illustrated).

Syrinx aruanus
L. 1758 *North Australia, up to 24in (600mm).*
Probably the world's largest gastropod. Heavy with angular,
rounded shoulders. Spirally ridged and axially threaded;
early whorls axially ribbed; later whorls nodulose at the
shoulder. Some ridges on body whorl larger than others.
Finely ridged lip; smooth columella; extended, open,
straight siphonal canal. Umbilicus is a narrow slit. Straw-
colored. The protoconch of some five-and-a-half whorls with
constricted sutures and axial ribs is normally lost in
adult shells. Illustration shows a juvenile with protoconch
still attached.

Syrinx aruanus

Oliva sayana

SUPERFAMILY: VOLUTACEA

FAMILY: OLIVIDAE

Variable in size, generally cylindrical, with short spire, a siphonal notch, the columella with folds anteriorly, and a fasciole. They are sand dwellers in all tropical and warm seas. Carnivorous, they feed at night and capture their prey by enfolding it in their large 'foot'. They have no periostracum or operculum, and their shells are very hard, shiny and usually brightly colored.

Oliva sayana

Ravenel 1834 *west Atlantic, 3in (80mm)*.
Rather extended spire; narrowly and deeply channeled suture; columella has numerous plaits. Fawn-gray with brown zigzag marks in two, generally spiral bands, and small, yellow tent marks; brown and yellow flecks at the suture; inner edge of lip brown shading into white and then violet; columella white. Variable in pattern and range of colors. The form *O.s. citrina* Johnson 1911 is a golden yellow.

| *Oliva sayana* form citrina | *Oliva reticularis* | *Oliva reticularis bifasciata* | *Oliva caribaeensis* form trujilloi | *Oliva flammulata* |

O. reticularis

Lamarck 1811 *West Indies, Florida Keys, 2.4in (60mm)*.
Rather long spire, narrowing sharply toward the anterior; channeled sutures. White, reticulated with pale or dark pinky brown; brown specks at suture; aperture white. *O.r. bifasciata* Küster 1878 has two red-brown bands, a narrow one in the middle of the body whorl, and a broad one anteriorly. Other forms include dark brown, pale yellow, white and red-brown, as well as variations in shape.

O. caribaeensis

Dall & Simpson 1901 *Caribbean, 1.6in (40mm)*.
More cylindrical than the above. Low spire and channeled suture. Color rather like that of *O. sayana*. Dark flecks below the suture; aperture purple. The form *trujilloi* Clench 1938 is rather narrow, red-brown, and has a light aperture.

Oliva spicata form fuscata

O. flammulata

Lamarck 1811 *West Africa, 1.4in (35mm).*
Similar in shape and color to *O. reticularis*. High spire and channeled suture. Usually pink-gray with red-brown, zigzag, axial markings and white or pale yellow tent marks; darker specks below suture; aperture white or with a purple tinge. Brown and yellow forms exist.

O. spicata

Röding 1798 *Tropical west America, 2.4in (60mm).*
Fairly high spire; a little concave, widest at the shoulder and narrowing anteriorly; deep narrow channel at the suture. Very variable in color. General form is pale yellow-gray; spotted or reticulated with brown or red-brown, denser at the suture; aperture white. Color forms vary from white to very dark red-brown. The common form *venulata* Lamarck 1811 is reticulated brown over a yellow-gray background. The form *fuscula* is shown.

Oliva spicata form venulata

O. porphyria

L. 1758 *Tropical west America, 4in (100mm).*
The largest of the genus, it has a low spire with a sharply pointed apex. The outline is a smooth curve from suture to fasciole, somewhat expanded at the shoulder. Narrow, deep channel at the suture; lip a little concave in the middle; columella strongly spirally ridged along its full length, except where it lacks a callus at the posterior end; strong fasciole. Violet-gray, covered profusely with tent marks of varying size outlined in dark brown-red; two indistinct bands of the same color; aperture and columella flesh; base of columella, outside edge of lip and siphonal notch violet; apex and early whorls also violet above the suture.

O. incrassata

Lightfoot 1786 T*ropical west America, 3.5in (90mm).*
Solid, heavy, angular; with very short callous spire; sharp apex; channeled suture. Ventricose, with a very angular shoulder for the genus, thickened before the lip. Callous columella with rather weak plaits anteriorly; heavy fasciole. Pale gray or yellow-gray; darker gray spots and dark brown, broken, axial bands of horizontal dashes, and sporadic spots and dashes; aperture white with pale pink or flesh tinge, especially on the columella. Gold, white and black forms are known.

Oliva porphyria

Oliva incrassata

205

Oliva splendidula

Oliva splendidula

Sowerby 1825 *Pacific coasts of Panama, Mexico, 2in (50mm).*
Short spire with pointed apex; channeled suture; cylindrical.
Markings comparatively constant. Pink-gray with small flesh-colored tent marks and dark red-brown spots; overall two, uneven, broad, broken bands of light brown; dark red-brown spots and fine lines below the suture; lip white; interior with a yellow tinge; columella and apex pale purple.

O. peruviana

Lamarck 1811 *Peru, Chile, 2in (50mm).*
Very variable in both color and shape. The typical form is short-spired; narrowly canaliculate suture; somewhat inflated posteriorly. Columella with plaited callus on anterior half; no callus posteriorly. Blue-gray to flesh-colored, profusely spotted with red-brown axial dashes and spots; aperture white with faint blue tinge; upper plaits of columella and fasciole cream, lower white. Varieties include all dark brown to white, sometimes with axial streaks; and variations in shape include a flatter spire with an angular shoulder and heavy callus at the posterior end of the columella, known as form *coniformis* Philippi 1848 (illustrated).

Oliva peruviana

Oliva peruviana form coniformis

O. tigrina

Lamarck 1811 *Indian Ocean, west Pacific, 2.4in (60mm).*
Short spire, sharp apex. Shallow sutural groove; slightly inflated body whorl. Columella plaited anteriorly. Typically white, well-spotted with blue-gray and some dark brown spots; aperture blue-white; base of columella with a red tinge. Sometimes dark brown almost black in form *fallax* Johnson 1910 (illustrated); or dark brown with white band or bands.

O. rufula

Duclos 1835 *Philippines, Moluccas, 1.4in (35mm).*
Very short spire; channeled suture; cylindrical, narrowing slightly. Thickened lip is very slightly flared. There is a callus on either side of the sutural channel where it ends on the body whorl. Columella callous and plaited anteriorly. Milk-chocolate, coarsely reticulated with darker chocolate and gray diagonal stripes, which become dark brown, almost black, on the edge of the lip; interior white; base of columella pale pink.

O. bulbosa

Röding 1798 *Indian Ocean, 2in (50mm).*
Short spire with pointed apex; inflated or bulbous body whorl. Lip more or less thickened before the edge. Columella with callus, sometimes very thin posteriorly and plaited anteriorly; a short sharp diagonal ridge at the top of the

fasciole. Many color varieties. Typical is brown with axial, wavy, dark brown lines. A common form *inflata* (not illustrated) Lamarck 1811 is pale blue-gray, profusely spotted with darker blue-gray; form *tuberosa* Röding 1798 is like *inflata* but with three broken bands of orange-brown; *fabagina* Lamarck 1811 with irregular brown blotches; form *bicingulata* Lamarck 1811 with two dark brown bands. There are other named and unnamed varieties.

Oliva tigrina form fallax

Oliva bulbosa form fabagina

Oliva bulbosa form bicingulata

Oliva bulbosa form tuberosa

O. tricolor

Lamarck 1811 *Indian Ocean, South China Sea, 2.4in (60mm)*. Short, callous spire and deeply channeled suture. Cylindrical, slightly inflated centrally. Heavily callous columella is plaited anteriorly. Cream profusely spotted with blue-green and gold spots, the blue-green showing particularly in two bands below the suture and in the middle of the body whorl; lip edge and spire tessellated with dark brown-black and gold; inside lip white; fasciole salmon pink, red blotch at base. The form *philantha* Duclos 1835 is a light form, with pale yellow, green and blue, spots, dashes and obscure bands.

Oliva rufula

Oliva tricolor form philantha

*Oliva
elegans*

*Oliva elegans
form flava*

Oliva episcopalis

*Oliva vidua form
albofasciata*

*Oliva vidua form
cinnemonea*

*Oliva vidua
form aurata*

Oliva elegans

Lamarck 1811 *Indo-Pacific, 1.6in (40mm)*.
Cylindrical, chubby, with very short spire, sharp apex and a narrow, deeply channeled suture. The lip is extended posteriorly to level with the apex, and the posterior end of the columella is extended to the same level. Columella plicated its full length. Pale yellow-green with a network of discontinuous oblique olive-green lines; two bands of darker marks on the shoulder and the middle of the body whorl; columella white with a pink tinge at the base; inside lip and interior pale blue-white. Very variable in color, from very dark to the golden from *flava* Marrat 1871, in which the aperture lacks the blue color.

O. episcopalis

Lamarck 1811 *Indo-Pacific, 2.4in (60mm)*.
High, callous spire; narrow, deep suture; slightly swollen centrally. Columella ridged posteriorly and plicate anteriorly. White, profusely spotted – except below the suture – with blue-gray and golden yellow, often together giving an overall green effect; the spots tend to join up in lines and are more dense in two faint bands; inside edge of lip and columella are white; fasciole has a yellow tinge; interior deep violet. There are a number of named forms of *O. episcopalis*, varying in color and shape.

O. vidua

Röding 1798 *Indo-Pacific, 2.4in (60mm)*.
Very short or flat spire; a little inflated posteriorly; deep narrow suture ending in raised callous projection as in *O. elegans* above. Columellar callus thin near posterior end, ridged throughout. This species has many named color forms, the typical being black with a white aperture. It is also well known by its synonym *O. maura* Lamarck 1811.

Form *albofasciata* Dautzenburg 1927 is brown with two darker broken bands; form *aurata* Röding 1798 is orange, gold or golden brown, without pattern; form *cinnemonea* Menke 1830 is cinnamon with darker, axial, wavy lines; other forms include gray backgrounds and dark, zigzag, axial lines and spiral bands.

O. reticulata
Röding 1798 *Indo-Pacific, 1.4in (35mm)*.
Fairly low spire; deep, narrow suture, callous near its end as in *O. Vidua*, but not as produced posteriorly. A little inflated; columellar callus weak posteriorly, obsoletely ridged centrally. Cream-white background, heavily covered with a network of dark gray-brown, two darker brown bands; aperture white; columella, plaits, and extreme edge of outer lip, red, giving it the name by which it was long known of *O. sanguinolenta* Lamarck 1811. The form *azona* Dautzenberg 1927 lacks the bands, and *evania* Duclos 1835 (illustrated) is paler and has a dense pattern. There are other named color forms.

Oliva reticulata form evania   *Oliva mustellina*

O. mustellina
Lamarck 1811 *India to Japan, 1.6in (40mm)*.
Rather narrow with moderate to short spire and channeled, deep, relatively wide suture. Shoulder rather square and high on the whorls, giving a somewhat oblong appearance. Columella weakly callous but plaited its full length, with a callus posteriorly bordering the end of the suture. Mustard yellow with an irregular network of purple-brown; columella blue-white; interior deep violet.

O. multiplicata
Reeve 1850 *Taiwan, 1.6in (40mm)*.
A high, very slightly convex spire, widest a little below the suture which is narrowly and deeply channeled. Narrows considerably toward the anterior end. Columella with many plaits as its name implies. Yellow-cream, heavily marked with pale purple-brown; darker purple-brown blotches at the anterior end, and with a few below the suture; the yellow-cream background shows as tent marks as in *O. porphyria* and many of the Conidae; columella and interior white.

Oliva multiplicata

Oliva oliva

O. oliva

L. 1758 *Indo-Pacific, 1.2in (30mm).*
Perhaps better known still by its synonym *O. ispid-ula* L. 1758. Short spire and narrow sutural groove. Columellar callus on the anterior two-thirds, which is unevenly plaited; rather narrow aperture. Color and pattern are extremely variable; white to black, through browns, chestnut, yellow, gray; with spots, zigzag lines, blotches, or without any markings; the columella is white and the interior usually brown, in some forms white or pink. Three forms are illustrated including the all-black *oriola* Lamarck 1811.

Oliva oliva

Oliva oliva form *oriola*

Oliva australis

O. australis

Duclos 1835 *Australia, New Guinea, 0.8in (20mm).*
Moderate to high spire and narrow sutural groove. Columella a little concave posteriorly; uneven plaits covering the whole columella. White, covered with fine, wavy, axial lines of cream-gray to gray; a row of purple-brown dashes at the suture; columella and aperture white.

O. caldania

Duclos 1835 *West and north Australia,
Indonesia, 0.9in (22mm).*
Similar to *O. australis* except that it has a much shorter spire. It may be a form of *O. australis.*

Oliva caldania

Oliva sidelia form *volvaroides*

O. sidelia

Duclos 1835 *Indo-Pacific, 0.8in (20mm).*
Narrow with a short spire which is covered by a callus except for the suture of the last whorl. The suture is deep and wide. Columella coarsely plaited along its full length. White with brown markings, generally tent-shaped. Columella and aperture white, sometimes with a violet tinge. The form *volvaroides* Duclos 1835 (illustrated) is all one color, either medium or dark brown or white.

O. carneola

Gmelin 1791 *Indo-Pacific,*
1in (25mm).
Short, almost flat spire; covered with a callus except for the deep sutural groove of the last whorl. Generally rather swollen and with a slightly angular shoulder. There are many color varieties and patterns but the shell is basically white, banded with orange, red or purple-red; many varieties are named.

Oliva carneola

O. paxillus

Oliva
paxillus

Oliva paxillus
form
sandwichiensis

Reeve 1850 *Guam, Fiji,*
1.1in (27mm).
High spire with narrow, deep sutural channel. Body whorl expanded at the shoulder and narrowing quite sharply toward the anterior. Columella with rather coarse plaits overall. Ivory white with faint, grayish-brown network below the shoulder; purple-brown, comma-shaped marks below the suture; aperture white; inside of lip sometimes with two or three, spiral, purple lines. A form from the Hawaiian Islands, named *sandwichiensis* Pease 1860 has a shorter spire, is less angular at the shoulder and has darker markings with two, obsolete, spiral bands.

O. tessellata

Lamarck 1811 *West Pacific, east Indian*
Oceans, 1.4in (35mm).
Short spire; rather callous with wide, shallow sutural channel. Body whorl a little expanded centrally; strongly plaited columella. Creamy yellow with rather evenly placed, purple-brown spots. Edge of lip and anterior end of fasciole white; aperture and columella rich, very deep violet.

Oliva tessellata

O. buloui

Oliva buloui

Sowerby 1887 *New Britain, 1.2in (30mm).*
Moderately high, callous spire. Body whorl a little expanded at the shoulder. Columella with coarse plaits. Spire and area below the suture, and anterior edge, pink; elsewhere apricot with brown-red streaks becoming more frequent and darker anteriorly.

O. miniacea

Röding 1798 *Indo-Pacific, 3.5in (90mm)*.
Heavy, solid, handsome, with moderate to short spire, deep, channeled suture and slightly inflated body whorl. Its color is very variable except for its characteristic rich orange interior. Typically it is a cream-yellow with irregular, wavy, brown-gray, axial lines, and two, broad, broken bands of dark chocolate, one below the suture and one in the middle of the body whorl; inner edge of lip brown with a cream band between it and the rich orange interior; columella white; fasciole band apricot; the axial streaks may be purple, brown, green or blue.

Oliva miniacea

O. tremulina

Lamarck 1811 *Indo-Pacific, 3.5in (90mm)*.
This may be a form of *O. miniacea*, from which it differs only in having a white interior. The color varieties are otherwise like those of *O. miniacea*. The form *oldi* Zeigler 1969 is pale gray with darker gray, close, wavy, axial lines, with dark bands at the shoulder and in the middle of the body whorl; columella with an orange tinge.

O. textilina

Lamarck 1811 *Indo-Pacific, 3.3in (85mm)*.
Short spire and deep, narrow, channeled suture. Top of columella with a strong callus rising above the suture on the penultimate whorl and broadening toward the end of the channel. White, more or less heavily marked with light or dark gray; some irregular, wavy, axial, gray-brown lines; usually a dark brown band below the suture and in the middle of the body whorl. An albino form is *O.t. albina* Melville and Standen 1897. The illustrated specimen is somewhere between this and the typical form.

*Oliva tremulina
form oldi*

O. ponderosa

Duclos 1835 *Indian Ocean, 3.3in (85mm)*.
Solid, heavy, with a short spire and a callous area at the top of the plaited

Oliva textilina   *Oliva ponderosa*

columella rising up as in *O. textilina*. White with a network of faint pale brown on much of the body whorl; streaks and spots of purple-brown below the suture, on the middle of the body whorl and the fasciole; aperture and columella pure white.

O. lignaria

Marrat 1868 *East Indian Ocean to Taiwan, north Australia, 2.6in (65mm).*

Long known by its synonym *O. ornata* Marrat 1867. Short spire is heavily callous; such of the sutural channel not covered is narrow and deep. Pale gray-cream, with dots and dashes of brown and light blue-gray, and sparse dashes of dark brown on two broken bands; aperture pale violet; columella tinged with red anteriorly. The golden

Oliva lignaria

Oliva lignaria form cryptospira

or orange form *cryptospira* Ford 1891 often has this color pattern showing faintly through the overlying color.

O. annulata

Gmelin 1791 *Indo-Pacific, 2.4in (60mm).* High spire and narrow, deep sutural channel. A little thickened before the edge of the lip and rather sharply shouldered for the genus; sometimes with a protruding ring around the center of the body whorl. The type form is an uncommon near white or cream color, while the more common form *amethystina* Röding 1798 is flesh-colored with pale purple spots and darker ones just below the suture; apex pale yellow. Form *intricata* Dautzenberg 1927 has a network of fine red-brown

Oliva annulata

Oliva annulata form mantichora

lines and sparse dark brown spots; aperture rich orange. The white form *mantichora* Duclos 1835 is similar but the posterior edge of the last whorl is more or less sharply angled. Variable like so many of the genus.

O. bulbiformis

Duclos 1835 *Indo-Pacific, 1.4in (35mm).* Short and rather bulbous. Short spire usually completely covered by a callus. Body whorl inflated especially posteriorly. Mustard or gray-yellow, more or less heavily reticulated with gray-brown and usually with two darker bands; one color variety is green-gray; columella may have a red tinge; interior usually violet-brown or chocolate brown.

Oliva bulbiformis

Ancilla lienardii

Ancilla albocallosa

Ancilla cingulata

Ancilla lienardii
Benardi 1821 *Brazil, 1.2in (30mm)*.
Chubby with moderate spire, swollen body whorl, concave columella, and deep, open, twisted umbilicus. Golden orange; aperture and columella white; narrow white band immediately above fasciole.

A. albocallosa
Lischke *Japan, 1.8in (45mm)*.
High, callous spire; inflated body whorl; wide aperture; no umbilicus. Fawn; brown band below suture and on fasciole, both edged white; aperture, columella, inner side of callus pink.

A. tankervillei
Swainson 1825 *West Indies to Brazil, 2.4in (60mm)*.
High spire and inflated, with deep narrow twisted umbilicus. Yellow; pink band below suture and above fasciole; aperture and columella white.

A. cingulata
Sowerby 1830 *East Australia, 3.5in (90mm)*.
Shiny; high spire; rounded apex; restricted suture; fine growth striae; folds on fasciole disappear into aperture. Fawn; white band above and below suture; narrow brown line on suture edge on last half of body whorl; penultimate whorl rich red-brown; antepenultimate paler; earlier whorls pink-white; interior fawn; columella, inner edge of siphonal notch white; fasciole has two red-brown bands, light band between.

A. australis
Sowerby 1830 *New Zealand, 1in (25mm)*.
Moderate spire; biangulate body whorl; suture entirely covered with transparent callus. Brown; broad, dark blue-brown band edged with white covering most of body whorl; interior dark brown; columella white; fasciole dark brown.

A. mucronata
Sowerby 1830 *New Zealand, 1.8in (45mm)*.
Solid, stubby, shiny; short, callous spire; wide aperture. Columella with central ridge, twisted anteriorly. Pink to brown; apex paler; fasciole darker; faint, pale line on shoulder.

Ancilla tankervillei

Ancilla australis

Ancilla mucronata

Olivancillaria urceus
Röding 1798 *Brazil to Uruguay, 1.6in (40mm).*
Solid and squat. Almost flat, broad, callous spire with sharp, pointed apex and wide, deep suture. Swollen just below suture then narrowing sharply. Aperture wide, especially anteriorly. Columella with large, heavily callous area posteriorly, plaited anteriorly and fasciole is very broad and callous. Lip extends beyond where it is attached to body whorl at end of sutural canal. White; profusely axially streaked with fawn; inside lip fawn; columella white; posterior half of callous area fawn; fasciole fawn-edged and clouded with brown.

Olivancillaria urceus

Olivancillaria vesica auricularia

O. vesica auricularia
Lamarck 1810 *Brazil to Argentina, 2in (50mm).*
Solid, coarse with very expanded body whorl. Very short spire, entirely covered with thick callus. Deeply channeled suture on dorsal side of body whorl, else-where covered by callus. Fine growth striae; lip extending further than its juncture with body whorl; smooth columella, plaited anteriorly; very broad, callous, fawn fasciole. Gray-white; columella and callous area white.

O. gibbosa
Born *Sri Lanka, 2in (50mm).*
Short spire and inflated body whorl; penultimate whorl callous almost to shallowly channeled suture. Columella smooth posteriorly, plaited over lower two-thirds, and curved convexly. Fasciole strong and raised, giving the effect of a 'dent' above it. Dark brown with light spots and axial dashes; white band low on body whorl; horn-colored band on fasciole; aperture, columella and callus white; creamy touches inside lip and base of columella. Sometimes pale yellow-green, heavily maculated with light brown.

Olivancillaria gibbosa

Agaronia testacea
Lamarck 1811 *Tropical west America, 2in (50mm).*
Slender, high, pointed spire; deeply channeled suture; wide aperture. Columella weakly callous posteriorly, strongly plaited and twisted anteriorly. Pale gray-green with uneven axial rows of gray-brown dots, dark below the suture; lip blue-gray lined with brown; columella white; fasciole clouded with dark brown, yellow and green.

Agaronia testacea

215

FAMILY: VASIDAE

A small family, most are moderately large shells. There are some twenty-five species, usually solid and heavy, spirally ridged, with a plaited columella. They are tropical, most living in shallow water on the reefs.

Vasum turbinellus

L. 1758 *Indo-Pacific, 3.3in (85mm).*

Moderate to short spire. Indistinct suture with two rows of more or less long blunt spines below it, the upper one on the shoulder being the larger; a discontinuous cord below these forms a row of small blunt nodules, then a rough ridge, two more rows of smaller blunt spines, the upper again the larger, and finally the fasciole ridge. The surface is generally malleate. The columella has three slightly oblique ridges with fine thin plaits between. Narrow, patterned parietal area; lip has coarse blunt teeth, some paired; open, short siphonal canal. White with dark brown maculations; aperture white; teeth dark brown; columella cream with brown marks round the edge.

Vasum turbinellus

V. rhinoceros

Gmelin 1791 *Kenya, Zanzibar, 3.3in (85mm).*
Rather short spire. Spirally ridged and corded with two rows of blunt spines/nodules, one pair below the suture and one pair above the fasciole, the posterior one in each pair is the larger, and overall finely lamellated axial striae. Thickened lip has teeth, generally in pairs, and one larger tooth posteriorly. Columella has three plaits; strong parietal callus; short siphonal canal; umbilicus may be open or sealed by the parietal callus. White maculated with brown; aperture white, some brown streaks within; columella cream, heavily clouded, especially on the parietal wall, with brown.

Vasum rhinoceros

V. capitellum

L. 1758 *West Indies, 2.6in (65mm).*
Fusiform with high spire and angulate. Fine spiral striae and coarse spiral ridges, about nine on body whorl; fine axial lamellate striae. Strongly crenulate lip is toothed within, some teeth bifid. Columella has three strong plaits and two obsolete ridges posteriorly; fasciole strong. White with brown clouding; aperture cream.

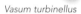

Vasum capitellum

V. ceramicum
L. 1758 *Indo-Pacific, 5.5in (140mm).*
Fusiform, solid and heavy with high spire. The sculpturing is the same as in *V. turbinellus,* though the shell is narrower for its length, and the two small plaits on the columella are not always present. White heavily maculated with dark brown-black; aperture white; teeth almost black: columella with dark brown marks on parietal wall.

V. tubiferum
Anton 1839 *Philippines, 4.5in (115mm).*
Very similar in shape and sculpture to *V. turbinellus,* but bigger spines on the two rows, and overall larger and stronger. Narrowly open umbilicus. White maculated with brown, not black; lip and teeth white; columella white with a pink tinge and a dark brown-purple blotch.

Tudicula armigera
A. Adams 1855 *Queensland, Australia, 2.9in (75mm).*
Delicate with rather short spire, large body whorl and long, narrow siphonal canal – rather like some of the Muricidae. Finely spirally corded with long, sharp, hollow spines on the shoulders – about eight on the body whorl – which show just above the suture on earlier whorls. Three cords on the body whorl are larger than the others and have sparse, short spines. There is a row of about five, long spines round the posterior end of the long siphonal canal and another of short ones below it. Finely dentate lip is ridged; columella has four plaits and a broad, partly free-standing parietal shield. White, cream or pale brown with brown clouding; aperture white.

Vasum ceramicum

Tudicula armigera

Vasum tubiferum

217

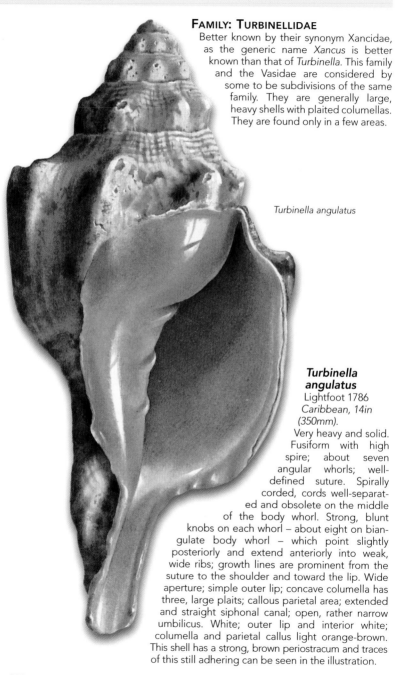

FAMILY: TURBINELLIDAE

Better known by their synonym Xancidae, as the generic name *Xancus* is better known than that of *Turbinella*. This family and the Vasidae are considered by some to be subdivisions of the same family. They are generally large, heavy shells with plaited columellas. They are found only in a few areas.

Turbinella angulatus

Turbinella angulatus

Lightfoot 1786
Caribbean, 14in (350mm).

Very heavy and solid. Fusiform with high spire; about seven angular whorls; well-defined suture. Spirally corded, cords well-separated and obsolete on the middle of the body whorl. Strong, blunt knobs on each whorl – about eight on biangulate body whorl – which point slightly posteriorly and extend anteriorly into weak, wide ribs; growth lines are prominent from the suture to the shoulder and toward the lip. Wide aperture; simple outer lip; concave columella has three, large plaits; callous parietal area; extended and straight siphonal canal; open, rather narrow umbilicus. White; outer lip and interior white; columella and parietal callus light orange-brown. This shell has a strong, brown periostracum and traces of this still adhering can be seen in the illustration.

T. pyrum

L. 1758 *Bay of Bengal, Sri Lanka, 6.75in (170mm).*
Very heavy. Moderate spire of about six whorls with adpressed sutures. Inflated body whorl; malleate surface; corded at the posterior end and on the short siphonal canal. Simple outer lip; columella with four plaits, the posterior one the largest, others decreasing toward the anterior; callous parietal wall. White; edge of lip, columella and parietal callus pale peach. This shell also has a thick heavy periostracum. It is a sacred object of the Hindus associated with Vishnu, and is frequently seen in Hindu and Buddhist temples, in sacred pictures, and so on. It is often carved with encircling grooves, and is drilled for use as a horn, and cut and carved into ornaments. Rare sinistral specimens are very valuable and most highly prized by Hindus.

Turbinella pyrum

T. laevigatus (not illustrated)

Anton 1839 *Brazil, 4.75in (120mm).*
Solid with bulbous body whorl. Spire tapering to heavy nucleus. Moderately elongated siphonal canal; columella with three strong plaits. White with a strong, brown periostracum. This is an uncommon shell even in its very restricted range.

FAMILY: HARPIDAE

A small family of two genera and some twelve species. Among them, to me, are the most beautiful of all shells. They have short spires, an inflated body whorl, a greater or lesser number of axial folds or ribs, wide aperture, no umbilicus and no operculum. Columella has no plaits and there is no periostracum. They live in and among coral, are active creatures and carnivorous. Most live in the Indo-Pacific region. Many of the harps are known as well or better by synonyms which have been given.

Harpa major

Harpa major

Röding 1798 *Indo-Pacific from East Africa to Hawaii, 4in (100mm).*
Moderate to low spire with sharp apex. Body whorl has about twelve ribs, some wide, some narrow, with small points on the subangulate shoulder; finely striate between ribs; earlier whorls callous; simple, blunt lip; large, callous parietal area; strong fasciole. White; ribs with transverse bands of shades of pale pink-brown; interstices scalloped axially with the same colors; penultimate whorl rosy pink over a purple background below the shoulder and yellow above to the pink apex; inside lip with red-brown marks at the end of the darker exterior bands, and inner aperture with golden brown clouding; outer side of columella and parietal area dark chocolate brown almost divided by a yellow wedge and with lighter brown areas on the anterior, inner half of the columella. Synonym *H. conoidalis* Lamarck 1843.

H. articularis (not illustrated)

Lamarck 1822 *Philippines and Indonesia to north Australia and Fiji, 3.75in (95mm).*

Moderate spire; sharp apex. Body whorl has about fourteen ribs, generally rather narrow, ending in small sharp points on the shoulder; finely axially striate; penultimate whorl callous below the shoulder. Simple lip; strong fasciole. Parietal area heavily glazed. Pink-flesh to tan with typical *Harpa* markings between the ribs. Bands of dark brown to black show on the ribs. Columella and parietal area dark brown, the ribs showing through in a lighter brown. Inside lip white, and interior light brown.

H. amouretta

Röding 1798 *Pacific, 2in (50mm).*

More slender than others of the family and with a higher spire. About thirteen, axial ribs, wider toward the aperture and finely pointed at the shoulder; finely axially striate between the ribs. Simple lip; parietal wall not very callous; long, rather narrow fasciole. White; ribs shiny and crossed by pairs of dark brown lines enclosing yellow-brown or gray-brown; the interstices are dull with profuse, brown, axial scalloping; the outside pattern shows obscurely through the outer lip; the columella is fawn anteriorly with a brown blotch in the middle and a brown spot near the anterior end, the posterior half continuing the pattern on the body whorl. Though this is the typical form, much less slender and more globose species are not uncommon, and the overall color can be more or less dark. The form *crassa* Krauss 1848 is heavier, coarser and more angulate; the ribs especially being heavier and sometimes more numerous. It is often lighter colored.

Harpa amouretta

H. crenata (not illustrated)

Swainson 1822 *West tropical America, 3.5in (90mm).*

Rather similar to *H. doris* but more inflated; lower spire; spines on the shoulder smaller but with two or sometimes three other rows of more or less obsolete spines below the shoulder. The markings are similar but it is generally lighter in color and the central band is purple-brown instead of orange-red.

Harpa amouretta

Harpa amouretta form crassa

221

Harpa davidis

H. davidis
Röding 1798 *Bay of Bengal, 3.5in (90mm).*
Light, moderate spire. Expanded body whorl with about eleven ribs, generally bigger toward aperture. Small, sharp spines on shoulder. Smooth lip; twisted fasciole. Fawn-pink; spiral bands of lighter pink scalloping and V-marks; ribs with single, red-brown lines; posterior of columella, parietal area dark brown, divided by >-shaped pale band; small, brown mark near anterior of columella.

H. kajiyamai
Rehder 1973
South Philippines, 2.8in (70mm).
Moderate spire; rather elongate. Twelve to seventeen ribs on body whorl bearing short, sharp spines on shoulder. A little inflated below shoulder. Early whorls with axial riblets and spiral cords. Penultimate whorl callous below shoulder. Concave between shoulder and suture with axial striae. Lip dentate anteriorly, obsoletely so posteriorly. Smooth, slightly concave columella; strong, heavily glazed fasciole. Flesh-pink with mauve-pink banding and white, mauve, pink and chestnut scalloping, the colors brighter and

Harpa kajiyamai

more vivid than in other Harpidae; blotches of red between alternate pairs of ribs spirally on periphery; red-brown lines in pairs or threes on ribs, which form dark brown marks on inside of lip; large mauve-brown blotch just above the fasciole on columella and parietal area, and small ones anteriorly and posteriorly; in the interior the outside colors show through the tan-white.

H. doris
Röding 1798 *Tropical west Africa, 2.9in (75mm).*
Body whorl more elongate and less inflated than in other species. About thirteen, low ribs. Short spines on the shoulder. Fine axial striae. Lip with teeth which are obsolete posteriorly. Rather dull coloring; pink-brown to tan, edge of ribs with thin, broken, dark brown line; narrow chestnut bands carrying white < marks end in teeth on lip; a more or less indistinct orange-red band on widest part of the body whorl; aperture pink-fawn with interrupted, darker, spiral bands; columella pale yellow anteriorly; posteriorly and on parietal area the basic pattern shows through the light glaze; large, dark chestnut blotch above fasciole running on to columella, a smaller one on anterior, outer edge of columella and a third smaller still where lip joins body whorl. Synonym *H. rosea* Lamarck 1822.

Harpa doris

H. harpa
L. 1758 *East Africa to Tonga, 2.9in (75mm).*
Ovate; moderate spire; square shoulder. Twelve axial ribs, bigger near aperture. Short, sharp spines on shoulder. Fine axial striae between ribs. Short, sharp teeth on posterior two-thirds of lip. Strong, twisted fasciole. Flesh-pink; ribs crossed by dark brown lines in twos, threes or fours; between ribs, axial scalloping in pink, white and red-brown, rows of dashes and V-shaped marks, the various colors and patterns forming bands only broken by the ribs; band on periphery of red-brown blotches between alternate pairs of ribs; lip with brown marks where groups of lines end on last rib; columella fawn with brown mark centrally, smaller blotch posteriorly on parietal wall and one smaller still at base of columella. Synonym *H. nobilis* Röding 1798.

Harpa harpa

H. costata
L. 1758 *The Imperial Harp, Mauritius, 3in (80mm).*
Almost flat spire with sharp, pointed apex. Body whorl with thirty to forty, close-set, axial ribs which project in short, sharp points on the shoulder, then cross a broad, shallow channel to the suture; posteriorly the ribs curve parallel with the lip and cross the fasciole forming lamellae. Simple lip; wide aperture. Columella with a faint ridge continuing the fasciole ridge into the interior. White, spirally banded with fawn and pink-brown; aperture white with yellow clouding, especially anteriorly; columella yellow with a large, triangular, dark red-brown area centrally; a lighter brown streak from it running toward the apex and with brown streaky blotches on the parietal area, Synonym *H. imperialis* Lamarck 1822.

Harpa costata

Family: Mitridae

The miters are a family of some ten genera and many species. They are large and small, generally fusiform and elongate, smooth or spirally ridged and some axially ridged or cancellate. Aperture is generally narrow, columella with plaits and siphonal canal has a notch. The animals live in sand or among coral and seaweed in intertidal and shallow areas. They are carnivorous and scavengers, and inhabit tropical and temperate seas worldwide.

Mitra papalis

L. 1758 *Indo-Pacific, 5in (125mm)*.
High spire. Punctate, spiral grooves becoming obsolete on the last two whorls which are coronated at the suture. Columella with about five plaits. White with dark red spots, generally rather square and in spiral rows; coronations white; aperture cream.

M. imperialis

Röding 1798 *Indo-Pacific, 2.6in (65mm)*.
Punctate, spiral grooves and small, blunt coronations at the suture. Columella with about six plaits; dentate lip. Yellow-brown with dark brown and white clouding; aperture orange-brown.

M. stictica

Link 1807 *Indo-Pacific, 2.9in (75mm)*.
High spire. Sharply angular, coronated shoulders; two rows of deep punctures on early whorls which disappear on the penultimate whorl. Slightly waisted body whorl with three spiral grooves anteriorly. Lip edge is parallel with the axis of the shell for most of its length and curves sharply through 90° to end at the siphonal notch; finely dentate lip; columella with about four plaits. White, with generally rather square red spots in spiral rows; aperture cream.

Mitra papalis

M. ambigua

Swainson 1829
Indo-Pacific, 2.9in (75mm).
Rather broad for its length; narrowly channeled suture. Spirally grooved; grooves obsolete on middle of body whorl. Lip coarsely dentate within; columella with about five plaits. Light red-brown with a wide cream band below the suture; aperture white.

Mitra imperialis

Mitra stictica

Mitra ambigua   Mitra cardinalis

M. cardinalis
Gmelin 1791 *Indo-Pacific, 2.9in (75mm)*.
High spire and simple suture. Spiral rows of small punctures, about twenty-five rows on body whorl. Lip with tiny blunt teeth; columella with about five plaits. White, with spiral rows of brown dashes and a few blotches of the same color on the spire; aperture cream-white.

M. coronata
Lamarck 1811 *Pacific, 1.2in (30mm)*.
High spire, coronated suture and cancellate sculpture. Finely toothed lip; columella with about five plaits. Dark brown; coronations and a single spiral ridge below the suture cream; aperture white.

Mitra coronata

Neocancilla papilio
Link 1807 *Indo-Pacific, 2.4in (60mm)*.
Spiral ridges a little elevated posteriorly, two or three smaller ridges between each of these; axial grooves divide the ridges to give the overall effect of scales. Columella with about five plaits; finely dentate lip. Creamy white with sparse purple-brown and red-brown spots, but profuse in two areas to form red-brown spiral bands; aperture cream-fawn.

Neocancilla papilio

225

Mitra fraga
Quoy & Gaimard 1833
Indo-Pacific, 1.2in (30mm).
Stoutly fusiform; sculptured with spiral
ridges divided by shallow channels in
which there are axial lirae. Near the lip,
the body whorl has axial grooves break-
ing the ridges into rows of nodules. Lip
toothed within; columella with about
five plaits; short, open siphonal canal.
Dark wine color with pale orange spots
on the ridges and nodules; aperture
pale brown.

Mitra fraga

M. lugubris
Swainson 1821
South Indo-Pacific,
1.6in (40mm).
Fusiform with high spire,
spiral ridges and axial
grooves. Obsolete corona-
tions at the suture and
shoulder. Finely dentate lip
is flared a little anteriorly;
columella with about five
plaits. Red-brown with a
white band from suture to
shoulder, spire therefore
being white with a little
brown showing above the
suture; aperture white; columella brown posteriorly, white
anteriorly including plaits.

Mitra lugubris

M. mitra
L. 1758 *Indo-Pacific, 5.5in (140mm).*
Largest of the miters, it has a high spire and
adpressed suture. Fine, punctate spiral lines
becoming obsolete and finally disappearing altogether on the last two whorls. Lip with short, sharp
spines anteriorly; columella with about four plaits.
Narrow columellar shield over fasciole area. White with
spiral rows of varying sized, generally rather oblong, red
spots; spots becoming large irregular blotches below the
suture; aperture creamy yellow.

M. eremitarum
Röding 1798 *Malaysia and Philippines across
the Pacific, 3.3in (85mm).*
High spire; coarse edging to adpressed suture. Spiral
grooves, pustulate on early whorls; axial striae. Dentate lip;
columella with about five plaits. Siphonal canal is short and a
little twisted. Light yellow-cream with irregular axial streaks
of dark and light browns.

Mitra mitra

Mitra eremitarum

Mitra incompta

M. incompta
Lightfoot 1786 *Indo-Pacific,*
4in (100mm).
Slender with a very high spire; adpressed suture and very
finely coronated. Obsolete axial riblets; spiral punctate
grooves. Finely dentate lip, sometimes recurved; columella with about five plaits; siphonal canal short and rather
straight, a little recurved. Cream or orange-cream with
dark brown axial streaks and a pale
band low on body whorl; aperture
creamy tan.

M. puncticulata
Lamarck 1811 *Indo-Pacific,*
2in (50mm).
Stubby with moderate spire. Suture
with small coronations; small axial
ribs are crossed by incised, deeply
punctate, spiral grooves. Finely dentate lip; columella with about four
plaits. Short siphonal canal is a little
twisted. White with two broad bands,
one below the suture and one anteriorly
of light orange-brown carrying dark
brown axial streaks, and a red-brown thread
in the middle of the central white band;
aperture cream.

Mitra puncticulata

227

Mitra chrysostoma

Mitra floridula

M. chrysostoma

Broderip 1836 *Indo-Pacific, 2in (50mm)*.
Rather broad with moderately high spire.
Adpressed, coarse sutures; axial riblets
and spiral grooves on early whorls; center of body whorl almost smooth,
grooves stronger anteriorly. Thickened lip; about five plaits on columella. White with broad, broken, brown
band below the suture and another
anteriorly; some splashes of the
same color across the central white
band and as axial streaks on the
spire; aperture dirty white.

M. isabella

Swainson 1831 *Japan, 4in (100mm)*.
Long and slender with a high
spire. Spiral ridges crossed by
axial threads. Narrow aperture;
finely dentate lip; columella with
about five plaits. Long and curved
siphonal canal with quite a strong
fasciole. White profusely clouded
and streaked with pale yellow-
brown; aperture pinky-cream.

M. floridula

Sowerby 1874 *South
Indo-Pacific, 2in (50mm)*.
Moderately high spire. Adpressed,
coronated suture; fine, spiral, punctate grooves becoming obsolete on
the middle of the body whorl. Finely

Mitra isabella

dentate lip; columella with about six plaits. Red or orange-
brown, with white blotches in a band below the suture, a row
of sparse white dots on the middle of the body whorl, and
white dashes and dots anteriorly; aperture white.

M. nubila

Gmelin 1791 *Pacific, 2.8in (70mm)*.
Solid with moderately high, slightly concave spire. Whorls
a little inflated; spiral punctate grooves. Dentate lip;
columella with about five plaits. White with red-brown
blotches in two indistinct bands; paler clouding and small
chalky white spots, partly edged with dark brown; aperture
and apex white.

M. cucumerina

Lamarck 1811 *Indo-Pacific, 1in (25mm)*.
Stubby with a moderate spire. Spiral ridges divided by
channels. Obsolete, broad, blunt axial ribs. Dentate lip;
columella with about four plaits. Red with a broad, central,
white band and white flecks elsewhere; aperture white.

Mitra cucumerina

Mitra nubila

Strigatella paupercula
L. 1758 *Indo-Pacific,*
1.2in (30mm).
Chubby with short spire and inflated at the shoulder of the body whorl, it looks like a member of the Columbellidae. Smooth except anteriorly where it has fine spiral threads. Lip slightly concave posteriorly; about five columellar plaits. Chocolate brown to black with wavy white axial streaks; lip and plaits white; interior deep brown.

Strigatella paupercula

S. litterata
Lamarck 1811 *Indo-Pacific, 1.2in (30mm).*
Short, fat with low spire and spiral punctate lines. Lip thickened and turned in, blunt tooth posteriorly; columella with about five plaits. Creamy white with brown, wavy, axial streaks and blotches, generally in three spiral rows; aperture blue-white.

S. scutulata
Gmelin 1791 *Indo-Pacific, 2in (50mm).*
Moderately high spire. Spiral cords, obsolete on the body whorl, and fine axial striae. Sinuate lip; columella with about four plaits. Dark brown-black; a narrow yellow band below the suture and white spots and short axial streaks; aperture blue-white.

Strigatella litterata

Strigatella scutulata

229

Swainsonia variegata

Neocancilla granatina

Neocancilla antoniae

Swainsonia variegata
Gmelin 1791 *Pacific, 1.8in (45mm).*
Solid, high-spired and slightly shouldered with axial ribs between shoulder and suture. Incised and punctate spiral lines, some fourteen on body whorl. Dentate lip; columella with about six plaits. Creamy gray with white blotches edged on the aperture side with wavy dark brown streaks; two obscure bands of pale and dark brown; aperture cream.

Neocancilla granatina
Lamarck 1811 *Indo-Pacific, 2.6in (65mm).*
High spire. Sculpture the same as *N. papilio* (see page 224). Columella has five plaits. Shiny white with spots and rather sparse, transverse dashes of magenta, rose, and orange, more profuse on two bands, one in the center and one at the anterior end of the body whorl; aperture cream to light tan.

N. antoniae
H. Adams 1870 *Indo-Pacific, 1.6in (40mm).*
Slightly inflated with nodulose spiral ridges, threads and axial incised lines. Lip dentate within; columella with about five folds. White with red-brown dashes on the rows of nodules; aperture pinky white.

Cancilla filaris

L. 1771 *Indo-Pacific, 1.2in (30mm).*
Fusiform with high spire and finely dentate lip. Columella with about four plaits. Surface somewhat cancellate; evenly spaced spiral cords crossed by vertical striae. The first cords is further below the suture than the distance between the other cords. White; spiral cords red; aperture white; cords showing through faintly but clearly at the edge.

C. praestantissima

Röding 1798 *Indo-Pacific, 1.6in (40mm).*
Very high spire. Sculpture similar to *C. filaris* but rather finer; lacking the extra width from suture to first cord. Color similar.

Cancilla filaris   *Cancilla praestantissima*

Imbricaria conularis

Lamarck 1811 *Indo-Pacific, 1in (25mm).*
Shaped and looks like a cone shell, except for the five or so columellar plaits. Moderate spire with high, sharp apex, sometimes with spiral lines of minute punctures. Lip uneven rather than dentate. Opaque white; chalky white squares; brown-red spiral lines and a central purple band which also carries the white squares; lip white; interior purple-brown; columella opaque and chalky white; apex purple-brown.

I. olivaeformis

Swainson 1821 *Pacific, 0.8in (20mm).*
Olive-shaped, hence its name. Low rounded spire with sharp, pointed apex; smooth or with obsolete spiral punctate lines. Smooth lip; columella with about five plaits. Green-yellow; apex and tip of columella purple.

Imbricaria conularis

Imbricaria olivaeformis

Imbricaria punctata

I. punctata

Swainson 1821 *South Indo-Pacific, 0.8in (20mm).*
Low, almost flat spire with sharp, pointed apex. Rounded shoulder narrowing to the suture and spiral, incised, punctate lines. Lip with very small, fine teeth; columella with about six plaits. Pale orange-yellow; paler on the spire and toward the lip; aperture pale cream-white.

Pterygia dactylus

Pterygia dactylus

L. 1767 *Indo-Pacific, 2in (50mm)*.
Solid and heavy with short spire and adpressed suture. Swollen at the rounded shoulders. Incised spiral lines and beveled lip. Columella has about seven strong plaits; small fasciole. White, heavily clouded with brown, on which three or four indistinct bands are discernible; aperture white; columella with sparse brown marks.

P. crenulata

Gmelin 1791 *Indo-Pacific, 1.6in (40mm)*.
Solid with short spire. Narrower than the above. Suture has a narrow ledge; rounded shoulder; finely reticulated. Lip faintly toothed within and columella has about eight plaits. White with light brown maculations; interior white.

Pterygia crenulata

P. nucea

Gmelin 1791 *Indo-Pacific, 2.4in (60mm)*.
Solid, heavy, with moderate spire and adpressed suture. Fine axial striae and faint spiral grooves. Lip has tiny nodules; columella has about five strong plaits; small but strong fasciole. White with three spiral rows of irregular dark brown dashes and spots and about six to eight rows of very small, lighter brown dots; nodules on the lip pale brown; aperture white.

Pterygia nucea

Vexillum taeniatum

Lamarck 1811 *Indo-Pacific, 2.9in (75mm).*
Narrow, fusiform, with high spire and sharply rounded shoulders below the suture. Axially ribbed, some ten ribs on body whorl; coarse spiral cords rather weak on middle of body whorl. Inside of lip lirate; columella with about five plaits; extended, open and recurved siphonal canal. White with three orange-red bands, one below the suture, one centrally on body whorl, and one anteriorly, all edged with strong black lines; with or without a narrow red line through the posterior white area; the bands show on the lip; aperture cream.

V. formosense

Sowerby 1890 *Western Pacific, 2.2in (55mm).*
Narrow, fusiform, with high spire and slightly constricted suture. Axial riblets, about twenty on body whorl, becoming obsolete on the last half of the body whorl. Spiral cords overall, but rather weak on middle of body whorl. Lirate inside lip; columella with about five plaits; open, slightly extended and recurved siphonal canal; small fasciole. Very dark brown with a narrow, white, spiral band, sometimes carrying a red thread; inside lip edged with dark purple-brown; columella brown; columellar plaits cream; interior violet.

Vexillum taeniatum

V. caffrum

L. 1758 *Indo-Pacific, 2in (50mm).*
Fusiform, and wider and heavier than the two preceding species. High spire and adpressed suture. Small crowded axial riblets become obsolete on middle of body whorl; spiral cords anteriorly on body whorl. Lirate lip is a little concave and inverted; columella has about four plaits; siphonal canal is open and a little recurved. Chocolate brown with two narrow yellow-white spiral bands; inside lip edge dark brown; columella brown; columellar plaits cream; interior cream.

Vexillum formosense

Vexillum caffrum

Vexillum
sanguisugum

Vexillum
melongena

Vexillum
stainforthi

Vexillum sanguisugum

L. 1758 *Indo-Pacific, 1.7in (42mm).*
Fusiform with high spire and about six whorls. Axial riblets are broken into nodules by fine, incised, spiral grooves. Very slightly concave lip; narrow aperture; columella with about four plaits. White; spiral rows of shiny white nodules divided into three groups of five by two rows of scarlet nodules; spiral grooves purple; aperture edged with purple-brown; columella brown; interior white; fasciole red-brown.

V. melongena

Lamarck 1811 *Singapore to Fiji, 2in (50mm).*
Narrow and fusiform with high spire and about eight whorls. Strong axial ribs and weak spiral ridges which do not cross the axial ribs. Narrow aperture; lirate lip; columella with about four folds; extended siphonal canal. Gray with a broad white band on the shoulder which is edged with purple and has a scarlet thread through the middle; two, narrow, brown bands anteriorly; aperture blue-white edged with purple-brown marks; columella pale brown; columellar folds white.

V. stainforthi

Reeve 1841 *West Pacific, China Seas, 2in (50mm).*
Narrow and fusiform with high spire and about eight whorls. Adpressed suture; widely spaced axial ribs, about ten on body whorl; fine spiral striae cross the ribs. Slightly concave lip; columella with about four plaits; small fasciole extended, slightly recurved siphonal canal. Cream; five scarlet bands which only appear on the axial ribs; inside and outside of lip with purple-brown marks where the bands end; columella brown anteriorly, rest of aperture white; apex and end of siphonal canal purple-brown.

Vexillum
exasperatum

V. exasperatum
Gmelin 1791 *Indo-Pacific, 1in (25mm)*.
High spire; about seven whorls; body whorl bi-angulate. Cancellate with finely nodulose axial ribs, the ribs protruding slightly at the shoulder. Lip with nodulose striae; columella with four plaits; small fasciole. White; a broad brown band between the upper and lower shoulders and one between the anterior shoulder and the fasciole, only show on the axial ribs; aperture white.

V. plicarium
L. 1758 *East Indian Ocean, southwest Pacific, 2in (50mm)*.
Broadly fusiform with a high spire, about eight whorls and adpressed suture Concave from suture to sharp shoulder. Fine axial striae, and spiral cords anteriorly. Strong axial ribs, about ten on body whorl, end in blunt knobs on the shoulder. Columella with about four plaits. White with a broad central blue-gray or brown band edged between the ribs with red-brown or black lines, and with a similar line below the shoulder and anteriorly; inside lip shows the banding; columella white; apex purple.

Vexillum plicarium

V. vulpecula
L. 1758 *Pacific, 2.2in (55mm)*.
Solid and fusiform with high spire, about seven whorls and narrowly channeled suture. Coarse axial ribs becoming obsolete near the aperture; narrow spiral grooves, and spiral cords anteriorly; the ribs are particularly strong at the angular shoulder. Slightly concave lip, lirate within; columella with about four plaits. Color variable cream, yellow or orange with three black or red-brown bands, one at the suture, one centrally and one anteriorly; siphonal canal and fasciole of the same color; lip carries the color band; interior white; columella white, with the black or red color anteriorly.

Vexillum vulpecula

Pusia microzonias
Lamarck 1811 *Indonesia to Polynesia, 1in (25mm)*.
Fusiform with about six whorls. Coarse, rounded axial ribs replaced by fine, nodulose spiral cords anteriorly. Lirate inside lip; columella with about four folds. Dark red-brown, with a row of white spots on the ribs joined by a white line on the middle of the body whorl; a pale spiral line below the ribs; aperture and columella white with brown showing through the lip.

Pusia microzonias

235

FAMILY: VOLUTIDAE

Some 200 species belong to this family and vary from large to fairly small. They are colorful, most having a reasonably simple sculpture. Most are carnivorous and live in sand in both shallow and deep water. Although found worldwide, Australia has far more than its fair share of species.

Ericusa sericata

Thornley 1951 *East Australia, 5in (125mm)*.
Solid and rather narrow. Moderate spire with large rounded protoconch forming the apex. About two-and-a-half whorls, nucleus eccentric; subsequent whorls about three-and-a-half. Lip slightly thickened and flared anteriorly. Columella is somewhat extended posteriorly and a little recurved, with four plaits. Siphonal notch is wide and rather shallow. Cream-tan, heavily covered with orange-brown, leaving tent marks of the base color; short orange-brown axial streaks below the suture; aperture cream-gray.

Ericusa sericata

Livonia mammilla

Livonia mammilla

Sowerby 1844 *Southeast Australia from Queensland to south Australia, north Tasmania, 12in (300mm)*.
Large and ovate. Short spire has very large, semiglobular protoconch of one whorl and three subsequent convex whorls. Very inflated body whorl; wide aperture; simple lip is extended posteriorly to a point on the penultimate whorl near the suture. Curved columella has three plaits and siphonal notch is wide but not deep. Weak fasciole and narrow callous parietal area. Cream or pale yellow-cream; two broad bands of sparse, dark brown-red, generally axial and oblique lines forming separate patterns; inside of lip, area at posterior end of lip and columella apricot; interior flesh-colored.

Fulgoraria mentiens

Fulton 1940 *South Japan, 8.5in (215mm).*
Fusiform; moderate protoconch of about two whorls, with eccentric nucleus; about five subsequent whorls. About sixteen axial ribs on penultimate whorl, becoming obsolete on body whorl, as also do the spiral striae which are strong on early whorls. Simple, slightly recurved lip; extended columella has about four plaits, the strongest anteriorly with a wide gap between it and the next; very shallow siphonal notch. Pale flesh, with three spiral bands, one below the suture, one centrally, and one anteriorly, of wavy, generally axial, dark red-brown lines, two of which show on earlier whorls; edge of lip white; interior pinky flesh.

Fulgoraria mentiens   Fulgoraria rupestris

F. rupestris

Gmelin 1791 *Taiwan, 5in (130mm).*
Fusiform and solid with moderate spire. Large protoconch has about two whorls with eccentric nucleus, and about three-and-a-half subsequent whorls. About fourteen axial ribs on penultimate whorl becoming obsolete on body whorl. Somewhat angular shoulders and strong, spiral, incised lines. Outer lip is a little thickened, beveled and slightly crenulated anteriorly. Extended columella is convex centrally with a ridge bearing about nine plaits. No siphonal notch. Creamy white to very pale creamy tan; brown wavy axial lines; aperture white; interior with a pale brown tinge.

F. delicata

Fulton 1940 *Southeast Japan, 2.2in (55mm).*
Small, narrow and fusiform with relatively high spire. Small protoconch has about two whorls, eccentric nucleus and about four subsequent whorls. About fifteen axial ribs on penultimate whorl becoming obsolete on body whorl. Constricted suture; very fine spiral striae; simple lip; columella has about two plaits; no siphonal notch. Creamy white.

Fulgoraria
delicata

Voluta ebraea
L. 1758 *North Brazil, 6in (150mm).*
Rounded protoconch; angular shoulders carry short spines at end of low ridges which disappear anteriorly. Uneven suture; thickened, sharply recurved lip. Recurved columella with five strong plaits and very weak plaits posteriorly. Narrow, callous parietal area; deep, narrow siphonal notch. Cream to tan; fine axial and spiral red-brown lines, mainly in two bands; faint purple marks on bands and strong fasciole; lip with twelve purple-brown spots; aperture, columella pale peach.

V. musica
L. 1758 *Northeast South America, east Caribbean, 3.5in (90mm).*
Blunt protoconch; shoulders carry heavy, pointed, laterally compressed knobs at end of low, wide ribs becoming obsolete anteriorly. Uneven suture; long aperture, wider anteriorly; thickened, recurved lip; straight columella, recurved anteriorly, five strong plaits anteriorly, strong lirae posteriorly. Parietal area narrow posteriorly, wider over part of strong fasciole; deep, narrow siphonal notch. Ivory or cream; spiral red-brown markings, especially in two bands; aperture cream. Variable; knobs more or less strong, color more or less heavy.

Voluta ebraea

Lyria mitraeformis
Lamarck 1811 *South Australia, 2.2in (55mm).*
Small, inflated, blunt protoconch; indented suture. Axial ribs, sixteen on body whorl. Aperture wide anteriorly. Concave columella with three plaits, low tooth posteriorly, lirae between. Shallow, narrow siphonal notch; small, partly callous fasciole. Cream heavily mottled with gray-brown spiral dashes, rectangular spots; lip with red-brown hair lines; aperture white; columella and notch with yellow tinge.

Lyria mitraeformis

Voluta musica

L. lyraeformis
Swainson 1821 *Kenya, 5.75in (145mm).*
Bulbous protoconch with spur at apex, convex, restricted at suture and slightly concave below. Axial ribs, eighteen on body whorl. Short aperture, wider anteriorly; thickened, beveled lip; columella has three plaits anteriorly, lirate centrally; parietal area and part of small strong fasciole callous; small siphonal notch. Creamy tan; three spiral bands of uneven red-brown edged with dark brown lines, broken in interstices of ribs, thin red-brown lines between; aperture pale orange.

L. delessertiana

Petit de la Saussaye 1842 *Madagascar, Comoro and Seychelle Islands, 2.2in (55mm).*
Small, rounded protoconch; close axial ribs, twenty on body. Indented, constricted suture. Narrow, long aperture. Thickened lip with a low ridge carrying three ribs. Concave columella has small plaits almost covering narrow parietal area; deep, narrow siphonal notch; weak fasciole. Pinky white clouded with orange-red; twelve, spiral, thin, red, broken lines; aperture white.

L. cumingii

Broderip 1832 *West Central America, 1.4in (35mm).*
Small, rounded protoconch; low shoulder; blunt, laterally compressed knobs at end of low ribs. Ten ribs on body whorl, obsolete anteriorly, enlarged in middle. Uneven suture; narrow aperture; thickened lip has axial ridge before beveled edge and small, blunt tooth centrally on inner edge. Concave columella, three plaits anteriorly, three or four weaker posteriorly; narrow parietal area; deep, narrow siphonal notch. Cream; brown clouding, especially in two spiral bands; aperture cream.

Volutocorbis abyssicola

H. Adams & Reeve 1848 *South Africa, 4in (100mm).*
Shallow, channeled suture; fine grooves. Thickened, slightly recurved lip; white columellar plaits, strongest anteriorly; wide, callous parietal area; wide, shallow siphonal notch; obsolete fasciole. Pale brown; long, narrow aperture is gray-brown.

Lyria lyraeformis

| Lyria delessertiana | Lyria cumingii | Volutocorbis boswellae |

V. boswellae

Rehder 1969 *South Africa, 2.4in (60mm).*
Rounded spire; strongly shouldered; channeled suture; close-set axial ribs. Shallow depression below suture forming two rows of sharp nodules, giving coronated effect at suture. Narrow aperture; thickened, faintly denticulate lip; ten columellar plaits, strongest anteriorly; shallow siphonal notch. Pale yellow-tan; aperture paler. The genus *Cymbium* is found only in the area from Portugal to the Gulf of Guinea in west Africa.

Volutocorbis abyssicola

239

Cymbium pepo

Lightfoot 1786 *Northwest Africa, 10.5in (270mm)*.
Large and globose, often more so than in the illustration. Concave spire; the later whorls extend beyond the apex which is usually callous; a wide channel separates the apex from the edge of shoulder; fine axial striae. Wide aperture; simple, flaring lip. Arched columella with three or four plaits; parietal area covered by this callus is very wide; wide, deep siphonal notch; wide, ridged fasciole. Gray-brown; aperture creamy pink; edge of lip and columella darker; plaits white.

Cymbium pepo   Cymbium olla

C. olla

L. 1758 *Portugal to Morocco, 4.5in (115mm)*.
The smallest of the genus. Very low spire, deeply channeled suture and rounded shoulder. Wide, flaring lip. Columella arched and with two plaits. Wide, very shallow siphonal notch; wide, ridged fasciole; fine axial growth lines; parietal area glazed, but not very wide. Pinky flesh; aperture paler and shiny; fasciole light red-tan.

C. cymbium

L. 1758 *Canary Islands to Senegal, west Africa, 6.1in (155mm)*.
Rather oblong in outline. The spire is flat or slightly concave. Apex has a heavy callus and a wide, flat platform dividing the suture from the sharply angled shoulder, which has a small uneven projecting ridge. Beveled lip with the anterior half flaring. Arched columella has three plaits; wide, deep siphonal notch; wide ridged fasciole. The surface is smooth but the whole shell, including the periostracum, is glazed so that grains of sand and small pieces of other matter get covered by the glaze giving a pustulate effect in places. Light brown; aperture and columella creamy brown.

Cymbium
cymbium

C. cucumis
Röding 1798 *Senegal, 6.25in (160mm)*.
Very similar to *C. cymbium* but not so wide from shoulder to protoconch which is much more pronounced, being long and protruding. Flaring, simple lip; columella with three plaits; deep siphonal notch. Light creamy tan; interior darker. Most gastropods when held with the anterior end downward and aperture toward one, have the aperture on the right; these are known as dextral shells. A very few genera have the aperture on the left and are known as sinistral shells. Rarely a normally dextral shell will be found in a sinistral form. I have in my collection a sinistral *C. cucumis* and have used this to illustrate the species and as an example of this abnormalcy.

Cymbium glans

Cymbium cucumis

C. glans
Gmelin 1791 *Senegal to Gulf of Guinea, west Africa, 13in (330mm)*.
The largest of the genus and the most graceful. Spire sunken and filled with callus, through which the protoconch is seen as a low knob. Sharp shoulder is curved up and out. Simple, flaring lip; arched columella with four plaits; wide fasciole; broad, rather shallow siphonal notch. The whole surface is covered with a thin glaze, often imprisoning many grains of sand. Pale cream-tan, with chocolate edge to the shoulder and streaked on the spire.

The genus *Melo* is found only in the area of Malaysia to Australia, where they are commonly known as balers, from their use for that purpose.

Melo miltonis

Griffiths & Pidgeon 1834 *Southwest and south coasts of Australia, 18in (450mm).*

Rather narrower in relation to its length than others of the genus. Large with rounded, protuberate protoconch of about three whorls; two-and-a-half subsequent whorls. Shoulders have sharp, hollow, even spines sloping inward; deep channel between shoulder and suture. Simple, expanded lip; arched columella with three strong plaits and some times a fourth weak one; base of columella curved forward; strong fasciole; wide but shallow siphonal canal. Creamy white, with purple-brown zigzag axial markings; two or three, broad, spiral bands; inside lip with a few purple marks and purple edging anteriorly; interior creamy brown to cream; columella apricot.

Melo miltonis

M. umbilicatus

Sowerby 1826 *Northeast and north coasts of Australia, 15in (400mm).*

Very inflated and subglobular with very widely flaring lip. Sunken spire with a large rounded protoconch of about three whorls; about two subsequent whorls. Shoulder with long, sharp, hollow spines which slope inward and in adult specimens almost obscure the spire. Simple lip; arched columella with three, strong plaits; strong fasciole; wide, shallow siphonal notch. Cream or brown-yellow with darker brown, axial zigzags and streaks, mainly forming two, interrupted, spiral bands, narrow and dark near the columella, wide, diffused and pale near the lip; spines dark brown, but paler near the lip; interior creamy tan; columella pale apricot. The illustrated specimen is not fully adult and the apex is only partly obscured.

M. aethiopica

L. 1758 *Indonesia, Malaysia, 10in (250mm).*

Large and heavy. Almost flat spire with large, rounded protoconch of about four whorls; about two-and-a-half subsequent whorls. Rather inflated body whorl; shoulders with rather close-set, short, solid, open spines, separated from the simple suture by a narrow, flat, lamellated area. Almost semicircular outer lip. Columella with three strong plaits and one weak one, straighter than most of the genus, and extending beyond the anterior end of the lip. Broad, shallow

Melo umbilicatus

siphonal notch; strong, ridged fasciole. Creamy with two rather faint, pale tan spiral bands, and an occasional, small, dark brown streak; aperture cream or peach; columella slightly darker.

M. amphora
Lightfoot 1786 *Northern half of Australia, south New Guinea, 18in (450mm).*
Very large and heavy. Almost flat spire, with low rounded protoconch of about four whorls, and three subsequent whorls. Shoulder spines are narrower, longer and more widely spaced than in *M. aethiopica* and disappear on the body whorl of adults. Flaring lip; slightly arched columella with three plaits; wide, shallow siphonal notch; strong fasciole. Creamy brown with white spots and blotches or darker, zigzag, axial lines; rather variable in color and often with two darker tan spiral bands, aperture peach; columella darker. A thin midbrown periostracum largely obscures the color and pattern, as in the illustration.

Melo amphora

Melo aethiopica

Melo melo

M. melo
Lightfoot 1786 *Strait of Malacca to South China Sea, 11in (275mm).*
Globose with spire and protoconch hidden beneath the body whorl, the shoulders of which meet at the apex, there being no suture or any spines or coronations. Inflated body whorl; almost semicircular, simple outer lip; arched columella with four plaits. Yellow, or sometimes almost white, with sparse small brown blotches in two spiral bands; aperture cream; periostracum medium brown.

Cymbiola aulica

Cymbiola aulica
Gray 1847 *South Philippines, 6in (150mm).*
Solid with a rather short spire. Large, blunt protoconch of about two-and-a-half smooth whorls; about three subsequent whorls with slightly angular shoulders carrying short laterally compressed spines at the end of ribs, which disappear anteriorly. Rather coarse growth lines; long aperture ending at the shoulder; simple, beveled lip, expanded anteriorly; slightly concave columella, with four, strong plaits and thickly callous; wide and moderately deep siphonal notch; callous fasciole. Pinky flesh with irregular, generally large, red blotches, mostly in two, broad spiral bands; aperture pinky flesh. This shell is variable in shape and color; the spines may be knobs or absent altogether, and the red may almost obscure the background color. A variety mottled with brown and white spots was known formerly as *C. cathcartiae* Reeve 1856. *C. aulica* is rather rare and a collectors' item.

C. flavicans
Gmelin 1791 *Northeast Australia, south New Guinea, 4in (100mm).*
Solid and heavy. Short, straight-sided spire with a small rounded protoconch of about three whorls; about four-and-a-half subsequent whorls with rounded shoulders, sometimes with a few, blunt, heavy knobs. Simple lip; almost straight columella with four strong plaits; deep, narrow siphonal notch; strong fasciole. Cream with blue and purple-brown irregular marks below the suture and irregular, wavy, axial splashes of the same

Cymbiola flavicans

color in two broad bands on the body whorl; inside lip cream with purple-brown marks; columella cream and interior pale blue-gray.

C. imperialis
Lightfoot 1786 *Philippines, 10in (250mm).*
Heavy and somewhat variable, with a low spire but a very large, blunt, rounded protoconch of about four-and-a-half, smooth, shiny whorls; about three subsequent whorls with sharply angled shoulders carrying long, sharp, hollow spines, generally curving a little inwards. Long aperture is wide anteriorly; simple lip is a little thickened; slightly concave columella with four strong plaits; deep, narrow siphonal notch; strong fasciole; callus on parietal area thin but wide; smooth except for growth lines. Protoconch red-brown; base color fleshy-pink, covered with many wavy axial lines of purple-brown and three, broken spiral bands of the same color through which the base color shows in large and small tent marks; aperture and columella pale apricot.

Cymbiola imperialis

*Cymbiola imperialis
form robinsona*

C. imperialis form robinsona
Burch 1954.
This is a form of the above which lacks the spiral bands.

C. nobilis
Lightfoot 1786 *South China Sea, 7.5in (190mm)*.
Variable. Solid and very heavy, usually having a short spire with a large, blunt, rounded protoconch of about three-and-a-half whorls; about two-and-a-half subsequent whorls. Angular, rounded shoulders are faintly knobbed; coarsely callous suture; wide aperture; thickened, simple lip extends a little posteriorly; slightly concave columella with four plaits; parietal area callous, very heavily in old specimens; a distinct posterior canal and a deep, narrow siphonal notch; strong, partly callous fasciole. Pale flesh color with axial, zigzag, purple-brown lines and three, broad, broken, spiral bands of the same color, one above the shoulder, two below. Edge of inside lip marked with the purple-brown of the spiral bands; aperture pale pink; parietal callus white. The color and pattern are very similar to that of *C. imperialis* and there is a form similar to *C. imperialis* form *robinsona* which lacks the spiral bands: However, it has no subspecific name.

Cymbiola nobilis

245

Cymbiolena magnifica
Gebauer 1802 *East Australia, 12in (300mm)*.

Large but light. Moderately short spire; large, blunt protoconch of three-and-a-half whorls and incised suture; about three-and-a-half subsequent whorls; indented suture; concave between suture and rounded shoulder. Body whorl shoulder may have blunt knobs near aperture. Thickened lip; four columellar plaits; deep, wide siphonal notch; parietal area with opaque callus. Pinky white base showing through heavy, pale brown, zigzag markings as axially flattened tent marks; brown overlay is darker with a purple tinge below suture, in three spiral bands on body whorl and bordering the strong fasciole; inside lip flesh; columella yellow-pink.

Aulicina deshayesi
Reeve 1855 *New Caledonia, 4in (100mm)*.

Solid. Fairly low spire; large, blunt protoconch of three-and-a-half whorls; faintly nodulose; two-and-a-half subsequent whorls. Shoulders with pointed nodules; a little concave between shoulder and suture. Fine axial growth lines. Thickened, beveled lip; straight columella with four strong plaits, curved sharply anteriorly; narrow, deep siphonal notch; very strong fasciole; narrow, callous parietal area. White; streaks of red forming spiral bands; aperture apricot.

A. sophiae
Gray 1846 *North coast of Australia, 2.9in (75mm)*.

Cymbiolena magnifica

Delicate with low spire and blunt apex. Protoconch of two-and-a-half axially ribbed whorls; two-and-a-half subsequent whorls. Very angular shoulders with short sharp spines, ten

Aulicina deshayesi

Aulicina sophiae

Aulicina nivosa

on body whorl. Long aperture; simple lip, expanded centrally, four columellar plaits; strong fasciole with sharp central
ridge; deep, narrow siphonal notch. Gray-white, heavily mottled with gray-brown, especially on two bands on body
whorl, each with two rows of thick black axial dashes, one at
each edge of the band; black lines radiate from suture
toward shoulder; lip gray-tan; interior gray; columella white;
fasciole white crossed by wavy dark brown lines.

A. nivosa
Lamarck 1804 *Western Australia, 3.3in (85mm).*
Variable. Generally moderate to short spire; blunt, rounded
protoconch of three whorls with obsolete nodules; two-and-
a-half subsequent whorls. A little concave between suture
and shoulder which is usually slightly angled. Smooth, long
aperture; rounded lip; four columellar plaits; strong fasciole
with ridge near posterior margin; deep, narrow siphonal
notch. Below shoulder white base shows through brown-
gray overlay as small white spots, and two bands of gray
with axial, dark brown streaks and dashes; from suture to
shoulder cream-white with brown blotches and profuse, dark
brown lines; inside lip brown; interior brown-gray; columella
pink-orange.

A. vespertilio
L. 1758 *North Australia, New Guinea, Philippines, Indonesia,
4.5in (115mm).*
Variable. Generally solid with short spire. Protoconch of
three axially ribbed whorls; three subsequent whorls with
short blunt spines extending a short way anteriorly as blunt
ribs (sometimes shoulders lack spines). Smooth; long, narrow aperture; slightly thickened, simple lip; four columellar
plaits; strong, callous fasciole; narrow, deep siphonal notch.
Pale tan; brown, red or olive, zigzag lines
creating tent marks; may be almost black.

A. rutila norrisii
Gray 1838 *East New Guinea to the
Solomons, 3.3in (85mm).*
Variable. Generally solid with
short, blunt spire. Rounded protoconch of three-and-a-half
whorls, obsolete nodules; three
subsequent whorls with low
blunt knobs on shoulder, ten on
body whorl which may appear
above suture on earlier whorls.
Simple, slightly thickened,
recurved lip; four columellar plaits;
strong fasciole; deep, narrow
siphonal notch. Creamy gray; irregular wavy black axial streaks and black
dots in three spiral bands. Color may
be cream-pink with red clouding.

Aulicina vespertilio   *Aulicina rutila norrisii*

Callipara bullatiana

Weaver & du Pont 1967 *South Africa, 2.8in (70mm).*
Low spire, indented suture, and long, rather narrow aperture. Simple, slightly thickened lip. Columella indented centrally, with two plaits anteriorly, sometimes a third. Very shallow siphonal notch; weak fasciole. Light brown, speckled with darker brown, thickly below suture and anteriorly, and forming five, indistinct, spiral lines on body whorl; very long aperture; inside lip white; columella and siphonal notch tan. No specimen of the species, the only one in the genus, is known to have been taken alive.

Callipara bullatiana

Cymbiolacca wisemani

Brazier 1870 *Queensland,
Australia, 3.3in (85mm).*
Moderate spire and blunt protoconch of three ribbed whorls. Axial ribs, posteriorly ending in sharp points on angular shoulders. Smooth with long, narrow aperture. Lip thickened with sharp edge; straight columella with four or five plaits. Narrow, deep siphonal notch; wide fasciole with central ridge. White to pink with pink-brown irregular blotches, generally in four bands; overall red-brown dots or short dashes in pale yellow surroundings; lip with pale yellow-brown clouding; interior, fasciole and columella white.

*Cymbiolacca
wisemani*

C. cracenta

McMichael 1963 *Queensland, Australia, 3in (80mm).*
Narrow; moderate to short spire; blunt protoconch of three-and-a-half ribbed whorls. Slightly angular shoulders have short, sharp spines, obsolete near long, narrow aperture.
Beveled lip; slightly concave columella with four plaits; deep, narrow siphonal notch; strong fasciole with central ridge. Pink; paler pink streaks and spots above spines and tent marks below; four bands of darker pink blotches and dark brown spots and axial dashes; lip pink; interior pinky gray; columella white.

*Cymbiolacca
cracenta*

C. pulchra

Sowerby 1825 *Queensland,
Australia, 3.5in (90mm).*
Very variable; typically with short spire and rounded protoconch of three-and-a-half ribbed whorls; ribs ending posteriorly in short, sharp

*Cymbiolacca pulchra
form woolacottae*

spines on slightly angular shoulders. Long, wide aperture; beveled lip; slightly concave columella with four plaits; deep, narrow siphonal notch; fasciole with low ridge. Pale red-brown; white tent marks; four darker bands bearing sparse chocolate dots and dashes. The form *woolacottae* (illustrated) is much paler, sometimes white with very pale yellow bands, chocolate dots and white aperture.

Zidona dufresnei

Donovan 1823 *East South America, 8in (200mm).*
Variable. Typically with moderately long, narrow spire; protoconch with pointed, clawlike projection of callus covering it. Early whorls convex but body whorl and penultimate whorl (less so) have very wide, rounded shoulders. Simple, slightly thickened lip; slightly concave columella with three plaits; wide fasciole; wide, shallow siphonal notch. Cream; axial, wavy, blue-gray or brown lines; lip, columella and very wide parietal callus apricot; interior cream. Grains of sand may be covered by the overall glaze.

Adelomelon ancilla

Adelomelon ancilla

Lightfoot 1786 *Southeast South America, 7.25in (185mm).*
Long, narrow; high spire; pointed protoconch of two whorls; early whorls sometimes ribbed. Long aperture; simple lip; slightly concave columella with three plaits; wide, deep siphonal notch; strong fasciole partly covered by callus. Cream; sparse, zigzag, axial, brown lines.

A. brasiliana

Lamarck 1811 *Southeast South America, 7in (180mm).*
Globose with short spire and blunt, rounded protoconch. Body whorl shouldered usually with ten, blunt, rounded protoconch. Body whorl shouldered usually with ten, blunt, axially pinched knobs. Wide aperture; slightly thickened, beveled lip; concave columella with two strong and one obsolete plaits; wide, rather shallow siphonal notch; wide, strong fasciole; parietal area with thick callus. Flesh to gray-white; brown clouding on knobs near lip; inside lip orange-pink; interior lighter; columella, parietal area rich pink-brown.

Zidona dufresnei

Adelomelon brasiliana

249

Volutoconus grossi
Iredale 1927 *Northeast Australia, 4.3in (110mm).*
Solid, heavy; moderate, bluntly pointed spire. Protoconch of three-and-a-half whorls; fine sharp point at apex; three subsequent whorls. Slightly concave below suture; smooth. Long, narrow aperture; simple, beveled lip; four columellar plaits, heavy callus posterior to last one. Deep, narrow siphonal notch; moderately strong fasciole. Pink-red; blue-white tent marks; sometimes four, more or less distinct, darker, spiral, red bands; aperture pink.

V. bednalli
Brazier 1878 *North Australia, 5in (130mm).*
Solid; moderate, rounded spire. Protoconch of three-and-a-half whorls; fine, sharp point at apex; three subsequent whorls. Slightly concave below suture; smooth; long aperture. Thickened lip; four columellar plaits; deep, narrow siphonal notch; moderately strong fasciole. Ivory or straw; latticed with dark purple-brown or chocolate lines.

Harpulina lapponica
L. 1767 *South India and north Sri Lanka, 4in (100mm).*
Solid, ovate; low spire. Prominent, globose protoconch of three whorls; five subsequent whorls. Low axial ribs on early whorls become obsolete on antepenultimate whorl; about ten, low, axially pinched nodules on body whorl become obsolete near lip. Uneven, faintly channeled suture; thickened, beveled lip; almost straight columella, three strong plaits anteriorly, four or five weak ones behind them. Narrow, deep siphonal notch; narrow anterior canal; callus partly covers fasciole. Cream; three spiral bands of pale brown

Volutoconus grossi

Volutoconus bednalli   *Harpulina lapponica*   *Alcithoe arabica*

250

blotches sometimes darker or absent, and overall spiral rows of dark brown dots and dashes except for a band below suture; aperture white edged with pale yellow; anterior end of columella, callus pale yellow-brown. Variable.

Alcithoe arabica
Gmelin 1791 *New Zealand, 195mm.*
Very variable. Moderate, concave spire; blunt, rounded protoconch of two-and-a-half whorls; five subsequent whorls. Usually angular with ribs on early whorls developing into blunt, pointed nodules on body whorl. Thickened lip, sometimes recurved; four strong columellar plaits and sometimes a weak one posteriorly; narrow, deep siphonal notch; parietal area and part of fasciole with callus. Yellow-gray or red-brown; fine, wavy, axial, brown lines and about four, broken, spiral bands of purple-brown, generally axial markings; lip, columella flesh-pink; interior gray-pink.

A. swainsoni
Marwick 1926 *New Zealand, 225mm.*
Like *A. arabica* above, of which it may be a form, it is variable. Usually solid with moderate spire. Rounded protoconch of two-and-a-half whorls; five-and-a-half subsequent whorls. Either smooth or with early whorls axially ribbed, ribs becoming obsolete and replaced by low blunt nodules on slightly angular shoulder; coarse, axial growth lines. Thickened recurved lip is projected a little posteriorly; almost straight columella with five strong plaits; deep, narrow siphonal canal; strong fasciole partly covered by shield of callus extending over parietal area. Light or dark red-brown; wavy, axial lines tending to be most obvious in three or four spiral bands; lip and parietal callus metallic pink; long aperture pink-white.

Alcithoe swainsoni

Odontocymbiola magellanica
Gmelin 1791 *Southern South America and the Falklands.*
Solid but rather light with moderately short spire. Small rounded protoconch of one-and-a-half whorls; three-and-a-half subsequent whorls; faint knobs on rounded shoulder. Body whorl a little inflated. Simple lip; slightly concave columella with three strong plaits; shallow, rather narrow siphonal notch; strong fasciole; lightly callous parietal area. Cream; wavy axial brown lines, forming three spiral bands; aperture pale creamy pink; columella darker.

Odontocymbiola magellanica

Amoria grayi

Ludbrook 1953 *West Australia, 4in (100mm).*
Large pointed protoconch of four to five whorls. Smooth; very long aperture; beveled lip, flaring anteriorly. Four columellar plaits; narrow, deep siphonal notch. Apex white; protoconch gray; subsequent whorls gray, axial chestnut lines at suture; lip gray-brown; interior rich brown; sometimes two, pale brown bands.

A. praetexta

Reeve 1849
Northwest Australia, 2.8in (70mm).
Protoconch of three whorls. Smooth with beveled lip. Three columellar plaits; narrow, shallow siphonal notch. Protoconch gray-white; subsequent whorls golden brown with fine, white tent marks; chestnut commas below suture; two rows of zigzag lines on body whorl; aperture white; interior pale brown.

A. maculata

Swainson 1822
East Australia, 2.9in (75mm).
Protoconch of four-and-a-half whorls. Smooth with beveled lip. Four columellar plaits; wide, shallow siphonal notch. Cream to brown; four bands of red-brown axial lines; aperture white; interior with brown tinge. Axial lines may form continuous bands.

A. damonii

Gray 1864 *North and west Australia, 5.5in (140mm).*
Variable. Protoconch of four-and-a-half whorls. Slightly shouldered and smooth with thickened, sharp-edged lip. Four columellar plaits; wide, deep siphonal notch broad, strong, fasciole with weak ridge. Apex white; protoconch whorls white at suture, opaque gray below; subsequent whorls with closely-set, blue axial streaks crossing on to callus covering suture; wide, brown-red band on penultimate whorl; body whorl cream-gray with light red-brown streaks and with two or three bands of purple-brown marks; lip brown; interior deeper brown; columella white edged with brown next to fasciole, which is white tipped with dark blue. Shell varies from narrow with high spire to inflated and broad with short spire; color from cream with thin red-brown lines to only red-brown markings.

Amoria grayi

Amoria praetexta

Amoria maculata

Amoria damonii

Amoria ellioti

Amoria benthalis

A. ellioti
Sowerby 1864
West Australia, 4.3in (110mm).
Protoconch of four-and-a-half whorls. Faintly shouldered, with a flaring, thickened, beveled lip and four columellar plaits. Strong fasciole; narrow, moderately deep siphonal notch. Protoconch opaque, very pale lemon; subsequent whorls rich cream; dark brown spots at suture and thin, brown axial lines, sometimes forming two spiral bands; lip white fading to pale brown interior; columella white.

A. benthalis
McMichael 1964
East Australia, 1.6in (40mm).
Protoconch of two, thinly callous whorls; suture with fine channel. Body whorl inflated at shoulder narrowing quickly toward anterior. Thickened, beveled lip; four columellar plaits; narrow, deep siphonal notch; weak fasciole. Rich cream; yellow-gold clouding in four broken bands obscured by close-set, axial, gold-brown lines with two waves in each; aperture white, and internal gray tinge.

Amoria canaliculata

A. canaliculata
McCoy 1864 *Queensland, Australia, 2.8in (70mm).*
Protoconch of three-and-a-half whorls; suture deeply channeled on body whorl which is inflated at shoulder. Smooth; beveled, expanded lip; four columellar plaits; narrow, deep siphonal notch. Shallow water form (illustrated) is white with five spiral bands of well-spaced, axial dashes of pale red-brown; protoconch, aperture white. Deep water form pink; large, red blotches; red axial lines.

Scaphella junonia
Lamarck 1804 *Florida, Gulf of Mexico, 5in (130mm).*
Protoconch of two whorls; four-and-a-half subsequent whorls; bi-angulate body whorl. Obsolete axial ribs on first two whorls, last two smooth. Thickened, beveled lip; four columellar plaits. White to pale yellow; nine spiral rows of rectangular, dark brown blotches, most dividing into two near lip; aperture white, brown tinge.

Amoria junonia

Amoria zebra

Amoria zebra

Leach 1814 *Northeast Australia, 2.2in (55mm).*
Ovate; short spire. Blunt, rounded protoconch of two-and-a-half whorls, three subsequent whorls. Indented suture; body whorl inflated at shoulder. Thickened lip; columella with four plaits, extended, curved at base; anterior canal; narrow, deep, oblique siphonal canal; fasciole with low ridge. Protoconch red; cream-yellow; wavy, axial, chocolate or orange-brown lines; aperture white; interior tinged pale brown.

A. undulata

Lamarck 1804 *Southeast and south Australia, Tasmania, 3.5in (90mm).*
Variable. Typically ovate with short, slightly concave spire. Small, slightly pointed protoconch of four whorls; three subsequent whorls. Smooth suture; round shoulder; a little concave between suture and shoulder. Thickened, crudely beveled lip; straight columella, four strong plaits, sometimes small plaits between; anterior canal a shallow notch; deep, narrow siphonal canal; fasciole with low ridge. Yellow-cream to white; sparse, brown blotches in four broken bands; axial, wavy, dark brown lines; inside lip white; interior, columella yellow-pink.

Amoria undulata

A. molleri

Iredale 1936 *North and southwest Australia, 4in (100mm).*
Elongate; moderate, slightly concave spire. Sharply pointed protoconch of four whorls; three subsequent whorls. Smooth; faint growth striae; long, narrow aperture; beveled inside lip with sharp, white ridge, becoming obsolete at ends; four, strong columellar plaits, sometimes weak plaits between; callous hump behind last plait; deep, narrow siphonal notch. Shiny pink-brown; paler below suture and at lip; inside lip pink; interior pink-brown; columella pink; fasciole weak, white.

Cymbiolista hunteri

Iredale 1931 *Central east Australia, 175mm.*
Light; low spire. Protuberant, conical protoconch of three whorls; three-and-a-half subsequent whorls with angular shoulders carrying short, sharp spines, twelve on body whorl. Slightly concave between shoulder and suture; a little inflated below shoulder; long, narrow aperture. Simple lip; four strong columellar plaits; deep, narrow siphonal notch. Commonly pale flesh; brown lines, especially across shoulder; three or four spiral bands of blue-gray marks generally edged on left with brown. Deep water form

Amoria molleri

is peach-colored, marks on bands orange-brown. Interior brown, darker farther from lip; columella pink; fasciole strong, white.

Neptuneopsis gilchristi
Sowerby 1898 *South Africa, 8in (200mm).*

Very high spire. Protoconch of two whorls; the first larger, conical and pointed off center; second narrower, shorter; six subsequent whorls. Inflated; constricted suture; fine, close, spiral striae. Wide, semi-circular aperture; thickened, beveled, slightly recurved lip; smooth, extended columella forming open siphonal canal; narrow parietal area with evenly curved edge, callous. Pink-white, with thin, brown periostracum (illustrated); protoconch, aperture, parietal area pink-white.

Teramachia tibiaeformis
Kuroda 1931 *South Japan, 3in (80mm).*

Light, elongate; very high spire. Small protoconch of two whorls; ten subsequent whorls closely axially ribbed except anteriorly, ribs becoming obsolete on penultimate whorl. Constricted at suture; narrow aperture. Flaring, semicircular lip; beveled, recurved edge. Slightly concave, smooth, extended columella. Gray-brown; darker brown band below suture on later whorls; aperture pink-gray, lighter at lip.

Neptuneopsis gilchristi

Cymbiolista hunteri

Teramachia tibiaeformis

Ampulla priamus
Gmelin 1791 *Portugal, Spanish Atlantic coast, 3in (80mm).*
Light, globose; moderate spire. Bluntly rounded protoconch of two-and-a-half whorls; three subsequent whorls. Inflated with indented suture; large aperture; flared, unevenly curved, simple lip; concave, smooth columella; wide, lightly callous parietal area; indistinct fasciole; wide, barely indented siphonal notch. Pink-brown; seven spiral rows of red-brown spots; inside lip edge pale, interior medium brown; columella pink; parietal area pale yellow-pink with red-brown spots.

Ampulla priamus

255

FAMILY: MARGINELLIDAE

The marginellas are a large family found worldwide in warm and tropical seas. There is one large member of the family, *Afrivoluta pringlei*, about 4.75in (120mm); two or three are about 2.8in (70mm); two or three are between 40 and 2in (50mm); a number between 20 and 1.2in (30mm); and a great many smaller.

Afrivoluta pringlei

Tomlin 1947 *East South Africa in deep water, 4.75in (120mm).* Light, rather delicate, with short, blunt spire and large, rounded protoconch. Body whorl is long and bi-angulate with fine growth lines. Coarse callus, very heavy on parietal area, covers most of spire, especially sutural area and much of anterior end of body whorl. Narrow aperture; thickened lip with edge recurved, straight along middle part; columella has four, very strong plaits anteriorly, one nearest anterior end smaller than other three. Light tan; darker brown periostracum; thin glaze overall.

Afrivoluta pringlei

Marginella glabella

L. 1758 *Northwest Africa,*
1.8in (45mm).
Solid with short, straight-sided spire and small, rounded protoconch. Body whorl a little inflated and roundly, though noticeably, shouldered. Moderately wide aperture; heavily thickened lip is recurved and faintly dentate; columella has four strong plaits. Cream with pale brown-pink overlay, stronger in two spiral bands; base color shows through as small dots; irregular blotches of brown-pink below suture; whole covered with thin glaze; inside lip and columella white; interior pale brown-pink.

Marginella glabella

M. desjardini

Marche-Marchaud 1957 *Ivory Coast, west Africa, 2in (50mm).*
Solid, elongate, with short, slightly convex spire. Small, rounded protoconch and rounded shoulders sloping to end of siphonal canal. Lip much thickened, recurved and finely dentate; columella has four plaits. Pale apricot; three darker bands; small white spots rather sparsely scattered over surface; short, white streaks radiating from suture; aperture white; interior with pink tinge.

Marginella desjardini

M. pseudofaba

Sowerby 1846 *Senegal, west Africa, 1.2in (30mm).*
Solid with moderately high spire. Shoulders of each whorl are sharply angled, with axially pinched knobs, about fourteen on body whorl. Knobbed shoulders of earlier whorls show above suture; some of knobs extend almost to siphonal canal but most cover only about one-third of body whorl. Narrow aperture; lip is thickened, recurved and dentate within; columella has four strong plaits; shallow anal canal; siphonal canal a little extended and recurved, sharply at lip. Ivory white; green-gray clouding, generally on two spiral bands; profusely spotted with black in spiral rows, about ten on body whorl; spots also generally aligned axially; inside lip, interior and plaits white; end of siphonal canal gray.

Marginella pseudofaba

Persicula cingulata

Dillwyn 1817 *West Africa, 0.8in (20mm).*
Flat spire, smooth, with body whorl a little inflated posteriorly. Narrow aperture; thickened lip extends slightly beyond apex. Convex columella has about seven small plaits, largest anteriorly and smallest posteriorly. Small, callous knob on parietal area opposite posterior end of lip. White or pink-cream; about twelve spiral red lines, two or three of which bifurcate away from lip; aperture white.

Persicula cingulata

257

Marginella rosea

Lamarck 1822 *East South Africa, 2in (50mm).*
Smooth with moderate spire and about two-and-a-half
shouldered whorls. Small rounded protoconch and thickened, recurved lip. Columella has four plaits. White; pale
pink, generally reticulate pattern; row of darker pink-brown
blotches between shoulder and suture; paler one at anterior
of body whorl; lip white, dark pink-brown spots on outer
edge; interior and columella white.

Marginella rosea

Marginella mosaica

Marginella piperata

M. mosaica

Sowerby 1846 *East South Africa, 1.2in (30mm).*
Similar in shape to above but slightly lower spire, more thickened lip, slightly extended and angled at shoulder. Creamy
white flecked with pale gray-brown; spiral rows – about
twelve on body whorl – of dark gray-brown spots and short
dashes; aperture white.

M. piperata

Hinds 1844 *East South Africa, 1in (25mm).*
Similar in shape to M. rosea, though smaller. White; slight
pale brown clouding; profusely speckled with tiny axial
dashes of red-brown; longer dashes of red-brown between
shoulder and suture; outer edge of lip with dark brown,
smudged spots; aperture white. There are a number of
named forms with different colors and patterns.

M. ventricosa

G. Fisher 1807 *Indonesia and Malaya, 1in (25mm).*
Smooth, shiny, with low spire and moderately wide aperture. Thickened, recurved lip runs round siphonal canal to
join fasciole, ending posteriorly in callous area on spire.
Columella has five plaits. Whole exterior is highly glazed.
Creamy gray; outer edge of lip darker with light brown-gray
rim; inside lip and plaits white. A well-known synonym is

Marginella ventricosa

M. *quinqueplicata* Lamarck.

M. adansoni
Kiener 1834 *Northwest Africa, 1.2in (30mm).*
Rather slender; shoulders with axially pinched knobs, about
sixteen on body whorl. Narrow aperture; thickened,
recurved lip with angular shoulder, thirteen teeth within.
Columella with four plaits, recurved at anterior end. Tan;
irregular darker brown marks on shoulder and more or less
conspicuous wavy axial brown lines; lip white with dark
brown spots; interior and columellar plaits white.

Marginella adansoni

Persicula persicula
L. 1758 *West Africa, 0.8in (20mm).*
Slightly sunken spire and a little
inflated at shoulder of body
whorl. Narrow aperture; thickened, recurved lip, extends
posteriorly beyond apex. Convex
columella with about nine plaits,
strong anteriorly becoming
smaller until barely perceptible
toward posterior. Large, blunt,
callous knob at top of parietal
wall. Pale cream; profuse pink-tan
spots, especially crowded in three
spiral bands; spire pink or red,
creamy glaze; aperture and
parietal knob white.

Persicula persicula

P. cornea
Lamarck 1822 *Northwest Africa, 1.2in (30mm).*
Graceful, slender, with very low spire covered with callus.
Narrow aperture; lip thickened and slightly concave centrally, extending posteriorly slightly above apex. Columella with
about ten small plaits, becoming smaller posteriorly. Cream;
three slightly darker spiral bands with a pink tinge; aperture
white; bands showing faintly through inside of lip.

Persicula cornea

P. elegans
Gmelin 1791 *Malay
Peninsula, 1in (25mm).*
Shaped like *M. ventricosa*
but chubbier and having
six strong plaits. Pale gray;
many darker gray spiral
bands, uneven in width and
distance apart, all broken
by many fine axial lines of
base color giving uneven,
reticulated color effect; lip
from callous area where it joins
spire, round end of siphonal
notch and on to lower end of
parietal area, orange-brown; interior
and plaits white.

*Persicula
elegans*

Marginella bullata

Born 1778 *Brazil, 2.8in (70mm).*

Sunken, glazed spire, apex just proud of surrounding area; smooth bar growth lines under glaze. Aperture widening anteriorly; thickened, recurved lip, slightly concave centrally, obsoletely dentate within; four columellar plaits; strong, glazed fasciole. Pale apricot; faint, darker, spiral bands; grains trapped under glaze give spotted appearance in places; outer edge of lip darker; inner edge, plaits and fasciole are shiny white; interior white with pale apricot tinge.

M. ornata

Redfield 1870 *South Africa, 1in (25mm).*

Chubby; moderate spire; sloping shoulder. Wide aperture; thickened, recurved lip is slightly angular at shoulder; four columellar plaits. Rose-brown; broad, central, pale band, narrow one either side, one on shoulder; central area may be stippled; lip white, dark rose-brown dots and dashes; interior mauve; columella, siphonal notch white.

Marginella bullata

Marginella
marginelloides

Marginella
ornata

M. marginelloides

Reeve *Philippines, 0.5in (12mm).*

Angular shoulders. Strong, axial ribs on all whorls. Finely spirally lirate. Narrow aperture; thickened lip with strong, internal, finely dentate ridge; columella and parietal area crossed by small ridges. Off-white to pale gray; dark brown blotch posteriorly within aperture, showing through on the shoulder on the dorsal side, especially between the ribs nearer, though not on, the lip.

M. philippinarum

Redfern 1848 *Philippines, 0.6in (15mm).*

Slender, small, solid with short spire. Smooth and shiny. Narrow aperture, wider anteriorly; thickened, turned-in,

Marginella
philippinarum

beveled lip; almost straight columella with four plaits. Slightly concave lip makes shell look a little bent. Pale tan or red-tan; three, broken, spiral bands of darker brown with gray flecks; suture white; lip cream externally, white on edge and within; interior red-tan; columella and plaits white.

M. avena
Kiener 1834 *Caribbean, 0.5in (12mm).*
Similar shape to above. Cream; three indistinct pale tan bands.

Marginella avena

Marginella cleryi

M. cleryi
Petit de la Saussaye 1836 *Northwest Africa, 0.8in (20mm).*
Fusiform; high spire. Slightly inflated; roundly shouldered. Narrow aperture; thickened, recurved, dentate lip; four columellar plaits. Green-cream; anterior end of body whorl with gray tinge; two, gray bands on body whorl, one just showing on spire whorls; axial, slightly wavy, sometimes bifurcating, dark chocolate lines at suture; lip, lower columella, plaits, interior white.

Marginella margarita

M. margarita
Kiener 1834 *Mozambique, 0.2in (5mm).*
Smooth, very shiny with low spire. Thickened lip, slightly concave centrally, some eighteen, small teeth on inner edge; four columellar teeth, middle two larger. Beautiful, shiny, very pale rose-cream; lip, aperture white.

Marginella apicina

M. apicina
Menke 1828 *Caribbean, Florida, 0.4in (10mm).*
Similar shape to above but less slender. White, cream to pink or banded pink; apex tan.

Prunum labiata
Kiener 1841 *Gulf of Mexico, 1.6in (40mm).*
Smooth, shiny; short spire; round shoulders. Thickened, dentate lip joins spire in thick, callous area, extending over spire almost to protoconch; four columellar plaits. Pale cream-pink; three, indistinct, darker bands; upper side of lip and callus near spire with strong yellow tinge; inside lip, interior, plaits white.

Prunum labiata

Persicula lilacina
Sowerby 1846 *Brazil, 0.8–1in (20–25mm).*
Sunken spire; slightly inflated body whorl; narrow aperture. Very thickened lip running to sunken apex; four columellar plaits; callous parietal area. Pale rose-gray; three broad darker bands; upper edge of lip orange; inner edge of lip, interior, columella and parietal area lilac; deep interior white.

Persicula lilacina

SUPERFAMILY: CONACEA

FAMILY: CANCELLARIIDAE

The nutmeg shells live in sand in tropical areas, mostly in west America.

Trigonostoma scalata

Sowerby 1832 *Indo-west Pacific, 1.2in (30mm).*
Shallow, wide channel from angular shoulder to slightly constricted suture. Weak, spiral cords; strong, axial ribs cross shoulder. Wide aperture; simple lip, tooth posteriorly, lirate within; three strong, one weak columellar plaits; lirate, narrow parietal shield. Brown-cream; sometimes brown banding; lip, columella white; interior brown.

Trigonostoma scalata

T. scalariformis

Lamarck 1822 *Indo-west Pacific, 1in (25mm).*
Similar to above but fewer, stronger axial ribs, nine on body whorl forming crenulations at shoulder. Weak, spiral striae cross ribs. Lip lirate within; three columellar plaits, shield almost closing umbilicus. Brown, gray or cream; white between shoulder and suture; white spiral band on body; narrow aperture, columella white; interior as exterior.

Trigonostoma scalariformis

Trigonostoma crenifera

Trigonostoma breve

T. crenifera

Sowerby 1832 *Japan, 1.2in (30mm).*
Similar to above but about fourteen ribs on body whorl. Three columellar plaits; obsolete tooth posterior of aperture; narrow, open umbilicus is partly covered by narrow columellar shield. Ivory white; brown clouding; central, spiral, pale band.

T. breve

Sowerby 1832 *Tropical west America, 0.8in (20mm).*
Flat or slightly concave between sharply angled shoulder and suture. Axial ribs form coronations from shoulder to suture; three, spiral ridges cross ribs forming nodules; fine striae between ridges; obsolete, axial riblets give cancellate surface. Dentate lip; three columellar folds; large umbilicus. Gray-white; brown flecks.

Cancellaria cassidiformis

Sowerby 1832 *Tropical west America, 1.6in (40mm).*
Globose; short spire; sharply angled shoulders. Oblique, axial ribs end in short spines. Deeply indented suture. Faint,

Cancellaria cassidiformis

spiral ridges cross coarse growth lines. Thickened lip, lirate within; three, white columellar plaits; heavily glazed palletal area. Off-white to tan; spiral white band forward on body whorl; may be spiral, red lines; lip, parietal glaze yellow-brown; interior white.

C. spengleriana
Deshayes 1830 *West Pacific, 2.2in (55mm)*.
High spire; shouldered. Spiral ridges; axial ribs; short, blunt spines. Lip strongly lirate within; two or three columellar folds; extended fasciole; no umbilicus. Flesh-tan; pink-brown flecks on shoulders; aperture cream-white.

C. reticulata
L. 1767 *Southeast USA, 1.4in (35mm)*.
Globose; inflated; sharp, narrow shoulders. Reticulated by axial and spiral ridges. Finely dentate lip, lirate within; one very strong, one weaker plait, spiral ridges posteriorly; strong fasciole; closed umbilicus. White; sparse, axial, brown streaks; two, broken, light brown, spiral bands; interior, plaits white.

Cancellaria spengleriana

Cancellaria reticulata   *Cancellaria asperella*

C. asperella
Lamarck 1822 *West Pacific, Indian Ocean, 1.6in (40mm)*.
Similar to above; less stout; narrower shoulders. Coarse, spiral and axial threads; rough growth lines. Lirate lip; three columellar plaits; callus, parietal area, columellar shield almost close umbilicus. Cream or pale yellow-brown; two or three, indistinct, pale brown, spiral bands; aperture white.

C. similis
Sowerby *Northwest Africa, 1.4in (35mm)*.
Solid; globose; slightly constricted suture. Cancellate; thin, spiral ridges; narrow, axial ribs. Scalloped lip, lirate within; three, curved columellar plaits, largest posteriorly; narrow umbilical chink usually open; narrower columellar shield; strong fasciole. White or pale gray; two brown-gray bands; aperture white.

Cancellaria similis

263

FAMILY: CONIDAE

GENUS: CONUS

For many shell collectors this is the most popular genus of all. The enormous variety of colors and patterns, as well as shapes within the general conical base shape, have a special fascination. The cones are carnivorous and most live in tropical waters. Only a few live in subtropical waters and they are small and less colorful. They live mainly in the intertidal area, between the reef and shore, in crevices in rock and coral, and in the sandy areas around the reef. They have a soft 'skin' covering the periostracum, which can be removed by soaking in a common household bleach for a few hours, and some have a small operculum. The sting with which they kill their prey can prove fatal to human beings in a few cases. *Conus geographus* is most notorious in this respect, but the *marmoreus* and *textile* groups are also dangerous. There are some 1,500 species of named cones, divided into some thirty subgenera.

SUBGENUS: CONUS

Conus marmoreus

L. 1758 *Indo-Pacific, 4in (100mm)*.
Flat, noduled spire Black or dark chocolate with white patches overall. Closely related are: *C. pseudomarmoreus* Cross 1875 which lacks the nodules on the spire and is endemic to New Caledonia; *C. bandanus* Hwass 1792 which has two indefinite bands where there are fewer white markings, giving the effect of black bands, and is found in the Maldive Islands, East Indies, Philippines and Melanesia to Hawaii; *C. nicobaricus* Hwass 1792 on which the banding is more marked than on *C. bandanus,* from East Indies and Philippines; *C. nocturnus* Solander 1786 which has broader and more conspicuous black bands and is found in the Philippines; and *C. vidua* Reeve 1843, the white markings forming a band at the shoulder and on the body whorl, also endemic to the Philippines. There are a few other, less common members of the group with the black or dark brown base color and white markings, all from the same area of east Indian and west Pacific Oceans.

SUBGENUS: RHOMBUS

C. imperialis

L. 1788 *Indo-Pacific, 4in (100mm)*.
It has an almost flat but noduled spire. White with two brown bands; body whorl is encircled by black and brown dots and dashes.

Conus marmoreus

Conus imperialis

The subgenus also includes: *C. zonatus* Hwass 1782 from the Maldives; *C. fuscatus* Born 1778 from Mauritius, which is a form of *C. imperialis,* as is *C. viridulus* Lamarck 1810 from east Africa.

SUBGENUS: LITHOCONUS

C. leopardus
Röding 1798 *Almost all of the Indo-Pacific, 8.75in (220mm).*
One of the largest and heaviest of the cones, it has a flat spire though more raised than its near relative *C. litteratus,* and rounded shoulders, the edges of the shoulders of the earlier whorls showing as ridges on the spire. White encircled with close-set markings of shades of blue and purple forming lines, some of dots, some of short axial lines, some of joined double dots, all slightly smudged. The tip is white, the surface rather dull, and the large, old, heavy specimens are often pitted and scarred.

C. litteratus
L. 1758 *Indo-Pacific, 4.75in (120mm).*
It has a flat spire with a rounded shoulder and is slightly waisted. White with more or less conspicuous bands of yellow, and overall, close-set bands of rectangular black or dark chocolate spots, larger and sometimes running together axially toward the shoulder.

Conus
leopardus

Conus litteratus

265

C. eburneus

Hwass 1792 *Throughout Indo-Pacific, 2.8in (70mm)*.

Varies a good deal over the large area. It has rounded shoulders and a flattened top with a small, pointed spire. There are two striae below the suture which show on the top when not worn away. White, sometimes with faint yellow bands, and squarish black or dark brown dots encircling the body whorl and spire. Specimens without the dark markings have been found. A small form of *C. eburneus, C. crassus* Sowerby 1857, is endemic to Fiji; and *C. polyglotta* A. Adams 1874 with heavier and larger black markings is found in the Philippines.

Conus eburneus

C. tessulatus

Born 1778 *Indo-Pacific, 2.8in (70mm)*.

Variable in shape and color, sometimes slightly waisted. It has a rather flat top and a short, very pointed spire with concave sides. The white background is covered with bands of squares and oblongs of red or orange, much more profuse than in *C. eburneus*; tip is often tinged with violet.

C. caracteristicus

G. Fischer 1807 *Indian Ocean and Philippines, 2in (50mm)*.

A chunky shell. White with two bands of wavy, brown-red lines, one on the upper part of the body whorl and one near the base; similar markings show on the apex and at the base.

There are two west African members of the subgenus: *C. pulcher* Lightfoot 1786 can grow bigger than any other cone, and is cream with brown and red markings in a pattern similar to others of the subgenus. *C. papilionaceus* Hwass 1792 is smaller but somewhat similar in color and pattern.

Conus tessulatus

Conus caracteristicus

Subgenus: Virroconus

C. ebraeus

L. 1758 *Indo-Pacific, 2in (50mm).*
A small, chunky, rather striking shell with a moderately elevated and coronated spire. Its white background is covered with three broad bands of black chevron-shaped markings, and black markings at the top and on the spire.

C. chaldaeus

Röding 1798 *Range similar to that of C. ebraeus, though it is less common, and not always found in the same places, 1in (25mm).*
Smaller and more angular than C. ebraeus with thick, black, wavy lines forming two broad bands. The lines often join up forming a 'Y' or inverted 'Y' or 'W' marking.

Conus ebraeus

Conus chaldaeus

Conus coronatus

Conus musicus

C. coronatus

Gmelin 1791 *Indo-Pacific, 1.4in (35mm).*
A variable species with a number of subspecies and very closely related species. It varies from slim with a well-elevated spire, to round and chunky. The color is also very variable, blue, gray, green, beige, with dark brown-red or olive dots and mottling, with coronations on the shoulder and spire. Allied species are: *C. abbreviatus* Reeve 1843 from Hawaii; *C. miliaris* Hwass 1792, Indo-Pacific; and C. taeniatus Hwass 1792, Red Sea.

C. musicus

Hwass 1792 *Indo-Pacific, 0.8in (20mm).*
It has a rather flat spire. White, with a pale blue-gray band on the middle of the body whorl and at the base, with dark blue at the very tip. It is encircled with lines of dark brown dots and dashes, two of which border the central band; and larger dark spots on the shoulder which show on the spire.

C. lividus

Hwass 1792 *East Indies and Pacific, 2in (50mm).*
Yellow-green with a white band and white coronated spire and purple tip.

Conus lividus

C. piperatus

Dillwyn 1817 *Indian Ocean,
1.2in (30mm).*
Light blue-gray with indistinct, pale brown banding and violet tip; dark brown spots between some coronations on the shoulder and spire.

C. distans

Hwass 1792
Indo-Pacific, 4in (100mm).
A large shell for the subgenus, it is slightly waisted. Light brown with a paler band at the waist and a darker tip, and shows rather conspicuous growth lines. Spire coronated and lighter.

*Conus
piperatus*

Other members of the subgenus include: *C. mus* Hwass 1810, West Indies; *C. scitulus* Reeve 1849, South Africa; *C. sponsalis* Hwass 1792, Pacific and Philippines; *C. nux* Broderip 1833, east Pacific; and *C. ceylanensis* Hwass 1792, Indo-Pacific.

SUBGENUS: PUNCTICULIS

C. arenatus

Hwass 1792
Indo-Pacific, 2.9in (75mm).
A solid, heavy shell, slightly inflated at the shoulders, with a twist at the base of the columella forming a plait or fold. The spire is slightly elevated and coronated. Its background color of white is speckled with small brown dots which tend to form two or three dark bands.

Conus distans

C. pulicarius

Hwass 1792 *Pacific and East Indies, 2.6in (65mm).*
In shape similar to *C. arenatus.* White with faint yellow blotches and marked with square-shaped, black or dark chocolate spots.

Conus arenatus

C. stercusmuscarum

L. 1758 *Indo-Pacific, 2in (50mm).*
A more slender member of the subgenus than the preceding two, with no coronations or very slight coronations

Conus pulicarius

Conus
stercusmuscarum

Conus zeylanicus

on the shoulders. Its white background is clouded with gray and it is profusely spotted with small black and some brown dots, so close in places as to form black patches.

C. zeylanicus

Gmelin 1791 *East Africa and Mauritius, 2in (50mm).*
Shape somewhat similar to *C. arenatus* but with rounded shoulders and without coronations, and with a small, pointed spire. Its pinky background color is covered with red-brown dots, darker and smaller blotches tending to form two bands. It has small, white areas mostly between the bands and on the top of the shell.

SUBGENUS: STEPHANOCONUS

C. regius

Gmelin 1791 *Florida to the West Indies, 2in (50mm).*
A common member of this subgenus, it is usually a chestnut brown with blue-white markings overall (not illustrated), but has other color variations in white and pale brown, and sometimes granulated (as illustrated). A variety *C. citrinus* Gmelin 1791 is yellow-brown only.

Conus regius

269

C. brunneus

Wood 1828 *Pacific coast of Central America and Galapagos Islands, 2in (50mm).*

A beautiful, rich, mahogany brown with sparse, white dots and splashes, mostly in an indiscrete band on the body whorl. Strong crenulations on the shoulder and spire, which are also white.

C. princeps

L. 1758 *Pacific coast of Mexico and Panama, 2.4in (60mm).* Pinky red with dark brown, axial streaks which cross the shoulder between the slight coronations. A variety, *C.p. lineolatus* Valenciennes 1832, has its dark markings as fine lines; and *C. apogrammatus* Dall 1910 has no markings.

C. varius

L. 1758 *Indo-Pacific, 1.6in (40mm).*
This shell is covered with small granulations giving it a very rough feel and appearance. Its crenulated spire, rising straight from the shoulder, forms slightly less than a right angle at the apex. Its white background color has dark brown blotches and sparse dots. A variety from Queensland, Australia, *hwassi* Weinkauff 1874, is illustrated.

Also in the subgenus: *C. klemae* Cotton 1953, Western Australia; *C. aurantius* Hwass 1792, rare, East Indies and Philippines; *C. gladiator* Broderip 1833, Gulf of California and Ecuador.

Conus brunneus

Conus princeps

Conus varius form *hwassi*

Conus purpurascens

SUBGENUS: CHELYCONUS

C. purpurascens

Sowerby 1833 *Pacific coast of Mexico and Panama, 2in (50mm).* A very variable shell but generally heavy and rather squat. Basically a blue-black color, but with white-blue cloudy markings and some brown markings.

C. achatinus

Gmelin 1791 *Indian and east Pacific Oceans, 2.2in (55mm).*
Variable throughout its range but invariably handsome.
It has convex sides, is lightly striated, has rounded shoulders
and a moderately high spire. The background color of pale
blue has dark brown clouding and the striations are a darker
brown, generally as dots across the blue and unbroken lines
across the brown.

C. catus

Hwass 1792 *Red Sea across the Indian and Pacific Oceans
to Hawaii, 1.6in (40mm).*
A common shell and naturally very variable, it is squat with
cloudy brown or olive-yellow markings on a pale or white
background. Two specimens are illustrated, one markedly
granulated which is from the Tuamotu Archipelago in the
south Pacific, and the other almost smooth from east Africa.

Other members of the subgenus include: *C. ranunculus*
Hwass 1792 from the West Indies, *C. fulmen* Reeve 1843
from Japan, *C. monachus* L. 1758 from the Pacific, *C. nigrop-
unctatus* Sowerby 1857 also from the Pacific – all these have
some resemblance to *C. achatinus;* and *C. orion* Broderip
1833 and *C. vittatus* Hwass 1792, both from the west Central
American coast and both with a central band of white with
dark markings on a variable background of white, orange
and lilac to brown, with dark markings on the spire.

Conus achatinus

Conus catus

SUBGENUS: LEPTOCONUS

C. sculletti

Marsh 1962, *1.6in (40mm).*
This recently discovered species from deep water off Cape
Moreton, Queensland, though rare, is included both as
an example of the fact that new species continue to be
discovered, and also for its unusual and attractive shape. It is
narrow for its length with sharp shoulders, and is slightly
waisted near the tip. It has a creamy white background
encircled with tan bands, dots and flamelike markings.

Conus sculletti

271

C. thalassiarchus

Sowerby 1834 *Philippines and north Borneo, 3.5in (90mm)*.
Like most of the subgenus, a very handsome shell.
It has a rather flat top and a small spire. The creamy
white background is closely patterned with wavy, axial
lines, usually light but sometimes dark brown, and
generally with cream bands at the shoulder and waist,
with a blue-black tip and dark markings on the top.

C. ammiralis

L. 1758 *East Indian and west
Pacific Oceans, 2.4in (60mm)*.
To me, the most beautiful of
the cones, though somewhat
variable. It is straight-sided
with a high, concave spire. The
body whorl is a rich red of
varying depths of color with
three bands of pale yellow,
one at the shoulder, one in
the middle, and one at the tip;
the whole is covered with pale
white tent marks, varying
from about 0.2in (5mm) across
down to minute; the shoulder is
white with red-brown markings
and the top has areas of pale
red-brown crossed with dark,
axial lines.

Conus thalassiarchus

Conus ammiralis

C. generalis

L. 1767 *Indo-Pacific, 3.5in (90mm)*.
A common species and very variable. Its rather
flat top carries a sharp, concave spire. It is darker
or lighter brown, with white markings, mostly
forming more or less a band at the waist and also
at the shoulder and tip; sometimes with dark
brown, axial lines; top is white with dark brown
streaks. Closely allied are *C. spirogloxus* Deshayes
1863 and *C. maldivus* Hwass 1792 from the west
Indian Ocean, both usually showing more white markings, the latter with a much flatter spire.

C. regularis

Sowerby 1833 *Pacific Central America, 2in (50mm)*.
A common member of the subgenus. Its blue-white back-
ground is covered with purple-gray markings reminiscent of
Arabic script, and it is encircled with rows of small red dots.

C. sozoni

Bartsch 1939 *Florida, 2.9in (75mm)*.
A high, pointed spire, straight sides and a very narrow tip
give this handsome shell an unusual appearance. The lip is
markedly convex. Its white background is encircled with

Conus generalis

Conus regularis

bands of pale yellow-brown and many rows of dots of darker brown which form flamelike markings on the spire.

C. recurvus
Broderip 1833 *Pacific Central America in deep water, 2.4in (60mm).*
Shaped like *C. sozoni* but with a flatter top, it has a white background color with large, dark brown, flamelike markings.

C. floridanus
Gabb 1868 *Florida, 1.6in (40mm).*
A shell similar in shape to the two preceding species though smaller. It is white with yellow to pale brown cloudy markings, and an indefinite white band with a row of dots running through the center.

C. jaspideus
Gmelin 1791 *Southeast coast of America and West Indies, 1in (25mm).*
High spire. Generally like *C. sozoni* in shape but with strong spiral grooves. Cream with irregular dark or light brown markings. Illustrated is a small form of *C. jaspideus*, pigmaeus Reeve 1844, about 0.5in (12mm), from the same area.

Conus jaspideus form pigmaeus

Conus recurvus

Conus floridanus

Conus sozoni

C. floridensis

Sowerby 1870 *Florida, 1.6in (40mm)*.
This is a color form of *C. floridanus* (see page 272) with spiral rows of dots and dashes, usually with much darker clouding than the specimen illustrated. The background color is also usually darker.

C. spurius

Gmelin 1791 *Florida and the Caribbean, 2.8in (70mm)*.
Has a rather flat top with a sharp spire. Its white background is encircled with rows of red dashes which sometimes run together vertically and horizontally. In *C.s. atlanticus* Clench 1942, the dashes do not run together, and sometimes some of the spots are blue-purple.

Conus floridensis

Other members of the subgenus include: *C. amadis* Gmelin 1791, Indian Ocean; *C. clarus* Smith 1881, Western Australia; *C. monile* Hwass 1792, Indian Ocean; *C. acuminatus* Hwass 1792, east Africa; *C. nobilis* L. 1758, Philippines; *C. virgatus* Reeve 1849, Central America; and *C. clerii* Reeve 1844, Brazil.

Conus spurius

Conus augur

Conus daucus

SUBGENUS: DAUCICONUS

C. augur

Solander 1786 *East Africa, 2.8in (70mm)*.
Solid, heavy, rather unlike any other of this subgenus. Flat spire. Oatmeal color, profusely banded with rows of very small dark purple-brown spots and two bands of irregular blotches of the same color.

C. daucus

Hwass 1792 *Caribbean, 2in (50mm)*.
Normally a red-yellow overall, but in its variety *C. luteus* Krebs 1864 it is much more yellow and shows a faint pale band. The specimen illustrated is a rare red form.

C. planorbis

Born 1780 *Pacific Ocean, 2.9in (75mm).*

Like others of the subgenus the shell varies considerably in color pattern and shape. It varies from a plain brown-yellow through bands of darker or lighter shades of this color (as illustrated) to specimens with much more striking banding and dark markings, not unlike *C. striatellus.* The tip is purple.

Conus planorbis

C. striatellus

Link 1807 *Indian Ocean, 2.9in (75mm).*
A synonym is *C. pulchrelineatus* Hopwood 1921. The name *C. lineatus* Hwass 1792 is also frequently used, but incorrectly as the name is preoccupied. Very variable but often a handsome shell. Generally white, with brown banding and dark flame markings on the shoulder and spire.

Conus striatellus

C. circumactus

Iredale 1929 *Pacific Ocean, 1.6in (40mm).*
Variable. Light brown, the shoulder and banding being white or with a pale mauve tinge; brown flame markings on or across the back and shoulders on to the rather flat spire.

Conus circumactus

275

C. litoglyphus

Hwass 1792 *Indo-Pacific, 2.6in (65mm).*
One of the most striking of the subgenus and less variable than most. The red-gold background has an irregular central band of pure white and another white band at the shoulder streaked with the background color, which also flecks the spire; anteriorly the body whorl has about five rows of granules; tip is purple. The specimen illustrated is a small one.

Also in the subgenus are: C. fulmineus Gmelin 1791, northeast Australia; C. furvus Reeve 1843, Philippines; and C. vitulinus Hwass 1792, Indo-Pacific.

Conus litoglyphus

SUBGENUS: PIONOCONUS

Mostly narrow shells which are striate anteriorly.

C. magus

L. 1758 *Indo-Pacific, centered on the Philippines, 3in (80mm).*
The cone collector's nightmare, with a very wide variety of forms in shape, color and pattern. Some have specific rank, while others are only varieties. Among them are *C. ustulatus* Reeve 1844, *C. raphanus* Hwass 1792 and *C. circae* Sowerby 1858.

C. suturatus

Reeve 1844 *Pacific from East Indies to Hawaii, 1.2in (30mm).*
Chubby, little shell with a rather flat top and sharp spire. Pale pink with three, broad, faint, yellow-brown bands and a violet tip.

Conus suturatus

Conus magus

Subgenus includes: *C. mercator* L. 1758, west Africa; *C. ximenes* Gray 1839 and *C. perplexus* Sowerby 1857, west Central America; *C. erythraeensis* Reeve 1843, Red Sea; *C. pertusus* Hwass 1792, Pacific; *C. consors* Sowerby 1833, Singapore; *C. mozambicus* Hwass 1792 and *C. simplex* Sowerby 1857/8, South Africa.

SUBGENUS: PHASMOCONUS

A small group from central and southwest Pacific plus one from the Indian Ocean and one from South Africa. They have an elevated striate spire, a body whorl usually of one color and are deeply grooved anteriorly.

C. carinatus

Swainson 1822 *Philippines, 3in (80mm).*
A species within the *C. magus* complex, despite its subgeneric placing. Brown-yellow with indiscrete white band and white blotches below shoulder.

Conus carinatus

Subgenus includes: *C. radiatus* Gmelin 1791, Philippines, New Guinea; *C. infrenatus* Reeve 1848, South Africa; *C. keatii* Sowerby 1858, Red Sea, Seychelles.

SUBGENUS: RHIZOCONUS
Large shells with broad shoulders, sometimes sharply angled, sometimes rounded; often nearly as wide as they are long.

C. vexillum
Gmelin 1791 *Indian Ocean and central and south Pacific, 7in (180mm).*
One of the large cones, somewhat variable in shape and markings. May have rounded or sharply angled shoulders. Basically brown with white bands on body whorl and shoulders usually broken up to form white blotches; sometimes streaked axially with black.

Conus capitaneus

Conus vexillum

C. capitaneus
L. 1758 *Indo-Pacific, 2.6in (65mm).*
Brown often with yellow or green tinge; white band on body whorl and shoulder; black and white checkered effect on spire spills over shoulders; lines of black spots encircle body whorl and border central white band but disappear toward purple tip.

C. rattus
Hwass 1792 *Most of Indo-Pacific, 1.6in (40mm).*
Variable. Shoulders either rounded or angled. Body whorl brown or green-brown with band, more or less discrete, of blue-white, horizontal flecks, blue-white shoulder band broken by blotches of body whorl color; spire checkered with both colors.

Conus rattus

277

Conus miles

C. miles

L. 1758 *Indo-Pacific, 3.5in (90mm).*
Much less variable than others of the subgenus. White background color is covered with fine, axial, wavy, light brown lines running from the apex to the base. It has a fairly narrow, dark band on the body whorl within a broader, very light brown band. The anterior quarter or fifth of the body whorl is almost black, bordered by progressively lighter bands up to one-third of its length.

Others in the subgenus include: *C. mustelinus* Hwass 1792, Indo-Pacific; *C. capitanellus* Fulton 1938, Japan; *C. namocanus* Hwass 1792 and *C. laevigatus* Sowerby 1857, Indian Ocean; and *C. trigonus* Reeve 1848, northwest Australia.

SUBGENUS: VIRGICONUS
Rather narrow shells. Body whorl slightly striate, especially anteriorly. One color with purple tinge at the base.

Conus virgo

L. 1758 *Indo-Pacific, 6in (150mm).*
A heavy shell, straight-sided, with a dull, almost matt surface. It is pale yellow with a purple tip, and is a sand dweller.

Conus virgo   *Conus emaciatus*   *Conus flavidus*

C. emaciatus

Reeve 1849 *Indo-Pacific, 2in (50mm).*
Has concave sides and the body whorl is finely ridged overall. It is pale yellow with a purple tip and is a reef dweller.

C. flavidus

Lamarck 1810 *Indo-Pacific, 2.6in (65mm).*
Usually a yellow-brown with a narrow white band and a pale top and shoulders. It has a purple tip and interior.

SUBGENUS: GASTRIDIUM

Thin, light shells with faint striae and a coronated spire. The lower half of the columella is concave making a very wide aperture anteriorly.

C. geographus

L. 1758 *Indo-Pacific, 6in (150mm).*
Its background brown color is clouded with some white tent marks and blotches; darker brown blotches, some forming two broken bands on body whorl. It has a poisonous sting known to have been fatal to man.

C. obscurus

Sowerby 1833 *Indo-Pacific, 2.6in (65mm).*
Shaped like a miniature *C. geographus* but shoulder often has small coronations. It is red-brown with very pale purple markings, roughly forming two bands. The Hawaiian variety is *C. halitropus* Bartsch, Rehder and Greene 1953.

Conus obscurus

SUBGENUS: REGICONUS

Large shells, cylindrical in shape with rounded shoulders and a turbinate spire. Their brown background color is covered with white tent marks.

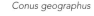

Conus geographus

C. aulicus

L. 1758 *Indo-Pacific, 5in (125mm).*
A very handsome shell, solid and somewhat inflated. Its dark or light brown background color is covered with small and/or large white tent marks.

Others in the subgenus include: *C. auratus* Hwass 1792 from Polynesia; and *C. aureus* Hwass 1792 from the east Pacific and Indian Oceans.

Conus aulicus

SUBGENUS: DARIOCONUS

The sides of the spire are more or less concave and the apex has a very small, sharp point. Markings are similar to those of the *Regiconus*.

C. omaria

Hwass 1792 *Pacific Ocean and the East Indies, 3in (80mm).*
Variable within the overall subgenus description both in shape of spire, color, size and number of tent marks.

C. episcopus

Hwass 1792 *3.5in (90mm).*
Long, narrow form of *C. omaria.* A synonym for those with high spire and red-tinged tent marks is *C. magnificus* Reeve 1843.

Conus omaria   Conus episcopus   Conus pennaceus

C. pennaceus

Born 1758 *Indo-Pacific, from the Red Sea to Hawaii, 2in (50mm).*
Variable both in shape, color and tent marks. The shell illustrated is a much lighter brown than the average.

Others in the subgenus include: *C. stellatus* Kiener 1849; *C.*

elisae Kiener 1849; and *C. praelatus* Born 1792 from east Africa.

SUBGENUS: CYLINDER

Cylindrical with a pointed, sharp spire. Background color golden yellow to red-brown, with dark wavy axial lines and white tent marks overall.

C. textile

L. 1758 *Indo-Pacific,*
3in (80mm).
Tends to be rather inflated below the shoulder and tapers to a narrow base. The illustrations show the wide variation in color and size of tentmarks. The latter leave random patches of the background color and axial lines. Closely related species are: *C. cholmondelyi* Melville 1800, east Africa; *C. archiepiscopus* Hwass 1792, east Australia west-ward across the Indian Ocean to east Africa; *C. verriculum* Reeve 1843, Indian Ocean; *C. scriptus* Sowerby 1858, east Africa; and *C. natalis* Sowerby, South Africa.

Conus textile

Conus textile

C. victoriae

Reeve 1843 *Western Australia to East Indies, 1.6in (40mm).*
A light, small shell with very fine, white tent marks leaving two bands of the back-ground red-brown color, and axial lines. Closely related are: *C. abbas* Hwass 1792, Indian Ocean; *C. complanatus* Sowerby 1866, Western Australia; *C. panniculus* Lamarck 1810, East Indies; and *C. dalli* Stearns 1873, west Central America. These shells are generally smaller than the preceding members, though otherwise similar.

Conus victoriae

C. tigrinus

Sowerby 1858 *Australasia and Melanesia, 2in (50mm).*
A heavy shiny shell with small tent marks and no axial lines. Other members of the subgenus closely related to *C. tigrinus* are *C. pyramidalis* Lamarck 1810, east Africa; and *C. legatus* Lamarck 1810 from the Admiralty Islands. Both are solid and have a high gloss.

Conus tigrinus

281

Conus retifer

C. retifer

Menke 1829 *Japan, the north Pacific to east Africa, 1.8in (45mm).*
Solid and rather pyriform. The background tan color has heavy, dark, axial lines and rather sparse, small tent marks, and an indiscrete darker band.

Also in the subgenus is *C. lucidus* Wood 1828 from the west Central American coast.

SUBGENUS: CLEOBULA

Heavy pyriform shells of one color or with lines of dots or dashes. Growth marks often conspicuous on the body whorl.

C. suratensis

Hwass 1792 *Philippines, 3.3in (85mm).*
Flesh-colored encircled with many lines of fine, dark, purple dots and dashes.

Conus suratensis

Conus genuanus

C. genuanus

L. 1758 *West Africa, 2.8in (70mm).*
Less wide at the shoulder in relation to its length than most of the subgenus. It is a most handsome shell with a clouded pink-mauve background color and two light brown bands. The encircling lines are made up alternately of small dots and dashes, and larger dashes, dots and blotches of black with white spaces between. Below the lower brown band the lines are only of small dots and dashes.

C. glaucus
L. 1758 *Philippines and New Guinea, 1.8in (45mm).*
A small member of the subgenus. Pale gray with many encircling lines of dark brown dashes.

C. figulinus
L. 1758 *Indo-Pacific, 3in (80mm).*
Typically shaped. Brown; darker on the spire; with many encircling, unbroken, darker brown lines.

C. betulinus
L. 1758 *Red Sea, Indian and Pacific Oceans, 6in (150mm).*
The largest of the subgenus. Its brown-yellow background color is overlaid with lines of sparse purple-brown dots.

Conus glaucus

Conus figulinus

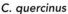

Conus betulinus

C. quercinus
Solander 1786 *Indo-Pacific, 2.9in (75mm).*
A heavy, solid and common shell. It is bright pale yellow to light tan, the color often varying on the same shell both axially and horizontally.

Also in the subgenus are: *C. patricius* Hinds 1843 and *C. fergusoni* Sowerby 1873 from west Central America; and *C. loroisii* Kiener 1847 from East Indies and Sri Lanka.

Conus quercinus

SUBGENUS: STRIOCONUS

Members of this group have channeled whorls on the spire and a tapered shoulder, striated body whorls and are colorful and brightly patterned.

C. striatus

L. 1758 *Indo-Pacific, 4.75in (120mm)*.
Common and variable within the subgeneric description. Pink-white with blotches of purple-gray or brown.

Others in the subgenus are: *C. gubernator* Hwass 1792 from east Africa; *C. terminus* Lamarck 1810 from the Red Sea; *C. floccatus* Sowerby 1839 from central Pacific; and *C. epistomium* Reeve 1844 from Mauritius.

SUBGENUS: TEXTILIA

Swollen, smooth shells; striae on the rather flat tops. Mostly uncommon.

Conus spectrum

L. 1758 *East Indies, east, north and west Australia, 2.6in (65mm)*.
Synonym *C. pica* A. Adams and Reeve 1848. White with brown or purple-brown markings covering the shell. These are sometimes as blotches, as in the illustration of the small form *pica,* and sometimes also with axial, wavy lines.

Conus striatus

Others in the subgenus are: *C. adamsonii* Broderip 1836 – perhaps better known as *C. rhododendron* – long one of the cones most coveted by the collector, from the Phoenix Islands; *C. bullatus* L. 1758 from midPacific to the Indian Ocean; *C. nimbosus* Hwass 1792 from the north Indian Ocean; *C. conspersus* Reeve 1844 from the Philippines and Australia; and *C. peronianus* Iredale 1931 from New South Wales.

Conus spectrum
form pica

Conus anemone

SUBGENUS: FLORACONUS

Short stocky shells from southeast, south and southwest Australia and South Africa.

Conus anemone

Lamarck 1810 *Victoria, south and Western Australia, 2in (50mm).* Often known in its banded form as *C. novaehollandiae* Adams 1854 from Western Australia. Variable in shape and color pattern, but basically with dark brown and pale blue, much intermingled.

Conus rosaceus

Dillwyn 1817 *Southeast Africa, 1.6in (40mm).*
A beautiful red color form of *C. tinianus* Hwass 1792 with a band of white, and darker red blotches.

Others in the subgenus are: *C. singletoni* Cotton 1945 and *C. segravei* Gatliff 1891 from Victoria to Western Australia; *C. apluster* Reeve 1843, *C. wallangra* Garrard 1961 and *C. papilliferus* Sowerby 1834 from New South Wales; *C. compressus* Sowerby 1866 from south Australia; *C. cyanostoma* A. Adams 1954 and *C. coxeni* Brazier 1875 from Queensland; and from South Africa *C. tinianus* Hwass 1792-of which *C. rosaceus, C. inflatus* Sowerby 1833, *C. aurora* Lamarck 1810 and *C. caffer* Krauss 1848 are all color forms.

Conus rosaceus

Conus nussatella

SUBGENUS: HERMES

Narrow, often spindle-shaped shells, with short spires and lirate body whorls – the lirae being finely granular.

Conus nussatella

L. 1758 *Indo-Pacific, 2.8in (70mm).*
Heavy for its size; short but acuminate spire. White-brown blotches and many rows of fine, red-brown dots and vertical dashes arranged in vertical and horizontal rows.

C. terebra

Born 1780 *Indian, west and central Pacific Oceans, 4in (100mm).*
Synonym *C. clavus* L. 1758. A large, heavy shell tapering to a narrow base and with coarse, horizontal ridges. White with two purple or pale yellow bands, a purple tip and purple lines below the sutures.

Others in the subgenus include: *C. tendineus* Hwass 1792, South Africa and its islands; *C. lautus* Reeve 1844, South Africa; *C. luteus* Sowerby 1833, north half of Australia; *C. auricomus* Hwass 1792 from the Indian Ocean-the only member of the subgenus to carry tent marks; *C. granulatus* L. 1758 from the Caribbean; *C. circumcisus* Born 1778 from the East Indies; and *C. aurisiacus* L. 1758, a most handsome shell also from the East Indies.

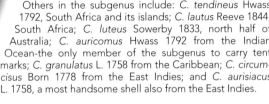

Conus terebra

Conus tulipa

SUBGENUS: TULIPARIA

Somewhat similar to the subgenus *Gastridium*. The shell is thin, swollen and smooth with a faintly coronated spire. The posterior half of the columella is concave, giving a wide lower half to the aperture.

Conus tulipa

L. 1758 *Central Pacific to Australia, 2.4in (60mm).*
It is sky blue with dark brown clouding, and encircling lines of tiny brown dots.

The only other member of the subgenus is *C. borbonicus* H. Adams 1808 from Mauritius to French Polynesia.

SUBGENUS: LAUTOCONUS

Conus ventricosus
Gmelin 1791 *Mediterranean, east Atlantic and the Red Sea, 1.6in (40mm).*
A very variable shell with many synonyms, but the only cone found in the Mediterranean Sea. Chunky, usually rather drab with brown markings over a pale background color.

Also in the subgenus is *C. californicus* Reeve 1844, off the Californian coast. Both these species occur in relatively cold waters for members of *Conus.*

SUBGENUS: LEPORICONUS
Somewhat similar to *Hermes*, but more pyriform. The body whorl bears coarse, granular lirae.

Conus ventricosus

Conus mitratus

Conus glans

Conus mitratus
Hwass 1792 *Indian Ocean to Queensland, 1.2in (30mm).*
Spindle-shaped and aptly named as it looks superficially like a miter shell. It has a very high spire, the whole being yellow-brown covered with three bands of smudged, dark brown, square blotches, which show on the whorls of the spire.

C. glans
Hwass 1792 *Indonesia and west Pacific, 2in (50mm).*
Rather variable but generally stubby and solid. Purple tip and streaks over a white background color and sometimes with cream-brown banding.

Others in the subgenus are: *C. tenuistriatus* Sowerby 1858 from East Indies; *C. coccineus* Gmelin 1791, a beautiful red-orange shell from southwest Pacific; *C. cylindraceus* Broderip and Sowerby 1830, Indo-Pacific, but rare; and *C. scrabriusculus* Dillwyn 1817, southwest Pacific.

SUBGENUS: ENDEMECONUS

Acute spire with a raised ridge on the sharply angled shoulder which forms a spiral ridge on the spire. Tapers to a narrow base.

Conus ione

Fulton 1938 *Japan, 2.6in (65mm).*
White encircled with rows of orange-brown dots and two bands of orange-brown blotches. The dots become lines across the shoulder and on the spire.

Conus sieboldi

Reeve 1848 *Japan, 3in (80mm).*
Larger than *C. ione* and much longer in relation to its shoulder width. It has the characteristic spire of the subgenus and is pure white with a few brown blotches, mainly forming a central

Conus ione

band on the body whorls and a more indefinite band below the shoulder.

Others in the subgenus are: *C. howelli* Iredale 1929 from New South Wales; and *C. villepinii* Fischer and Bernardi 1857 from the Gulf of Mexico.

SUBGENUS: CONASPRELLA

A high pointed spire and a sharply angled shoulder, tapering to a narrow base. The body whorl is encircled with grooves and fine axial striations.

Conus cancellatus

Hwass 1792 *Japan, 1.8in (45mm).*
The body whorl white and slightly swollen below the shoulder. From the shoulder to the preceding whorl on the spire it is concave, so forming a spiral groove to the apex. This groove has brown blotches.

C. acutangulus

Lamarck 1810 *Philippines to Hawaii, 1in (25mm).*

Conus sieboldi

A solid, little shell, sharply pointed at both ends. The spire is about one-third the length of the shell. White flecked with brown, forming spiral broken bands.

Conus cancellatus

Conus acutangulus　　　　*Conus sowerbii*

C. sowerbii
Reeve 1849 *Philippines, 1.2in (30mm).*
Spire almost as long as the body whorl. Brown encircled with rows of white dots and dashes.

Also in the subgenus are: *C. austini* Rehder and Abbott 1951 from east Central America; *C. kieneri* Reeve 1849 from Japan; and *C. verrucosus* Hwass 1792 from the Caribbean.

SUBGENUS: ASPRELLA
Sharp spire; edges of the whorls ridged; sharply angled shoulders. Body whorl tapering to a point and encircled with grooves.

Conus orbignyi
Audouin 1831 *Japan, 2.8in (70mm).*
The shoulder angle carries small tubercles which on the earlier whorls show on the spire. It is deeply grooved and is a medium brown with some dark brown banding.

Conus orbignyi

Others in the subgenus are: *C. sulatus* Hwass 1792 from southeast Asia; *C. australis* Holten 1820 from North China Sea; *C. laterculatus* Sowerby 1870 from Australia and East Indies.

SUBGENUS: DYRASPIS
Contains one species.

Conus dorreensis
Peron 1807 *Western Australia, 1in (25mm).*
Better known by its synonym *C. pontificalis* Lamarck 1810. It is unlike any other cone, being short, stubby and heavy for its size. The shoulder and spire are heavily coronated. The tip and coronations are a dull white; the remainder green.

Conus dorreensis

Terebra crenulata　　　*Terebra areolata*

FAMILY: TEREBRIDAE

The auger shells; of which there are some 150 species, are all long and narrow with a high, pointed spire and many whorls. They have rather small apertures with a simple lip and usually a plait on the columella. The sculpture is variable from smooth to ribbed, curved or noduled. They have thin horny opercula. The animals live in sand and are carnivorous, inhabiting tropical and semitropical seas. They often move just below the surface of the sand, leaving well-defined trails, and a handful of sand scooped up at the end of such a trail will usually reward the collector. They have no periostracum, and moving through sand they are clean and shiny when taken alive.

Terebra crenulata

L. 1758 *Indo-Pacific, 4.75in (120mm).* Solid. Shoulders with small nodules, about fifteen on body whorl, and a slight constriction below the nodules which becomes obsolete on the later whorls; early whorls with axial plicae giving way to fine growth lines anteriorly. Almost smooth columella; short but strong fasciole. Uneven oatmeal color; nodules white; three or four spiral rows of red-brown dots on body whorl, two showing on other whorls; small fine streaks of the same color between the nodules.

T. subulata

L. 1767 *Indo-Pacific, 6in (150mm).* Slender with some twenty-five whorls; two rows of small nodules divided by a fine groove immediately below the suture on early whorls; these become obsolete on later whorls. Otherwise smooth and shiny apart from fine growth lines. Twisted columella; small fasciole. Cream with three spiral rows of squarish, dark brown blotches on the body whorl, two of which show on the others.

T. areolata

Link 1807 *Indo-Pacific, 4.75in (120mm).* Less slender than the preceding species. About twenty whorls, earlier axially plicate, later with faint growth lines. A slight constriction below the suture forms a second 'shoulder' on each whorl and divides the whorls into approximately one-third above and two-thirds below the constriction. Aperture less 'square' than that of *T. subulata*; small but strong fasciole. Cream with four spiral rows of squarish, medium brown blotches on body whorl, three showing on other whorls; the squares in the anterior row are about four times the size of the others.

T. dimidiata
L. 1758 *Indo-Pacific, 4.75in (120mm)*.
Fairly solid and smooth and shiny. About twenty whorls, early whorls axially plicate, later ones with fine growth striae. A groove below the suture as in *T. areolata*. Rather elongate aperture and lip a little flared anteriorly. Columella with a weak plait and rather straight; strong fasciole. Orange-red with wavy white streaks, often bifurcating posteriorly.

T. guttata
Röding 1798 *Indo-Pacific, 5.5in (140mm)*.
Solid with about twenty-one whorls. A ridge and a fine groove bordering it below the suture in the early whorls giving way to blunt, very low knobs on later whorls, and a similar row on anterior end of the body whorl. Rectangular aperture; weak fasciole. Cream brown; early ridge and later knobs white.

Terebra subulata

Terebra dimidiata

Terebra guttata

291

Terebra commaculata

Gmelin 1791 *North and east Indian Ocean and west Pacific, 3in (80mm).*

Long and narrow with twenty-five or more whorls. Two bands of nodules below the suture are divided by a narrow groove; below these are smaller, spiral ridges – about eighteen on the penultimate whorl – and smaller, rather curved axial riblets, giving a somewhat cancellate effect. Rectangular aperture; parietal wall at almost 90° to columella. White with axial, rather rectangular, brown flame marks, about six per whorl anteriorly, the number reducing to three in about a dozen whorls, beyond which they become indistinct.

T. variegata

Gray 1834 *Tropical west America, 3.3in (85mm).*

Quite a stout, strong shell with an overall malleate appearance. Below the suture a band of uneven, rather coarse nodules, below which are weak, uneven, axial riblets, with or without spiral grooves. Aperture is scimitar-shaped and columella recurved with two plaits. Blue-gray with axial, brown dashes split by a white band which may just show above the suture on early whorls; subsutural band white with square brown blotches.

T. maculata

L. 1758 *Indo-Pacific, 10in (250mm).*

The largest of the genus, strong and heavy. About eighteen whorls, the early ones axially plicate, the later ones smooth except for growth lines. Rather wide aperture; parietal wall at about 120° to the columella, which has a weak fold; small but strong fasciole with a central groove. White with spiral bands – about five on body whorl – of pale tan, axially aligned, rectangular blotches and two spiral bands of irregular, purple-brown blotches on the posterior half of each whorl – that part which shows above the suture.

Terebra commaculata

Terebra variegata

Terebra maculata

T. robusta

Hinds 1844 *Baja California, Panama and the Galapagos, 5.5in (140mm).*
More or less narrow. Early whorls with nodulose, subsutural band and axial plications, all of which become obsolete on later whorls and are replaced by faint spiral striae and axial growth lines. Somewhat rectangular aperture; twisted, recurved columella. White with creamy clouding; about four spiral rows of axially aligned, dark brown rectangular blotches which may merge to form two or even one row on spire whorls.

T. strigata

Sowerby 1825 *Gulf of California and Galapagos, 4.75in (120mm).*
The largest of the west American augers, it is solid and heavy. Angle at apex is wide, though not as great as in *T. maculata.* Early whorls with slightly wavy, axial plications and subsutural groove; plications disappear well before the body whorl and groove becomes obsolete. Coarse growth lines; body whorl rather long, as is the aperture; smooth columella is only at a slight angle to the parietal wall; rather coarse fasciole. Creamy white with dark chestnut axial flames.

Duplicaria duplicata

L. 1758 *Indo-west Pacific, 3.5in (90mm).*
Moderately narrow with many whorls; axial plicae on early whorls become flattish ribs on later whorls which may also be slightly inflated. Sharply defined subsutural groove, giving a broad subsutural band. Wide aperture with a deep narrow notch; slightly recurved columella; fasciole with a strong ridge. Variable in color; may be as illustrated – blue-gray, rusty brown clouding and faint, short, axial streaks of darker gray – or unicolored, dark brown, orange-pink, cream or white, or varieties of these with other markings, but usually with a rather opaque shine.

Terebra robusta

Duplicaria duplicata

Terebra strigata

293

Terebra monilis

Quoy & Gaimard 1832 *West Pacific, 2in (50mm).*
Subsutural row of nodules bounded by a sharply incised line; rest of surface smooth but uneven; rectangular aperture. Pale orange tan; nodules white. Note: W. O. Cernohorsky has pointed out that *monilis* is preoccupied and should be replaced.

T. nebulosa

Sowerby 1825 *Indo-Pacific, 2.9in (75mm).*
Subsutural groove; slightly wavy, tight-set, axial grooves; much smaller, spiral grooves; rectangular aperture. White; irregular, squarish, orange-red blotches; band of same color at anterior end of body whorl; aperture same.

Terebra monilis

Terebra nebulosa

Terebra ornata

Terebra felina

Terebra succincta

Terebra pertusa

T. ornata

Gray 1834 *Gulf of California and Galapagos, 3in (80mm).*
Groove below suture; early whorls nodulose above suture; columella twisted with two plicae. Brown-cream; spiral rows of squarish, dark brown spots on body whorl, two or sometimes three showing on earlier whorls; top row between groove and suture.

T. felina

Dillwyn 1817 *Indo-Pacific, 3.5in (90mm).*
Groove below suture becoming obsolete on last whorls, as does fine, axial ribbing. Cream or white; row of well-spaced, small, brown spots above suture; row of small spots anteriorly on body whorl.

Terebra anilis

T. succincta

Gmelin 1791 *Pacific and Indonesia, 1.2in (30mm).*
Groove below suture, nodulose between; axially ribbed; fasciole with low ridge. Dark brown; shiny nodules a shade lighter.

T. pertusa
Born 1780 *Indo-Pacific, 2.9in (75mm)*.
Nodulose band below suture; early whorls axially ribbed; on last whorls ribs become obsolete; spiral, incised lines in interstices on early whorls giving cancellate structure with obsolete ribs on last whorls. Pale yellow to orange; sutural band white; short purple streaks between many of nodules; light band anteriorly on body whorl.

T. anilis
Röding 1798 *Philippines to Samoa, 2.9in (75mm)*.
Row of strong, oblique nodules; second row of small nodules below suture; weak, axial ribbing is cut by spiral grooves, about seven on penultimate whorl. Tan; rows of nodules lighter.

Duplicaria bernardi
Deshayes 1857 *East Australia, 1.6in (40mm)*.
Deeply indented suture and subsutural groove; axial ribs overall. Red-brown; blue-white band on center of body whorls shows just above sutures on earlier whorls; ribs on sutural band, especially near suture, blue-white.

Duplicaria bernardi

Hastula lanceata
L. 1767 *Indo-Pacific, 2.4in (60mm)*.
Slender, graceful; axial ribs on early whorls become obsolete anteriorly. Narrow aperture; columella concave posteriorly, recurved anteriorly; weak fasciole. Shiny white; thin, wavy, axial, red-brown lines, broken on body whorl by white band.

Hastula lanceata

Hastula diversa

H. diversa
E. A. Smith 1901 *Pacific, 1.2in (30mm)*.
Axial ribs. Purple-brown to orange with white band below suture on which there are dark brown spots, about eight on body whorl; narrow, white band at posterior end of body whorl.

Impages hectica
L. 1758 *Indo-Pacific, 3in (80mm)*.
Smooth; callous near suture; smooth columella; fasciole with central groove. White or cream; slightly broken purple band below suture; columella brown.

Impages confusa

Impages confusa
Smith *Northwest Pacific, 0.8in (20mm)*.
Growth lines and weak ribs below suture. Combination of purple and waxy white, from nearly all purple to nearly all white; when purple, a small white area with tiny purple spots below suture.

Impages hectica

FAMILY: TURRIDAE

The turrids form one of the biggest families of mollusks; some 1200 species are known. Found in all seas in deep and shallow water. Many are very small. Generally have a turret-shaped spire, extended siphonal canal, and a notch, slit or sinus in the posterior half of the lip. Like the Conidae and Terebridae they use a dartlike tooth to harpoon and poison their prey.

Micantapex lühdorfi

Micantapex lühdorfi

Lischke 1872 *Japan, 1.6in (40mm).*
Moderate spire; short, broad siphonal canal. Shoulder has rounded nodules, row of smaller ones below suture; about three, fine, spiral ridges in concave area between rows of nodules. About eight, larger, spiral ridges from shoulder to top of siphonal canal, twelve, small ones from there to tip of canal; sinus at end of shoulder ridge; thin lip. Light brown; interior, columella white.

Turris crispa

Lamarck 1816 *Madagascar to Fiji, including India, Japan, Indonesia, Philippines, north Australia, 6in (150mm).*
High spire; long siphonal canal. Posterior end of aperture is marginally nearer anterior end than apex of spire. Sculptured with spiral ridges of varying height and width, that ending in sinus flat, others pointed; fine, lamellate, spiral threads in interstices. White or cream profusely covered with axial, dull chocolate dashes, tending to align themselves especially on body whorl and siphonal canal; in older specimens axial dashes tend to form wider blotches and lose the axially lined effect; aperture white. Shell is variable and gives rise to subspecies: *T.c. variegata* Kiener 1839, India; *T.c. yeddoensis* Joussaume 1883, Japan; *T.c. intricata* Powell 1964.

Turris crispa

Lophiotoma acuta

Perry 1811 *Indo-Pacific, 2.6in (65mm).*
Synonym tigrina Lamarck 1822. Variable, typically with high spire and long, straight canal – relatively shorter than *T. crispa*. Spirally ridged; two, strong ridges with narrow, dividing channel on shoulder protruding strongly, and moderately large ones either side of deep suture; other ridges and threads generally small and finely beaded. Sinus at end of strong shoulder ridge. White speckled with small, dark brown dots, most prominent on main ridges but with smaller specks on lesser ridges and threads; aperture creamy white.

Thatcheria mirabilis

Angas 1877 *Japan, 4in (100mm).*
One of the most fascinating of all shells. About eight whorls with very angular shoulders and small carina. Wide area from shoulder to suture is slightly concave and angle at suture is close to 90°; this presutural area spirals up the shell like a ramp. Body narrows sharply to wide, open siphonal canal.

Lophiotoma acuta

Thatcheria mirabilis   *Polystira albida*   *Turricula javana*

Wide aperture; simple, thin lip; and slightly concave and extended columella. Smooth but with very fine, spiral threads and weak growth lines. Pinky tan to tan; interior white.

Polystira albida
Perry 1811 *Gulf of Mexico and West Indies, 4in (100mm).*
High spire and long siphonal canal. Strong, spiral ridges and threads; largest ridge is at shoulder, ending at short sinus. White; thin, brown periostracum.

Turricula javana
L. 1767 *North Indian Ocean and South China Sea, 2.9in (75mm).*
High spire and moderately long. At times rather twisted siphonal canal. Shoulder carries obliquely set nodules, longer than wide. Two, small, spiral ridges below suture. Strong spiral threads from shoulder to end of siphonal canal. Wide sinus from shoulder to suture. Light tan to dark purple-brown; nodules lighter.

Drillia suturalis
Gray *Southeast Asia, 1.4in (35mm).*
High spire, short siphonal canal. Shoulders with slightly oblique nodules, longer than wide. Small ridge below suture; strong, spiral threads overall. Brown; nodules, threads white.

Drillia suturalis

SUPERFAMILY: ACTEONACEA

FAMILY: HYDATINIDAE

Thin, fragile with sunken apex. Large, inflated body whorl. Sand dwellers.

Hydatina velum

Gmelin 1790 *South Africa and Mauritius, 2in (50mm).*
Very fragile with flat spire. Suture a deep groove; fine growth lines; wide aperture; thin lip; smooth, slightly callous columella. Waxy white; two, very broad, spiral bands of oblique, axial, close-set, brown lines, both edged on each side with an unbroken, darker brown line; gap between the two bands is narrow.

Hydatina velum

H. albocincta

Van der Hoeven 1839 *Indo-west Pacific, 2.4in (60mm).*
Very thin, fragile; concave spire. Very large aperture; lip extends beyond apex; smooth, thinly callous columella. White or very pale brown; four, broad, spiral bands of curved, axial, brown lines; bands may be edged with narrow lines of brown on white, or white on brown; aperture white; outer color shows through.

Hydatina albocincta

SUPERFAMILY: PHILINACEA

FAMILY: SCAPHANDRIDAE

Scaphander lignarius

L. 1758 *Mediterranean, 2.8in (70mm).*
Thin, moderately strong; sunken apex. Body whorl contracting toward apex and expanding anteriorly; spiral incised lines; fine growth lines. Thin lip, flared anteriorly; smooth, thinly callous columella. Pale yellow-brown; darker periostracum.

Scaphander lignarius

SUPERFAMILY: BULLACE

ATYIDAE

Thin shells with deeply sunken spire. Sand dwellers.

Atys cylindricus

Atys cylindricus

Hinds 1779 *Indo-Pacific, 1.2in (30mm)*. Thin, fragile, subcylindrical with sunken spire. Lip extends beyond apex of shell. Body whorl with incised spiral lines at each end, smooth in middle; fine growth lines. Aperture narrow posteriorly, wide anteriorly; thin lip; smooth columella. White or very light brown and may have a few, axial, brown hair lines.

FAMILY: BULLIDAE

Bubble shells, related to Atyidae, have a deep narrow umbilicus at the apex.

Bulla ampulla

L. 1758 *Indo-Pacific, 2.4in (60mm)*. Thin, moderately solid, globose; expanded body whorl. Simple lip, extended posteriorly beyond apex, slightly constricted centrally and expanded anteriorly. Columella, reversed 'S' shape, smooth and thinly callous. Cream; blotches of dark purple-brown; overall clouding of light brown, rarely with two spiral bands; aperture, columellar callus white.

Bulla ampulla

B. striata

Bruguière 1792 *Mediterranean, 1.2in (30mm)*. Thin, delicate, rather narrow. Aperture narrow posteriorly, wide anteriorly. Incised spiral lines at ends of body whorl; smooth centrally bar fine growth lines. Thin lip, slightly constricted centrally, extends beyond apex. Brown-gray; darker, smudged dots and dashes; aperture and smooth, thin columellar callus white.

Bulla striata

B. punctulata

A. Adams 1850 *Pacific, 1.2in (30mm)*.
Similar shape to *B. ampulla* but smaller and more cylindrical. Cream; clouding of brown or gray in two to four spiral bands, generally spotted with squarish chocolate dots smudged to the left and bordered to the right by white spots; aperture, columellar callus white.

Bulla punctulata

Mollusks that have two valves or shells. This and the following pages give just a few examples of this class of mollusks to show something of the variety of shape, size and coloration within the class.

FAMILY: PINNIDAE

Large, fragile shells. The animals live in sand or muddy sand, point anchored into the substrate by a series of hairs called the byssus. Most are long in relation to width, as illustrated, but others are more rounded.

Pinna incurva

Gmelin 1791 *Northeast Indian Ocean and South China Sea to north Australia, 12in (300mm).* Thin, fragile and translucent. Inner layer of the shell is partly nacreous.

FAMILY: ISOGNOMONIDAE

Flattened shells. Hinges have rows of pits into which the joining ligaments fit. They are found in the Indo-Pacific and Atlantic Oceans.

Isognomon isognomum

L. 1758 *Indo-Pacific, 4.75in (120mm).* Both valves very flat. Shape very variable. Blue-gray, usually heavily encrusted; interior pearly white. Strongly anchored by a byssus to mangrove roots, coral and so on.

FAMILY: PTERIIDAE

The wing oysters. Flattened and fragile with hinge projected both ways. Pearly interior. They are edible and rarely produce pearls. They live in tropical to temperate regions and anchor themselves to the bottom.

Pteria levanti

Dunker *Indo-Pacific, 3in (80mm).* Rather inflated on the ventral side. Edge very fragile. Outline like a bird. Light brown with a fine periostracum.

Pinna incurva

FAMILY: ARCIDAE

The ark shells are usually rather oblong with a long, straight hinge on which there are very many, small, subequal, fine teeth. The beaks are hooked and separated from each other. Most anchor themselves by a byssus of hairs. They live worldwide and are edible.

Trisidos tortuosa

L. 1758 *Indo-Pacific, 4.75in (120mm)*.
This shell is unusual and interesting as it is
twisted so that the extremities are at 90°
to each other. There are many fine radial
threads. White.

Anadara maculosa

Reeve *Indo-Pacific, 2.4in (60mm)*.
It is a more normal ark shell. Strongly ribbed and
solid with a thick periostracum as shown in the illustration.

Trisidos tortuosa

Isognomon isognomum

Pteria levanti

FAMILY: GLYCYMERIDAE

Solid, equivalved and rather circular in outline, with a porcellaneous
interior. Always have many teeth on
the curved hinge, larger laterally.
They have a thick periostracum and
are not attached by a byssus. They
are found world-wide and are
generally edible.

Anadara maculosa

Glycymeris glycymeris

L. 1758 *The Dog Cockle,
British and European waters,
up to 2.4in (60mm)*.
Indistinct radial sculpture. Cream
with dark blotches of red-brown,
often in zigzag pattern; variable.

Glycymeris glycymeris

Family: Pectinidae

The scallop shells include many species, often very colorful. They are usually regular in outline either with the right valve convex and the left flat or slightly concave, or more or less equivalved. They are generally sculptured with radiating ribs which sometimes carry small spines. The beak generally has an 'ear' on each side, the anterior larger. They are found worldwide and some species are highly prized as food. They are one of the most popular mollusks to appear in art and used as the symbol of the Royal Dutch/Shell Group are recognized worldwide. They swim, apparently haphazardly, by a rapid opening and shutting of their valves, especially to escape their main predators, starfish.

Decatopecten striatus

Schumacher *Indo-Pacific, 1in (25mm).*
Solid, inflated, somewhat triangular, with about five rather large ribs and many fine radial cords. Unequal ears. White usually marked with pink-brown.

Pecten tranquebaricus

Gmelin 1790 *South China Sea, 1.6in (40mm).*
About twenty radial ribs; not very inflated; uneven ears. White, sometimes with red clouding, and irregular, generally horizontal, black banding.

Decatopecten striatus

Pecten tranquebaricus

Chlamys swifti

Bernardi 1858 *North Pacific, 4in (100mm).*
Large, solid, with five broad ribs which are nodulose where they cross heavy, concentric ridges and fine radial riblets. Somewhat inflated with unequal ears. Attached to rocks by a byssus. Left valve usually shades of purple-red, darker at the nodules; right valve much paler or white with pink bands.

Aequipecten opercularis

L. 1758
The Queen Scallop, Europe, 3in (80mm).
Very rounded, with about twenty ribs. Ears are almost equal. Color variable, yellow, orange, brown, red, pink or purple, and often blotched or spotted.

Chlamys swifti

FAMILY: LIMIDAE

The file clams are generally ovate and somewhat compressed. The anterior side is straighter and the ear smaller. The posterior side is more rounded and the valves usually gape. They are generally radially ribbed and white in color. The Limidae swim quite rapidly by opening and closing their valves and using the long filaments which extend from the margin of the animal.

Lima sowerbyi

Deshayes *Indo-Pacific, 1.6in (40mm)*.
It has about twenty, radial, scaly ribs. White.

Lithophaga teres

Aequipecten opercularis

Lima sowerbyi

FAMILY: MYTILIDAE

The mussels are generally rather elongate, oval or roundly triangular, and fairly thin-shelled. The valves are equal, inflated and have a thick periostracum. The interior is nacreous. They are found worldwide, usually attached by a byssus to rock or other material and often in thick clusters. Some bore into soft rock or coral and some into quite hard material such as limestone. Some species are eaten, especially in the Mediterranean.

Lithophaga teres

Philippi *Indo-Pacific, 2.4in (60mm)*.
Despite boring into rock and coral, it is very thin and fragile. Rather cylindrical with the beaks near the anterior end. It is white with a dark brown periostracum, as illustrated.

Perna viridis

L. *South China Sea, 2in (50mm)*.
A solid shell with a rich, deep green periostracum, a little lighter near the beak where the underlying white of the shell shows through.

Perna viridis

Mytilus perna

L. 1758 *East coast of South Africa, 2.8in (70mm)*.
South Africa's common mussel. Beaks pointed and a little down-turned. Purple-brown; interior blue or yellow.

Mytilus perna

303

FAMILY: CARDIIDAE

The cockles are usually ovate and nearly globular, with radial ribs sometimes carrying lamellae or short spines. The hinge has two central teeth and there are usually one or two lateral teeth on each side of the hinge. They are very active and move about with their long, strong foot. They are found worldwide. Like other burrowing bivalves they provide food for many predators.

Discors lyratum

Discors lyratum

Sowerby 1841 *Indo-Pacific, 2in (50mm)*.
Solid, swollen with strange sculpture in that it has radial riblets, stronger posteriorly, and clear, oblique ridges restricted to the anterior half. The color is also unusual, a rich, slightly purple-red periostracum; white spots more frequent near the white beaks; interior white and yellow; pink in the umbo area.

Cardium costatum

L. 1758 *West Africa, 4in (100mm)*.
Has about ten, strong, hollow, elevated, quite sharp, radiating ribs ending abruptly at the edge of the valves. Posterior end of the shell – the corselet – is rather flattened, has smaller, very rough-topped ribs, and does not close, but 'gapes'. White or off-white; brown or orange between ribs near umbo.

Cardium costatum

Cerastoderma edule

L. 1758 *The European Cockle, Europe, 2.4in (60mm)*.
Equivalved with twenty-five ribs and strong growth lines. Yellow-white to orange-brown; sometimes darker rings. Eaten by man, bird and fish.

FAMILY: GLOSSIDAE

(see also page 308)
These are even more heart-shaped in anterior view than the Cardiidae, with the beaks twisting in a spiral and turning toward the anterior.

Meiocardia moltkiana

Cerastoderma edule

Gmelin 1791 *Pacific, 1.6in (40mm)*.
Delicate and handsome, with a strong ridge or carina running from the beak to the posterior edge of the shell; small, concentric, incised lines in front of the carina, smooth behind it. Cream-white.

Meiocardia moltkiana

FAMILY: SPONDYLIDAE

The thorny oysters are perhaps the most popular bivalves among collectors. Attractive in sculpture and color. The surface is sculptured with radiating ribs which generally bear more or less long, spatulate or pointed spines. They cement themselves to rock or coral by the right valve which is strongly convex; the left is usually flatter. Their 'ears' are small or obsolete and they have no byssus. There are some 100 species.

Spondylus regius

L. 1758 *Japan and southeast Asia, 8in (200mm)*.
One of the most splendid of the thorny oysters. It is almost equivalved with seven, strong, elevated, radial ribs bearing long, erect, strong spines. Between the large ribs it has small, prickly, radial riblets. Rose-pink, the spines are lighter.

Spondylus regius

S. barbatus

Reeve 1856 *Japan and southeast Asia, 2.8in (70mm)*.
The radial ribs carry some broad, rather spatulate spines. The right valve is flat or slightly concave. The color varies, generally purple-red stained with rose and deep red near the beaks, or pinky mauve, as illustrated.

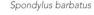

Spondylus barbatus

FAMILY: OSTREIDAE

The oysters, of which there are many species, mostly edible, are found worldwide. They are generally rather dull. One of the more interesting is:

Lopha cristagalli

L. 1758
The Cock's-comb Oyster, Indo-Pacific, 2.8in (70mm).
The edge of the shell is zigzag; surface rough like a piece of coarse leather. A dull purple. It cements itself firmly to rock or coral, as illustrated.

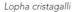

Lopha cristagalli

FAMILY: VENERIDAE

The venus shells are a large family, found worldwide. They generally have a strong shell and are often colorful. They are equivalved, with the beaks more or less central and directed forward and inwards. They live usually a little below the sediment surface. Many species are used for food.

Hysteroconcha lupanaria

Chione paphia

Hysteroconcha lupanaria

Lesson 1830 The Comb Venus, tropical west America, 3in (80mm). It is one of the most spectacular of the family. A row of strong spines runs from the beak to the posterior edge of the shell on both valves. The spines increase in size away from the beak. In front of the spines are sharp, concentric ridges and the corselet is smooth. Gray, with purple spots at the base of the spines; purple radial streaks near the posterior margin.

Chione paphia

L. The Key Venus, Caribbean, 1.6in (40mm).
It has ten, strong, coarse, heavy, concentric ridges undercut on the beak side and strongly grooved between. On the rear quarter of the shell the ridges end sharply and continue as thin flanges. Off-white or cream with red-brown zigzag lines and dark brown escutcheon.

Paphia amabilis

Philippi Indo-Pacific, 2.9in (75mm).
Rather elongated, concave in front of the beaks; close concentric ridges. Cream with fine, zigzag, light brown lines and four, darker brown radial rays.

Paphia amabilis

Lioconcha castrensis

L. 1758 Indo-Pacific, 1.6in (40mm).
Solid and inflated with round outline. Smooth except for fine growth lines. Cream with some gray shading and dark brown-black, zigzag lines.

Lioconcha castrensis

Anomalodiscus squamosus
L. 1758 *Indo-Pacific, 1.2in (30mm).*
Inflated and extended posteriorly into a beak. Radially ribbed; strong concentric ridges; edges strongly crenulate. White with some yellow or yellow-brown clouding.

Anomalodiscus squamosus

FAMILY: TRIDACNIDAE
The giant clams. The family contains six species all from the Indo-Pacific.

Tridacna gigas (not illustrated)
L. 1758 *The largest living shelled mollusk. It can grow up to 53in (1,350mm) and weigh over 570lb (260kg).*
Often embedded in rock and coral. The brightly colored blue, green and yellow mantles of the animals are very conspicuous.

Hippopus hippopus
L. 1758 *12in (300mm).*
Equivalved with strong carina from umbo to anterior edge. Rather triangular with several broad, low, strong radial ridges with close riblets between; the ribs bear a few short scales. The ribbed area in front of the carina is wide. Generally flattened but concave near the beaks. The ventral margin is strongly undulating. This genus has a very small byssal gape. Creamy white with purple-brown and white blotches.

Tridacna squamosa
Lamarck 1819, *300mm.*
Equivalved and elongate with about five, strong, low, rounded radial ridges, each carrying curved, fluted scales growing larger further from the beak. It has a large byssal gape, typical of this genus. White, becoming lemon yellow toward the margin.

Tridacna squamosa

Hippopus hippopus

FAMILY: GLOSSIDAE (SEE PAGE 304)

Glossus humanus
L. 1758 *Northeast Atlantic and Mediterranean, 4in (100mm).*
The Heart Cockle, though not in fact a cockle (Cardiidae). Equi-valved and solid, but not heavy; very inflated. Beaks which do not touch each other coil forward, outward and downward like a pair of horns. Off-white; thick brown or dark green periostracum.

FAMILY: MACTRIDAE
The otter and trough shells. Generally thin, smooth, light shells and most have a triangular-shaped pit in the hinge to which the ligament is attached. Most live burrowed well into the sand. Some are used for food, but they are not as tasty as most of the edible bivalves.

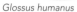

Glossus humanus

Spisula elliptica
Brown 1827 *Northeast Atlantic, 1.2in (30mm).*
Equivalved, oval and fairly solid. Smooth except for growth lines. Dirty white but sometimes stained with blue, green or yellow concentric rings (as illustrated). Lives in muddy sand or gravel.

FAMILY: LUCINIDAE
Found worldwide, they are generally circular and often thin-shelled. White predominates as color.

Spisula elliptica

Codakia orbicularis
L. 1758 *The Tiger Lucina, southeast USA and the West Indies, 3.5in (90mm).*
Almost circular. Smooth close to the beaks, otherwise with fine concentric ridges and radial riblets giving a cancellate sculpture. White; interior with a pale yellow tinge, often with a rose tinge on the hinge.

FAMILY: TELLINIDAE
The tellins generally have rather flat, thin shells. The posterior end is often a little twisted to the right. They burrow quickly and deeply and are often very brightly colored.

Codakia orbicularis

Tellina radiata
L. 1758 *Southeast USA and West Indies, 4in (100mm).*
Elongate, smooth and shiny with faint growth lines. Shallow groove from beak to near posterior. White or white with

pink-red or yellow rays and/or concentric bands; beaks usually with red tips; interior may have a pale yellow clouding.

T. rostrata

Tellina radiata

L. *Malaysia, 3in (80mm).* Elongate and flattened; strongly twisted posteriorly. Pointed posterior. Concentric fine ridges becoming oblique posteriorly. Each valve has a low, spined ridge running from the beak to each extremity; below each posterior ridge is a flattened furrow. White.

Tellina rostrata

Donax vittatus

Donax serra

FAMILY: DONACIDAE

The wedge shells are generally triangular, medium to small, fairly solid shells, rather similar to the tellins. They are found worldwide.

Donax vittatus

da Costa 1778 *Europe from Norway to the Mediterranean, 1.6in (40mm).*
Wedge-shaped, smooth and shiny with very fine growth lines. Somewhat inflated. Inside edge strongly but finely toothed. Brown, purple-brown or yellow, usually with white rays; interior mostly purple.

D. serra

Röding 1798 *South Africa, 2.6in (65mm).*
Posterior end truncated with wavy concentric ridges. Otherwise smooth with fine growth lines and very faint radial grooves. Inside edge of shell serrated. Purple-brown, yellow-brown or white with narrow, darker, concentric bands; interior purple, white or both.

Solecurtus strigillatus

FAMILY: SOLECURTIDAE
Oblong and rectangular, gaping at both ends. Rather similar to the tellins.

Solecurtus strigillatus
L. 1758 *Portugal to Senegal and Mediterranean, 6in (150mm)*.
Inflated, it has strong, some coarse, growth lines, and fine oblique striae. Pale tan with a pinky tinge and a few pale rays; interior white with pink tinge at the edges.

FAMILY: SOLENIDAE
The razor shells are long, narrow, and open at each end. They burrow a foot or more into the sand. They are found worldwide and many of the species are used for food.

Solen marginatus

Solen marginatus
Pulteney 1799 *North Europe to Morocco, 5in (130mm)*.
Straight and square-ended, gaping widely at each end. Rather delicate with growth lines becoming coarse posteriorly. Beak at anterior with furrow running just inside anterior margin. The illustration shows some of the periostracum still attached to the shell. Color pale tan.

FAMILY: PHOLADIDAE
The piddocks are boring mollusks. They have thin, fragile shells, gaping at each end, with filelike ridges anteriorly enabling them to bore into rock or clay. Beaks are obscured by reflected shell margin. Inside each valve, under the beak, they have a rod or spoonlike projection, and there is a variable number of accessory plates between the valves which protect the muscles holding the two valves together – a function of the ligament in almost all other bivalves.

Cyrtopleura costata
L. 1758 *Angel Wings, east North America and West Indies, 8in (200mm)*.
The largest of the family. Elongate and rather fragile with strong radiating ribs carrying short spines, strongest anteriorly; the ribs show internally as grooves – pitted beneath the spines. The illustration shows the spoonlike projection and an accessory plate.

FAMILY: CLAVAGELLIDAE
The watering pot shells start life as small, typical-looking bivalves, but develop a shelly tube. The original valves can be seen in the illustration. The bottom of the tube is buried in the sand or mud. The base of the tube has many tiny holes, hence the name watering pot.

Cyrtopleura costata

Penicillus penis

L. 1758 *Indo-Pacific, 8in (200mm).*
Tube tapering from base. Smooth with indistinct growth lines. No attached foreign matter. Domed base is surrounded by a flat, thin frill of many radiating, fine tubules; dome with narrow, central slit and fine, raised grooves. Elongate shells, situated just above the fringe, not noticeably sunken. White to pale gray.

P. cumingianum

Australia, 4.75in (120mm).
Tube somewhat uneven, not tapered, becoming slightly flared at top. Upper one-third has conspicuous growth lines and plated ruffles. Small granules of foreign matter cemented to lower two-thirds of tube; larger pieces cemented to base. Base rough, obscured by foreign matter and consists of scattered, relatively wide, elevated tubules which also form a rough fringe. Valves sunken near base of tube (see illustration) and almost equi-dimensional, wide at top. Fringes white; base of tubes orange-brown; shells white.

Penicillus penis

Penicillus cumingianum

Includes the octopus, cuttlefish, spirula, squid and nautilus. Active carnivores.

Nautilus pompilius

L. 1758 *The Pearly Nautilus, Indo-Pacific, 8in (200mm).*
Shell coiled in flat spiral with both umbilici covered. Large aperture, nacreous interior.Smooth, apart from distinct growth striae. Area of shell facing aperture with thin black callus. Cream or white with red-brown radial bands narrowing toward umbilical area. Other species, much rarer, are very similar but have a more or less deep umbilicus. The interiors of all these shells have chambers serving as buoyancy tanks allowing the animal to change depth.

Nautilus pompilius

Argonauta hians

Spirula spirula

Argonauta hians

Dillwyn 1817 *All warm seas, 2.9in (75mm).*
Very thin and fragile. Coiled in a flat plane and lacking umbilici. Radial ridges and angular shoulders with two rows of knobs on either side of a flat, smooth periphery. Brown; nodules darker, becoming paler toward the aperture.

The females of the *Argonautidae* all produce a somewhat similar delicate structure, which is not chambered, in which to deposit and incubate their eggs. Other species are *A. argo* L. 1758, 12in (300mm) and *A. nodosa* Lightfoot 1786, 5in (125mm). Both white.

Spirula spirula

L. 1758 *All warm seas, 1.4in (35mm).*
The only species in the superfamily Spirulacea. The shell is a free coil and has chambers like the nautilus. It is almost completely embedded within the animal, rather like a squid. The shell is very finely reticulated. White; interior nacreous.

CLASS: SCAPHOPODA

Tusk shells are hollow, tusk-shaped shells but open at both ends, often with a notch or slit at the narrow end. Some are very small and most are white. They are found in most seas and live on protozoa.

Dentalium vernedei
Sowerby 1860 *Japan, 4.75in (120mm)*.
Fine, close-set, longitudinal threads. White, irregularly banded usually with light yellow or brown.

Dentalium vernedei

D. elephantinum
L. 1758 *Indo-Pacific, 3in (80mm)*.
This species is strongly longitudinally ridged – about nine ridges – and banded with shades of green, darker at the wider end; white at the lip.

Dentalium elephantinum

CLASS: AMPHINEURA

Chitons are nearly all flattened and oval-shaped, rather like a wood louse. They have eight plates which overlap and are kept together by a surrounding girdle. They live on rocks and other hard surfaces and are vegetarians. There are about 550 species in a number of families and numerous genera. Illustrated is a typical example and also the eight plates separated. The largest, *Amicula stelleri* Middendorff 1847 west North America, grows to 10in (250mm).

Chiton

Chiton

CLASS: MONOPLACOPHORA

These are the most primitive of the mollusks. They have no eyes or tentacles and unlike all other mollusks they have segmented bodies (see illustration). Their fragile shells look like that of a limpet, but have a series of paired muscle scars inside. The apex is close to the anterior end and it has fine, concentric, uneven ridges. They were known only as fossils until the 1950s and have only been found in very deep water. The illustration shows the inside of the shell with the animal, *Neopilina adenensis* Tebble.

Neopilina adenensis

INDEX